US Hegemony and International Legitimacy

This book examines US hegemony and international legitimacy in the post-Cold War era, focusing on its leadership in the two wars on Iraq.

The preference for unilateral action in foreign policy under the Bush Administration, culminating in the use of force against Iraq in 2003, has unquestionably created a crisis in the legitimacy of US global leadership. Of central concern is the ability of the United States to act without regard for the values and interests of its allies or for international law on the use of force, raising the question: does international legitimacy truly matter in an international system dominated by a lone superpower?

US Hegemony and International Legitimacy explores the relationship between international legitimacy and hegemonic power through an in-depth examination of two case studies – the Gulf Crisis of 1990–1991 and the Iraq Crisis of 2002–2003 – and examines the extent to which normative beliefs about legitimate behaviour influenced the decisions of states to follow or reject US leadership. The findings of this book demonstrate that subordinate states play a crucial role in consenting to US leadership and endorsing it as legitimate, and have a significant impact on the ability of a hegemonic state to maintain order with least cost. Understanding of the importance of legitimacy will be vital to any attempt to rehabilitate the global leadership credentials of the United States under the Obama Administration.

This book will be of much interest to students of US foreign policy, IR theory and security studies.

Lavina Rajendram Lee is a lecturer in the Department of Modern History, Politics and International Relations at Macquarie University, Australia, and has a PhD in International Relations from the University of Sydney.

Contemporary security studies
Series Editors: James Gow and Rachel Kerr
King's College London

This series focuses on new research across the spectrum of international peace and security, in an era where each year throws up multiple examples of conflicts that present new security challenges in the world around them.

NATO's Secret Armies
Operation Gladio and terrorism in Western Europe
Daniele Ganser

The US, NATO and Military Burden-Sharing
Peter Kent Forster and Stephen J. Cimbala

Russian Governance in the Twenty-First Century
Geo-strategy, geopolitics and new governance
Irina Isakova

The Foreign Office and Finland 1938–1940
Diplomatic sideshow
Craig Gerrard

Rethinking the Nature of War
Edited by Isabelle Duyvesteyn and Jan Angstrom

Perception and Reality in the Modern Yugoslav Conflict
Myth, falsehood and deceit 1991–1995
Brendan O'Shea

The Political Economy of Peacebuilding in Post-Dayton Bosnia
Tim Donais

The Distracted Eagle
The rift between America and old Europe
Peter H. Merkl

The Iraq War
European perspectives on politics, strategy, and operations
Edited by Jan Hallenberg and Håkan Karlsson

Strategic Contest
Weapons proliferation and war in the greater Middle East
Richard L. Russell

Propaganda, the Press and Conflict
The Gulf War and Kosovo
David R. Willcox

Missile Defence
International, regional and national implications
Edited by Bertel Heurlin and Sten Rynning

Globalising Justice for Mass Atrocities
A revolution in accountability
Chandra Lekha Sriram

Ethnic Conflict and Terrorism
The origins and dynamics of civil wars
Joseph L. Soeters

Globalisation and the Future of Terrorism
Patterns and predictions
Brynjar Lia

Nuclear Weapons and Strategy
The evolution of American nuclear policy
Stephen J. Cimbala

Nasser and the Missile Age in the Middle East
Owen L. Sirrs

War as Risk Management
Strategy and conflict in an age of globalised risks
Yee-Kuang Heng

Military Nanotechnology
Potential applications and preventive arms control
Jurgen Altmann

NATO and Weapons of Mass Destruction
Regional alliance, global threats
Eric R. Terzuolo

Europeanisation of National Security Identity
The EU and the changing security identities of the Nordic states
Pernille Rieker

International Conflict Prevention and Peace-Building
Sustaining the peace in post conflict societies
Edited by T. David Mason and James D. Meernik

Controlling the Weapons of War
Politics, persuasion, and the prohibition of inhumanity
Brian Rappert

Changing Transatlantic Security Relations
Do the U.S., the EU and Russia form a new strategic triangle?
Edited by Jan Hallenberg and Håkan Karlsson

Theoretical Roots of US Foreign Policy
Machiavelli and American unilateralism
Thomas M. Kane

Corporate Soldiers and International Security
The rise of private military companies
Christopher Kinsey

Transforming European Militaries
Coalition operations and the technology gap
Gordon Adams and Guy Ben-Ari

Globalization and Conflict
National security in a 'new' strategic era
Edited by Robert G. Patman

Military Forces in 21st Century Peace Operations
No job for a soldier?
James V. Arbuckle

The Political Road to War with Iraq
Bush, 9/11 and the drive to overthrow Saddam
Nick Ritchie and Paul Rogers

Bosnian Security After Dayton
New perspectives
Edited by Michael A. Innes

Kennedy, Johnson and NATO
Britain, America and the Dynamics of Alliance, 1962–68
Andrew Priest

Small Arms and Security
New emerging international norms
Denise Garcia

The United States and Europe
Beyond the neo-conservative divide?
Edited by John Baylis and Jon Roper

Russia, NATO and Cooperative Security
Bridging the gap
Lionel Ponsard

International Law and International Relations
Bridging theory and practice
Edited by Tom Bierstecker, Peter Spiro, Chandra Lekha Sriram and Veronica Raffo

Deterring International Terrorism and Rogue States
US national security policy after 9/11
James H. Lebovic

Vietnam in Iraq
Tactics, lessons, legacies and ghosts
Edited by John Dumbrell and David Ryan

Understanding Victory and Defeat in Contemporary War
Edited by Jan Angstrom and Isabelle Duyvesteyn

Propaganda and Information Warfare in the Twenty-First Century
Altered images and deception operations
Scot Macdonald

Governance in Post-conflict Societies
Rebuilding fragile states
Edited by Derick W. Brinkerhoff

European Security in the Twenty-First Century
The challenge of multipolarity
Adrian Hyde-Price

Ethics, Technology and the American Way of War
Cruise missiles and US security policy
Reuben E. Brigety II

International Law and the Use of Armed Force
The UN charter and the major powers
Joel H. Westra

Disease and Security
Natural plagues and biological weapons in East Asia
Christian Enermark

Explaining War and Peace
Case studies and necessary condition counterfactuals
Jack Levy and Gary Goertz

War, Image and Legitimacy
Viewing contemporary conflict
James Gow and Milena Michalski

Information Strategy and Warfare
A guide to theory and practice
John Arquilla and Douglas A. Borer

Countering the Proliferation of Weapons of Mass Destruction
NATO and EU options in the Mediterranean and the Middle East
Thanos P. Dokos

Security and the War on Terror
Edited by Alex J. Bellamy, Roland Bleiker, Sara E. Davies and Richard Devetak

The European Union and Strategy
An emerging actor
Edited by Jan Hallenberg and Kjell Engelbrekt

Causes and Consequences of International Conflict
Data, methods and theory
Edited by Glenn Palmer

Russian Energy Policy and Military Power
Putin's quest for greatness
Pavel Baev

The Baltic Question During the Cold War
Edited by John Hiden, Vahur Made, and David J. Smith

America, the EU and Strategic Culture
Renegotiating the transatlantic bargain
Asle Toje

Afghanistan, Arms and Conflict
Post-9/11 security and insurgency
Michael Bhatia and Mark Sedra

Punishment, Justice and International Relations
Ethics and order after the Cold War
Anthony F. Lang, Jr.

Intra-State Conflict, Governments and Security
Dilemmas of deterrence and assurance
Edited by Stephen M. Saideman and Marie-Joëlle J. Zahar

Democracy and Security
Preferences, norms and policy-making
Edited by Matthew Evangelista, Harald Müller and Niklas Schörnig

The Homeland Security Dilemma
Fear, failure and the future of American security
Frank P. Harvey

Military Transformation and Strategy
Revolutions in military affairs and small states
Edited by Bernard Loo

Peace Operations and International Criminal Justice
Building peace after mass atrocities
Majbritt Lyck

NATO, Security and Risk Management
From Kosovo to Khandahar
M.J. Williams

Cyber-Conflict and Global Politics
Edited by Athina Karatzogianni

Globalisation and Defence in the Asia-Pacific
Arms across Asia
Edited by Geoffrey Till, Emrys Chew and Joshua Ho

Security Strategies and American World Order
Lost power
Birthe Hansen, Peter Toft and Anders Wivel

War, Torture and Terrorism
Rethinking the rules of international security
Edited by Anthony F. Lang, Jr. and Amanda Russell Beattie

America and Iraq
Policy making, intervention and regional politics
Edited by David Ryan and Patrick Kiely

European Security in a Global Context
Internal and external dynamics
Edited by Thierry Tardy

Women and Political Violence
Female combatants in ethno-national conflict
Miranda H. Alison

Justice, Intervention and Force in International Relations
Reassessing just war theory in the 21st century
Kimberley A. Hudson

Clinton's Foreign Policy
Between the Bushes, 1992–2000
John Dumbrell

Aggression, Crime and International Security
Moral, political and legal dimensions of international relations
Page Wilson

European Security Governance
The European Union in a Westphalian world
Charlotte Wagnsson, James Sperling and Jan Hallenberg

Private Security and the Reconstruction of Iraq
Christopher Kinsey

US Foreign Policy and Iran
American–Iranian relations since the Islamic Revolution
Donette Murray

Legitimising the Use of Force in International Relations
Kosovo, Iraq and the ethics of intervention
Corneliu Bjola

The EU and European Security Order
Interfacing security actors
Rikard Bengtsson

US Counter-Terrorism Strategy and al-Qaeda
Signalling and the terrorist world-view
Joshua Alexander Geltzer

Global Biosecurity
Threats and responses
Edited by Peter Katona, John P. Sullivan and Michael D. Intriligator

US Hegemony and International Legitimacy
Norms, power and followership in the wars on Iraq
Lavina Rajendram Lee

US Hegemony and International Legitimacy

Norms, power and followership in the wars on Iraq

Lavina Rajendram Lee

LONDON AND NEW YORK

First published 2010
by Routledge
2 Park Square, Milton Park, Abingdon, Oxon OX14 4RN

Simultaneously published in the USA and Canada
by Routledge
711 Third Avenue, New York, NY 10017

Routledge is an imprint of the Taylor & Francis Group, an informa business

© 2010 Lavina Rajendram Lee

Typeset in Times by Wearset Ltd, Boldon, Tyne and Wear

All rights reserved. No part of this book may be reprinted or reproduced or utilised in any form or by any electronic, mechanical, or other means, now known or hereafter invented, including photocopying and recording, or in any information storage or retrieval system, without permission in writing from the publishers.

British Library Cataloguing in Publication Data
A catalogue record for this book is available from the British Library

Library of Congress Cataloging-in-Publication Data
Lee, Lavina.
US hegemony and international legitimacy: norms, power and followership in the wars on Iraq/Lavina Lee.
p. cm.
1. Hegemony–Case studies. 2. Legitimacy of governments–Case studies. 3. Persian Gulf War, 1991–Diplomatic history. 4. Iraq War, 2003–Diplomatic history. I. Title. II. Title: U.S. hegemony and international legitimacy.
JZ1312.L44 2010
327.73–dc22

2009031782

First issued in paperback 2013

ISBN13: 978-0-415-72430-2 (pbk)
ISBN13: 978-0-415-55236-3 (hbk)
ISBN13: 978-0-203-85949-0 (ebk)

Contents

List of illustrations   x
Acknowledgements   xii

1   Introduction and theoretical framework   1

2   Legitimacy and hegemony in the Gulf Crisis   24

3   Material factors and followership in the Gulf Crisis   49

4   Legitimacy and hegemony in the Iraq Crisis   75

5   Material factors and followership in the Iraq Crisis   106

6   Comparing and contrasting the Gulf Crisis and the Iraq Crisis   134

7   Conclusion   155

Notes   161
Index   192

Illustrations

Figures

3.1	Financial contributions to the Gulf War	53
3.2	Military contributions to the Gulf War	54

Tables

2.1	Support for goals and rationale	46–47
2.2	Support for means and normative justification	48
3.1	Contributions pledged in 1990 and 1991 to the United States to offset US costs, commitments and receipts through to May 1992	52
3.2	Operation Desert Storm – comparative totals	53
3.3	Japanese contributions to the anti-Saddam coalition	59
3.4	The UK contribution to the Gulf coalition	67
3.5	Oil dependency and followership	71
3.6	Alliance dependence and followership	71
3.7	The balance of threat and followership	72
3.8	Countries participating in the military coalition	74
4.1	Resolution 1441 – goals, means and justifications – views of the Security Council	97
4.2	Summary of views of members of the Security Council	98
4.3	Views of the wider membership – states against the use of force	99–101
4.4	Views of the wider UN membership – states in support of the use of force	102
4.5	Views of the Security Council on the legitimacy of the use of force	103
4.6	Views on the use of force expressed at the open meeting of the Security Council	104–105
5.1	Non-US troop and financial contributions to post-war stabilisation and reconstruction in Iraq	110–111
5.2	The UK military contribution to the war in Iraq	124

5.3	Normative threat assessment – threat to international order	129
5.4	Material assessment of threat	129
5.5	Alliance dependence	129
5.6	The oil factor	129
6.1	Persuasiveness of the oil dependency factor	135
6.2	Persuasiveness of the alliance dependence factor	137
6.3	Material assessments of the Iraqi threat	139
6.4	Normative perceptions of the Iraqi threat	140

Acknowledgements

This book would not have been possible without the efforts of a number of people. Huge thanks must go first to Jason Sharman for all his valuable comments on various drafts of the manuscript, for giving me an encouraging nudge when I needed it, and for spurring me to do more. To the anonymous reviewers, your comments have been extremely helpful and have undoubtedly improved the final product. Deep thanks also must go to James Gow for his inspirational teaching and research, and all his guidance over the years. I want to also thank my parents for their love and support and for teaching me the value of education and scholarship. Finally, I owe so much to John Lee for his love, patience and persistence in spurring me to do more than I think I can. I could not have finished this book without him.

The authors and publishers would like to thank the following for permission to reproduce their material:

Edward Foster and Dr Rosemary Hollis, 'War in the Gulf: Sovereignty, Oil and Security', *Whitehall Paper 8* (1992) p. 174 © The Royal United Services Institute for Defence and Security Studies, reprinted by permission of (Taylor & Francis Ltd, www.tandf.co.uk/journals) on behalf of The Royal United Services Institute for Defence and Security Studies.

1 Introduction and theoretical framework

Interest in the impact of US hegemony is not new among scholars of international relations. During the 1970s, scholars became absorbed with the possible linkage between the perceived decline in US power and instability in key institutions of the post-Second World War international order.[1] A heated debate then ensued in the 1980s over the reality or fiction of US hegemonic decline;[2] one that was decisively put to rest with the end of the Cold War and the steady expansion of US power over the course of the following decade. What has sparked a third wave of interest in examining the nature of US hegemony, and particularly the limits or lack thereof of US power, was the increasingly unilateralist approach taken to the formation of foreign policy, a trend which reached its apogee during the tenure of the administration of George W. Bush.

The preference for unilateral action first became evident during the tenure of the Clinton Administration in the context of waning support within the UN Security Council for the application of a containment strategy against Iraq. Of note were the effectively unilateral military strikes on Iraqi air defences in 1996[3] to police the 'no-fly zones', and on alleged Iraqi WMD sites in December 1998 (known as 'Operation Desert Fox') after the expulsion of UNSCOM inspectors by Saddam Hussein. Prior UN Security Council authorisation was not forthcoming in either case. This tendency clearly accelerated under the leadership of the Bush Administration, demonstrated among other things by the refusal to ratify the Kyoto Protocol and the Rome Statute establishing the International Criminal Court, opposition to the creation of an additional protocol strengthening the 1972 Biological and Toxin Weapons Convention and US withdrawal from the Anti-Ballistic Missile Treaty. The high point for this go-it-alone strategy came in the form of an ambitious military operation to effect regime change in Iraq in 2003, without UN Security Council authorisation, nor significant backing from many long-standing allies.

The unilateralist character of the Bush Administration's foreign policy has been argued to derive from a combination of unique forces and views. September 11, 2001, revealed the existence of a new and formidable terrorist threat to US national security which succeeded in exploiting the openness of US society to effect real damage to the homeland with relatively meagre material resources. Whilst any government would be under a duty to counter to such a threat, the response taken was highly influenced by the Administration's understanding of the significance of the 'unipolar moment'[4] and the unique opportunity this afforded to the US to re-shape the rules and norms of international order, with or without the support of long-standing allies.

Normatively, the Administration became convinced that the existing rules and norms on the use of force in self-defence needed significant revision to take into account the revealed aims and methods of terrorist organisations, and the potential magnification of the terrorist threat should alliances be formed with 'rogue' states. Further, the war on Iraq demonstrated a strong ideological conviction that the promotion of liberal democracy, through forceful and non-forceful means, provided the best means of addressing the root causes of terrorism and conflict. At the same time, the 'unipolar moment' provided the US with a unique opportunity to pursue and defend national interests and values, which were believed to be benevolent,[5] unfettered by the need to take into account the views and interests of other states, whether those of rivals or allies.

The increasing trend towards unilateralism in US foreign policy, during the tenure of both Administrations, has turned attention towards the broader implications of the emergence of a hegemonic state in the system on international order. The Bush Administration's lack of faith in institutional solutions to common problems, and selective observance of international legal or normative constraints, raises the question of whether hegemonic power can be limited by the rules and norms of international order. Does it in fact matter whether a hegemonic state's behaviour is viewed as illegitimate by international society? Do questions of international legitimacy significantly influence the behaviour and interests of hegemonic states or other states in their response to a hegemon in the system? If not, does the emergence of a unilateralist and revolutionary hegemon constitute a threat to the continued existence of a pluralistic international order and society?[6]

This book enters into the debate over whether international legitimacy truly matters in an international system dominated by a lone superpower. It does so with two key aims. First, I seek to examine the nature of the relationship between hegemony and international legitimacy as theoretical concepts. Within the literature, two broad approaches to hegemony can be discerned. Materialist approaches (realist in orientation, including hegemonic stability theory) define hegemony as a relationship of dominance in which a hegemon maintains international order by using its predominant material resources to reward and coerce subordinate states. Questions of international legitimacy are second order concerns. In contrast, normative approaches (Gramscian and constructivist) characterise hegemony as a socially recognised leadership role based primarily upon a hegemon's ability to lead international society by engendering consent and consensus around an ideological programme for the achievement of common goals. A hegemon is able to maintain order without relying heavily on coercion and bribery, as followership by subordinate states is largely spurred by the internal acceptance of the legitimacy of international order. In sum, the book's first objective is to evaluate whether hegemony in the post-Cold War era is best conceptualised as a relation of dominance or of leadership.

The second aim of the book is to empirically evaluate the opposing theoretical conceptualisations of hegemony through an examination of two case studies – the Gulf Crisis of 1990–1991 ('the Gulf Crisis') and the Iraq Crisis of 2002–2003 ('The Iraq Crisis') – in which the US sought to lead international society to resolve a threat to international peace and security. Three questions are addressed. First, what kinds of hegemony – hegemony as dominance or hegemony as leadership – are in evidence in the Gulf Crisis and the Iraq Crisis respectively? Second, to what extent was US hegemony and action seen as legitimate by international society, and can this be related to the decisions by states to follow or reject US leadership in each case? Third, through which theoretical approach – realism or constructivism – do we acquire the best explanation of US hegemony in this period?

The question of whether international legitimacy significantly constrains and enables the exercise of hegemonic power is important to both policy and theory. In policy terms, the question concerns the nature of US hegemony in the post-Cold War era and the forces that shape and define it. The book hopes to offer insights into the factors that affect the political influence and power of the United States and the stability of international order. If it can be shown that states were significantly motivated to follow US leadership or to reject it on normative grounds, this has important implications for both policy-makers within the United States as well as those from potential 'follower' states. For decision-makers within the US, a recognition that legitimacy itself is a form of power would imply that a greater effort should be given to persuading subordinate states that the US 'vision' for international order is proper, rightful and appropriate. Success in this endeavour would be instrumentally advantageous, because it would be a much less costly means of maintaining international order.

In theoretical terms, the book seeks to evaluate the conceptualisations of hegemony put forward by realist, Gramscian and constructivist approaches and to assess which conceptualisation fares better vis-à-vis the actual practice of hegemony in our two case studies. At issue are distinctive characterisations of the nature of power in international politics, and the impact of international rules and norms on the formation of interests and strategies by states. Ultimately, an evaluation of these theoretical approaches involves a judgement as to which is better able to account for events in international politics. I have chosen to focus on the use of force because realism and its variants claim to provide superior accounts of the use of force by state actors which has always been core to the study of international relations generally. It is in this area that the greatest degree of scepticism exists about the efficacy of norms in changing the behaviour of states, and is therefore precisely the ground on which to evaluate whether a norms-based approach can add to accounts of these events. If we are to address the question of whether legitimacy really matters in a hegemonic international system, it is important to first define just how the terms 'international legitimacy' and 'hegemony' will be used.

Whilst the concept of legitimacy – its meaning, sources and implications – has long been of interest to scholars seeking to explain the stability or otherwise of domestic political orders, until recently it has been largely neglected in the study of international relations.[7] This is largely explained by the relative dominance of material and rationalist approaches to the study of international relations, which have to a large extent excluded or downplayed the role of norms, rules and institutions as having first-order causal or constitutive effects (discussed further below, pp. 6–11). In this book we are intentionally challenging this viewpoint by putting legitimacy at the centre of our enquiry about the operation of hegemonic systems of order.

What do we mean then by the concept of legitimacy? Mark Suchman puts forward a very useful definition of legitimacy as 'a generalised perception or assumption that the actions of an entity are desirable, proper, or appropriate within some socially constructed system of norms, values, beliefs and definitions'.[8] This definition is equally applicable to an assessment of the legitimacy of a rule or to a social role or institution, and draws attention to two essential aspects of legitimacy: that it is an individual normative judgement; and that this judgement is drawn from shared understandings of appropriate behaviour within a particular political community. Thus, any conception of legitimacy presupposes the existence of a society in which its subjects come to view themselves to be bound to one another in the observance of certain normative standards of behaviour.

In this book we take seriously the position that an international society of states exists in the international system, authoritatively defined by Hedley Bull as 'a group of states' which become 'conscious of certain common interests and common values' and which 'form a society in the sense that they conceive themselves to be bound by a common set of rules in their relations with one another, and share in the working of common institutions'.[9] Whilst it is the sense of obligation – the self-conception of being bound – which proves the existence of international society,[10] it is the standards of legitimacy accepted at a particular historical epoch that provides the character of that society, principally in relation to standards of appropriate membership and of appropriate behaviour between the members of international society. It is important to note that any conception of legitimacy should not be a static one. Whilst these standards become entrenched within the system structure, agents can and do challenge and contest conceptions of legitimacy leading to change or evolution in the character of international society over time.

Questions of legitimacy are particularly pertinent where political order emerges based on a relation of unequal power distribution within a society, an arrangement which naturally gives rise to questions of equity and fairness. As Beetham has observed:

> Those who are subordinate experience [the exercise of power over them] as constraining, often humiliating and sometimes life-threatening; and many would escape it if they could. Those who hold power, or seek to do so, are themselves frequently at odds with one another over the scope of their power and the control over their subordinates, with potentially damaging consequences.[11]

As a result, in most, if not all, societies rules are developed to control the use of power which is viewed as legitimate 'to the extent that the rules of power can be justified in terms of [normative] beliefs shared by both dominant and subordinate'.[12] In this book our aim is to elucidate what international standards of legitimacy have emerged and have gained acceptance in international society in relation to the exercise of leadership over the collective, and how they impact upon the ability of the United States to restore or maintain international order. This issue of the relationship between legitimacy and hegemonic power is the subject of constructivist approaches to hegemony and will be discussed further below (pp. 13–18).

In comparison to legitimacy, the concept of hegemony is more prominent in the study of international relations. The term 'hegemony' has become the subject of a substantial literature and as such there are wide varieties of conceptualisations of the term which differ in terms of their 'theoretical emphases, use of history, characteristic methodologies, normative bases, and implications for the future'.[13] This has resulted in 'hegemony' or 'hegemonic leadership' being categorised as an 'essentially contested concept', meaning

> the concept involved is appraisive in that the state of affairs it describes is a valued achievement, when the practice described is internally complex in that its characterisation involves reference to several dimensions, and when the agreed and contested rules of application are relatively open ...[14]

When one surveys IR scholarship, despite the best intentions to remain true to value-free enquiry, there are clear appraisals made about the value or otherwise of the existence of hegemony in the international system, differing stances on the factors or dimensions underpinning hegemony, as well as what factors enable us to distinguish hegemony from other forms of social relations in human history.

For our limited purposes we need not discuss the various normative implications of particular conceptualisations of hegemony,[15] nor the arguments for or against labelling particular states or periods of history as hegemonic. The most illuminating aspect of contestation with respect to the concept of 'hegemony' concerns its internal complexity. As Rapkin has noted, theoreticians use multiple connotations of the term 'hegemony' and base these connotations on various related concepts which are also somewhat contested, such as power, international order, public goods, regimes and ideology.[16] As such, the term 'hegemony' is used by scholars within the discipline to mean primacy, dominance, preponderance of power, leadership or all four.

What is common to all approaches is an agreement that, by definition, a hegemon must possess a predominance of power capabilities compared to other actors within the international system. However, whilst all conceptualisations characterise hegemony as a power relationship, important differences arise in relation to the emphasis or lack of emphasis placed on the realm of norms and ideas in the operation of hegemonic systems, i.e. the extent to which legitimacy really matters. These differences stem from assumptions about the nature of international structures, power and the forms of power able to be utilised by a hegemon to maintain order. I have categorised these conceptualisations on a spectrum, with one end occupied by the 'materialist' approaches which in broad terms put forward a conceptualisation of hegemony as a dominance relationship. On the other end of the spectrum are 'normative' approaches which put forward, to varying degrees, a conceptualisation of hegemony as a relationship of leadership and followership, with a hegemon occupying a socially defined and constituted leadership role of international society.

Materialist approaches to hegemony

Within International Relations scholarship, realist conceptions of hegemony provide the dominant materialist understandings of the subject. What makes these approaches primarily materialist in orientation is their emphasis on the material nature of international structures, power and power relationships between a hegemon and subordinate states. The approaches taken to hegemony by scholars within this broad categorisation fall on a continuum between those who ascribe relatively little role for rules, norms and institutions and beliefs as drivers of state action to those who acknowledge some limited independent role for the ideational realm. I have placed structural realists on one end of this spectrum, classical realists at the other and hegemonic stability theorists falling somewhere in between.

Structural realism

The structural realist approach to hegemony can be represented by the influential works of two major theorists, Kenneth Waltz and John Mearsheimer. In the seminal work of Kenneth Waltz, international structure is defined by three parameters: the organising principle of the system, the function or character of the units and the distribution of capabilities.[17] Under Waltz's theory, it is the third dimension of international system structure, the distribution of capabilities defined materially, which is used to explain state behaviour and outcomes.[18] The distribution of ideas or knowledge within the system is not included in Waltz's definition of structure. International systems are therefore characterised by the levels of concentration of power – whether bipolar, multi-polar or unipolar – with power being defined as material capabilities. For Waltz, hegemony is synonymous with unipolarity.

John Mearsheimer puts forward an offensive form of structural realism which argues that, in a self-help system, as intentions, future shifts in the balance of power and the relative power needed to ensure survival are all difficult to gauge with accuracy,[19] the optimal strategy for ensuring state survival is to become the most powerful state in the system. Thus all states seek to become hegemonic, with hegemony defined as the predominance of power relative to other states.[20] What makes Mearsheimer's theory offensive is that he argues that 'the pursuit of power stops only when hegemony is achieved'.[21]

Whilst the offensive nature of Mearsheimer's theory separates him from Waltz's defensive structural theory, both scholars share common ground in their conceptualisation of hegemony. First, both share a definition of hegemony as describing an international system in which there was a unipolar concentration of material capabilities. In other words hegemony is defined as a type of international system in which a single state possesses a preponderance of material capabilities as compared to other states within the system.[22]

Second, both would agree that hegemony, when it occurred, would be a brief and unstable condition in the system because the imperatives of anarchy would compel states to balance against the hegemon to prevent it from potentially extinguishing their survival as independent sovereign entities.[23] Thus, in a situation where two coalitions form, '[s]econdary states, if they are free to choose, flock to the weaker side; for it is the stronger side that threatens them'.[24]

Third, whilst hegemony is likely to be relatively short lived, this does not preclude the emergence of a hegemonic order of sorts embodied in rules, norms and institutions. However, for structural realists the content of these rules, norms and institutions reflect the underlying distribution of power. In Waltz's words, 'whatever elements of authority emerge internationally are barely once removed from the capability that provides the foundation for the appearance of those elements. Authority quickly reduces to a particular expression of capability.'[25] Mearsheimer suggests that great powers cooperate to build an international order, but do so not because they value it, but in order to maximise their shares of world power.[26] International rules, norms and institutions are therefore essentially instruments to be used to institutionalise the relative power positions of hegemonic states (or great powers) and will be discarded when they no longer serve their purpose.

Fourth, both structural realists share a similar definition of power termed the 'elements of national power' approach,[27] in which power is equated with the possession of material capabilities, with special emphasis on economic and military capabilities which impact upon a state's capacity to wage war. In taking this approach, both refute the challenge put forward by the 'relational power' approach exemplified by Robert Dahl's famous definition of power as a type of causation.[28] Here Dahl conceives of power as a 'relationship in which the behaviour of actor A at least partially causes a change in the behaviour of actor B'.[29] For both theorists, this definition confuses means with ends by allowing for the existence of power only when a state exercises control or influence, which can only be measured after interaction is complete.[30] For Mearsheimer, power should not be equated with outcomes because 'sometimes this leads to implausible conclusions'[31] because in some cases the state with inferior material capabilities may in fact win out in a dispute. Non-material factors, such as strategy, intelligence, resolve, weather and disease, are cited as giving one combatant, who may have less material capabilities than her opponent, a decisive advantage nevertheless.[32]

Whilst both forms of structural realism appear to reject the relational definition of power, elements of each theorist's argument do in fact rely on such a definition. Mearsheimer's contention that the optimal strategy for ensuring state survival is to seek hegemony shows an understanding of power in terms of the ability of a state to use material capabilities to impose its will on other states or resist attempts by others to do the same. Similarly, while railing against the relational view of power as 'practically and logically untenable', towards the end of *Theory of International Politics*, Waltz puts forward, somewhat inconsistently, a definition of power which is in fact relational: 'an agent is powerful to the extent that he affects others more than they affect him.'[33] Implied by the work of both theorists is the view that the possession of material capabilities, particularly resources that can be utilised in war, allows a state to influence the behaviour and actions of other states, i.e. to exercise power over another.

Whilst rules, norms and institutions do play a part in hegemonic systems in structural realist accounts, their role is purely as an instrumental tool to cement the interests of the powerful. Neither great powers nor subordinate states adhere to rules and norms of an international order out of a true sense of normative obligation, but do so only through threat of sanction or out of self-interest. As such, legitimacy is an instrumental form of power rather than a social form which activates rights, duties and obligations on the part of both hegemon and follower states.

Hegemonic stability theory

The second major theory within the 'realist' tradition which speaks on the topic of hegemony is the aptly named hegemonic stability theory (HST).[34] The central problem that HST sought to answer was under what conditions public goods, such as international economic infrastructure, would be provided in the international system. In the influential work *The World in Depression 1929–1939*,[35] Charles Kindleberger argued that because of the problem of free riding, the public good of international economic stability would not be provided unless a single state existed that was sufficiently large relative to all others such that it was able to capture a share of the benefits of international economic stability larger than the entire cost of providing it.[36] Hegemony here was benevolent because it is smaller states that benefit most by the presence of a hegemon able to bear the costs of maintaining the economic infrastructure necessary for stability.[37]

Taking a more pessimistic view of hegemony, Robert Gilpin argues that the presence of a hegemonic power is indeed central to the preservation of international order, a public good, but that it does so for its own self-interest. Hegemonic states do indeed provide the public good of order, but use their power to extract contributions or taxes from other states to pay for it. The legitimacy of a hegemon's leadership is dependent upon whether subordinate states still benefit more from the provision of the public good than they need to pay the hegemon to provide them.[38] However, as Snidal has argued, Gilpin's version of hegemonic stability theory is coercive because the hegemon is in a position to exploit subordinate states by imposing costs greater than the benefits received from the provision of the good.[39]

Introduction and theoretical framework 9

The main tenets of hegemonic stability theory have come under strong criticism on two main grounds. First, scholars such as Snidal have shown that it is possible for a small group of states to obtain sufficient net benefits from the provision of an international public good to consider doing so. Hegemony may not then be so necessary for the provision of public goods.[40] Second, Kindleberger's further hypothesis that '[t]he decline of hegemonic structures of power can be expected to presage a decline in the strength of corresponding international economic regimes'[41] has also been attacked by neoliberal writers such as Robert Keohane who argue that 'cooperation does not necessarily require the existence of a hegemonic leader after international regimes have been established. Post hegemonic cooperation is also possible.'[42]

Whilst these criticisms are important for an assessment of the validity of hegemonic stability theory as a theory, for our purposes it is important to draw out precisely how 'hegemony' as a concept is developed. Hegemonic stability theory as proposed by its major adherents, Kindleberger, Gilpin and Keohane, is essentially a realist theory of hegemony. I include Keohane in this group because his revision of the theory is a partial one, which still accepts that international cooperation is more likely in the presence of a hegemon that is willing and able to enforce the rules of the system.

First, similar to structural realism, the hypothesis behind hegemonic stability theory itself is dependent on a material view of power. Hegemony is defined as preponderance of material resources, particularly control over raw materials, sources of capital, markets, the production of highly valued goods as well as military and technological capabilities.[43] Gilpin describes a hegemonic international structure as one in which 'a single powerful state controls or dominates the lesser states in the system'.[44]

Second, the behaviour of states is deemed to be conditioned by the distribution of capabilities in the system at any one time. Stability is caused by the concentration of material power in the system, and instability caused by its dissipation. For Gilpin, the materially powerful states govern the international system and 'establish and enforce the basic rules and rights that influence their own behaviour and that of the lesser states in the system'.[45]

Where there is some departure from the assumptions of structural realists is in terms of the role of non-material factors in affecting the governance of the system by a hegemonic state. Gilpin, for example, argues that hegemonic states are able to exercise control through the role of prestige, which he likens to the function of authority within domestic systems. The legitimacy of a hegemon's 'right to rule' is said to rest on three factors: 'its demonstrated ability to enforce its will on other states' through victory in the last hegemonic war; its provision of public goods such as international security and economic order, and on the 'ideological, religious, or other values common to a set of states'[46] which justify its domination. However, Gilpin clearly states that these normative influences on order are 'usually weak or nonexistent'.[47] Rather, prestige rests primarily on a state's reputation for being willing to use its economic and military capabilities to enforce the rules of order to its advantage.[48] Rules, norms and institutions have at best second-order effects on the stability of international order.

Robert Keohane's modified hegemonic stability theory is more supportive of the role of rules, norms and institutions in the maintenance of international order. However, Keohane still takes an instrumental view of the role of norms,[49] stating that 'norms and rules of regimes can exert an effect on behaviour even if they do not embody common ideals but are used by self-interested states and corporations engaging in a process of mutual adjustment'. They are '"intervening variables", between fundamental characteristics of world politics such as the international distribution of power on the one hand and the behaviour of states and non-state actors such as multinational corporations on the other'.[50] Keohane's theory does not propose that state goals or interests might be influenced by normative beliefs or that state action might be motivated by beliefs about appropriate, proper and rightful behaviour. This would involve acknowledging a constitutive role for norms rather than just an instrumental one. This leaves hegemonic stability theory as a material approach to hegemony, but one that acknowledges a limited instrumental role for international rules, norms and institutions.

Classical realism

The materialist theory which is most accommodating of the role of international rules and norms, and the idea of legitimate power is that of classical realism. Whilst emphasising material capabilities as the source and measuring stick of state power, Hans Morgenthau appreciated that power could be derived also from 'the respect or love for men or institutions',[51] and noted the instrumental advantages of wielding legitimate power:

> Legitimate power which can invoke a moral or legal justification for its exercise, is likely to be more effective than equivalent illegitimate power, which cannot be so justified. That is to say, legitimate power has a better chance to influence the will of its objects than equivalent illegitimate power. Power exercised in self-defence or in the name of the United Nations has a better chance to succeed than equivalent power exercised by an 'aggressor' nation or in violation of international law.[52]

Elsewhere he recognises that norms guide action by internally influencing beliefs and thereby circumscribing both the means by which states pursue their national interest, as well as the goals they seek 'not because in light of expediency they appear impractical or unwise but because certain moral rules interpose an absolute barrier'.[53] Even hegemonic states would be constrained by shared beliefs that certain goals and means are 'off limits', including the prohibition on mass extermination, use of political assassinations, protection of civilians and combatants unable or unwilling to fight in times of war, and the restriction of war as an instrument of foreign policy as an evil to be avoided rather than used on the grounds of expediency.[54]

Introduction and theoretical framework 11

However, whilst Morgenthau is more expansive in his acknowledgement of the role of rules and norms in international life than other realist theorists, ultimately classical realism is still a theory of power in which moral action for a rational decision-maker may require the subordination of normative beliefs where the survival of the state is at stake:

> while the individual has a moral right to sacrifice himself in defense of such a moral principle, the state has no right to let its moral disapprobation of the infringement of liberty get in the way of successful political action, itself inspired by the moral principle of national survival.[55]

In practice, moral restraints, much like the legal restraints of international law, become subject to the realities of a decentralised system of international relations. For Morgenthau, in an anarchical system the successful operation of international law, and implicitly international norms more generally, is dependent upon the existence of 'complementary interests of individual states' and the 'distribution of power among them'.[56] Whilst hegemony specifically is not addressed by Morgenthau, we can surmise that he would have viewed legitimacy as an instrumentally useful form of power for a hegemon but that the power of norms to constrain would and should give way in matters of state survival.

Normative approaches to hegemony

There are two major approaches to hegemony with a normative focus which derive from the work of Antonio Gramsci and that of constructivists. Both challenge the materialist approaches that have been discussed so far by placing legitimacy at the centre of the relationship between a hegemon and subordinate states. Whilst it is agreed that a hegemonic state by definition must possess a predominance of material resources relative to other states, both approaches argue that material resources alone do not bestow the entitlement or right to lead and cannot ensure that a stable and sustainable political order is created or maintained.

Antonio Gramsci

Gramsci's *Prison Notebooks* (1929–1935)[57] introduced a new concept of 'hegemony' to Marxist literature in an attempt to explain why it had proven so difficult to create the conditions for a socialist revolution in central and western European states, unlike the Bolshevik experience in Tsarist Russia. The term 'hegemony' for Gramsci[58] described the supremacy of a ruling class maintained by cultivating a belief among the ruled classes that the inequality of power relations was in fact legitimate.[59] Such orders are described as consensual in the sense that social control is exerted by moulding the internal normative belief systems of the ruled, and not primarily through the use of external incentives such as force or bribery.[60] It was legitimacy that accounted for the stability and longevity of bourgeois supremacy in Western capitalist societies.

Important to the rise of a hegemonic order was the construction of an ideology justifying the division of power within society which was accepted and fostered by the institutions of civil society, such as the press, political parties, churches and schools. It was through the practices of societal institutions in spreading and reinforcing this dominant ideology that the moral, political and cultural values of the ruling class achieved the status of common sense. Given Gramsci's belief that capitalist economic and social relations were essentially exploitative of the working classes, he argued that the hegemony of the capitalist class was achieved by deception in the sense that the ruled classes suffered under a 'false consciousness'. In terms of the modern 'faces of power' debate, the ruling class was able to exercise power over the ruled by influencing their beliefs and preferences for their own benefit.[61]

Following the ideas of Gramsci, Robert Cox introduced a conception of hegemony to international relations as the hegemony of a social class and an associated mode of production within the state which expands beyond state boundaries through a process of emulation.[62] Supremacy here is also maintained primarily through consent, through the construction an ideology capable of universal application, i.e. an order which is not directly exploitative of other classes but one which most states 'could find compatible with their interests'.[63] Whilst this departs somewhat from the idea of a 'false consciousness', like Gramsci, Cox argues that international institutions and the forces of global civil society facilitate hegemony by spreading the dominant ideology to elites and absorbing 'counter-hegemonic ideas' that challenge the spread of the dominant mode of production.[64]

Apart from the centrality of legitimacy to any understanding of hegemony, Gramscian approaches also depart from materialist understandings of system structure. Gramsci was motivated by a desire to advance the Marxist cause in the bourgeois-led capitalist regimes of Western Europe, which had not crumbled beneath the weight of their inherent contradictions.[65] Particularly, Gramsci was keen to overturn the assumption that the economic base or relations of production determined the superstructures of society, or the political and social relations embedded in civil society. Gramsci argued that economic structures 'should not be treated as natural, law-like regularities to be passively accepted as fact'. Rather, such structures were socially constructed which, over time and through practice, were perceived to be natural, permanent, legitimate and unchangeable. Central to his revision of the base/superstructure Marxist model is the concept of 'historic bloc' in which the base economic relations of production and the super-structural levels of the state and civil society are 'organically linked' or mutually interdependent and reciprocal, rather than the latter being determined by the former.[66] Similarly, Robert Cox argues that hegemony consists of a historical structure in which three categories of forces – ideas, material capabilities and institutions – are congruent. In his words, '[i]deas and material conditions are always bound together, mutually influencing one another, and not reducible one to the other'.[67]

This aspect of Gramscian thought separates it from the materialist theories we have examined thus far. Whilst Gramsci still viewed social relations as highly influenced by material structures, in this case as structured by the social relations of production in the economic base, political and cultural practices at the level of the superstructure were crucial in stabilising and strengthening a given order. Rules, norms and institutions were not simply derivative of material power relations, but rather could potentially sustain a change and transformation in the material power relations of a particular society. In terms of the relationship between hegemony and legitimacy, the latter was seen as an integral form of power which sustained the supremacy of a ruling class, and it was through the waging of ideological war that a change to the relations of productions might be effected.

The Gramscian approaches to hegemony we have discussed so far provide a valuable counterpoint to realist conceptions of hegemony. Whilst realist approaches are predominantly materialist in nature, Gramscian approaches put forward a stronger role for ideology, institutions and normative belief systems in explaining the longevity and stability of political orders. We cannot, however, place these approaches at the same point on the spectrum as constructivists. Whilst Gramsci puts forward the idea that there is a mutually constitutive relationship between base and superstructure, we cannot discount the fact that for Gramsci social relations are essentially defined in terms of the economic relations of production that exist within a particular society. Ideas are used as a tool by dominant social classes and revolutionary agents to control the 'ordinary man' who is incapable of knowing objectively what his interests are. What we can and should take away from Gramsci's approach to hegemony is the possibility that the stability of hegemonic orders derives largely from the acceptance by the ruled of the legitimacy of existing social relations. Whether this acceptance is based on false premises or not is another matter and one that is specific to time and place. Constructivists share this focus on legitimacy as integral to the sustainability of a political order but go further by focusing more deeply on constitutive role of norms in international social life and how this impacts upon the relationship between a hegemon and the rest of international society.

Constructivism

Constructivism is a social theory that 'makes claims about the social world and social life' but of itself is not a substantive theory of international politics.[68] As such we cannot speak of a constructivist theory of hegemony as we have done with respect to the theoretical approaches we have examined so far. However, what we have chosen to do in this book is to take some of the central premises shared by all constructivists, as well as insights by scholars who have been described as modernist (or conservative) constructivists[69] to build a constructivist conceptualisation of hegemony in international relations. As the name would suggest, constructivists share an anti-foundationalist ontology, or the position that the world does not exist independently of our knowledge of it.[70]

There are two main tenets of constructivist thought, according to Alexander Wendt. First, constructivists hold 'that the structures of human association are determined primarily by shared ideas rather than material forces'.[71] Material forces are acknowledged to have some independent effects on international politics,[72] because ideas must be based on and limited to some extent by material reality.[73] What is argued, however, is that 'material resources only acquire meaning for human action through the structure of shared knowledge in which they are embedded'.[74] Structure cannot be material only or even mainly because material factors cannot constitute themselves as causes of action independent of the meaning given to them.[75]

Second, constructivists argue that the shared knowledge, understandings and expectations that make up the social structure of international politics does more than regulate and constrain the behaviour of actors whose interests are pre-existing. Normative structures also constitute state identities and interests.[76] Norms by definition are intimately tied to identity as they specify collective expectations of proper behaviour for a given identity. That is, in some instances they have constitutive effects by defining the identity of an actor and delineating the actions that 'cause' other relevant actors to recognise that identity and respond accordingly. Norms may also have regulative effects by specifying the standards of legitimate or proper behaviour associated with an already defined identity.[77] In combination, 'norms establish expectations about who the actors will be in a particular environment and about how these particular actors will behave'.[78]

Before moving on to an elaboration of a constructivist conceptualisation of hegemony it is important to differentiate between the 'logic of action' emphasised by materialist and normative theories of hegemony respectively. Materialist theories assume that rational state decision-makers choose between alternative courses of action based on what March and Olsen characterise as the 'logic of expected consequences'. Under this logic, actors 'choose among alternatives by evaluating their likely consequences for personal or collective objectives, conscious that other actors are doing likewise'.[79] Political order arises through cooperation where each actor rationally calculates that there might be gains from coordination in terms of their individual pre-given preferences through processes of bargaining and negotiation.[80] The social context in which actors interact is not given any independent role in the decision-making process with norms also approached in terms of utility maximisation. 'Actors construct and conform to norms because norms help them get what they want',[81] and not because they might be motivated by a belief in the legitimacy of the norm.

In contrast, constructivists draw attention to an alternative 'logic of action' which captures the process by which norms constitute identity and interest. Here action is rule-based and 'involves invoking an identity or role and matching the obligations of that identity or role to a specific situation'.[82] Drawing from the normative structure in which they act, actors internalise identities and rules associated with these identities and act in accordance with these prescriptions, not for instrumental purposes but because they understand the behaviour to be legitimate, or desirable, proper or appropriate in the circumstances.[83] Rather than being agent driven, the 'logic of appropriateness' necessarily posits a strong role for social structure in driving action. Whilst norms do not determine behaviour, the reasoning process involved is different from the logic of consequences in that an actor does not choose on the basis of expected utility but on the basis of which role or identity is called upon in a given situation.[84]

Given the position taken by constructivists on the nature of structure and the effects of structure on the formation of actor identities, interests and behaviour, how would constructivists approach the concept of hegemony? For constructivists, any understanding of the meaning of hegemony would require an inquiry into the cultural–institutional context in which states act which constitutes as well as regulates the identities and interests of all states. Whilst hegemony may be thought of as the existence of a materially dominant state in the system, it is the rules, institutions and norms of international society at a particular time which give meaning to hegemony.

As Wendt has argued, many different types of anarchy are possible depending on the identities and interests which form through the interaction between states over time.[85] One type of anarchy may resemble a realist world where states are self-regarding egoists who have learned through interaction to assume the worst about other states' intentions and to assume that states adhere to norms not because they value them, but because doing so achieves their self-defined interests. Thus, where a materially dominant state emerges, we can expect that international order is maintained, and can only be maintained, through the exercise of force or coercion, or the provision of material incentives as all actors essentially act under a logic of expected consequences.

This realist conception of hegemony is, however, but one possibility. Wendt argues that it is possible that through processes of interaction states may develop less egoistic and more positive identification with other states, such that security threats are not perceived to be a private matter but a collective responsibility.[86] In an international system inhabited by other-regarding states, the meaning attached to a unipolar distribution of material capabilities could involve a relationship between a hegemon and other states that was more akin to leadership than of dominance. This presupposes the development and acknowledgment of some sense of common identity and common interests, i.e. that an international society of states exists in which states conceive of themselves to be bound to observe certain standards of behaviour in their conduct with one another. Without a sense of collective interest and collective values, less-powerful states would have little need for a 'leader' that could take the initiative in terms of the achievement of common goals.

Before moving on to a discussion of the role prescription associated with 'hegemonic leadership', an important distinction must be made between materialist and constructivist approaches to hegemony in terms of the role of power in maintaining the stability of international order. The materialist conceptualisations of hegemony put forward a model of order in which the rules of order reflect the interests of the dominant states and are imposed upon the subordinate states in the system. Secondary states 'obey' the rules of order for two reasons: because they fear the sanction of the hegemon and/or because they calculate that obedience is within their self-interest defined materially. In March and Olsen's terms, within a realist hegemonic order states act upon a logic of expected consequences.

Such an order is both costly to maintain and highly unstable for a number of reasons. As Ian Hurd has argued, a system of order dependent on coercion is maintained at high cost because it requires substantial resources to both monitor and enforce compliance. Additionally, a coercive system is likely to generate resistance and resentment over time which suggests that such orders are prone to instability.[87] A system of order based on the provision of inducements is also likely to be costly to maintain and highly unstable because compliance is dependent upon a hegemon being capable of providing secondary states with 'a positive stream of benefits'.[88]

Further, for classical and structural realists, hegemonic systems are highly unstable and short-lived phenomena because either the structure of the international system or the vagaries of human nature cause states to balance against predominant power.[89] Regardless of how benevolent a dominant state may appear to be, the shadow of the future looms large for all states in the system. All states will seek to limit their vulnerability to exploitation through balancing behaviour to guard against the possibility that a hegemonic state might display less benevolent intentions in the future.[90] Thus under materialist conceptualisations of hegemony, a hegemonic order is costly to maintain, highly unstable and is likely to be short-lived in duration.

In contrast, a constructivist approach to hegemony is able to explain how a hegemonic system may in fact achieve longevity and stability based on a social view of power.[91] From this perspective, whilst a hegemon may in some cases need to coerce or bribe states to conform, where its leadership role and the rules and norms of the international order it promotes are accepted as legitimate, international order becomes self-enforcing in accordance with the logic of appropriateness. That is, subordinate states will conform to the norms of international order because of a belief that doing so is rightful, proper and appropriate.[92] In instrumental terms, a hegemon that is able to engender a belief in the legitimacy of its leadership role and the norms of order, is able to maintain order with less effort and cost than one that is not socially recognised. Where this occurs, subordinate states effectively redefine the meaning of 'self-interest' to include a commitment to the standards, laws, rules and norms present in international society at the intersubjective level.[93]

The link between the stability of order and legitimacy is however a double-edged sword: legitimacy acts as both a form of hegemonic power as well as a constraint on that power. Norms constitute hegemonic power by defining the range of legitimate behaviour that will cause other actors to recognise a state's identity as a leader. So, to be recognised as a leader, a dominant state must act in accordance with the expectations of proper behaviour associated with that role, and in doing so is entitled to expect that other states will act towards it in accordance with their own role prescriptions. If a hegemonic state is able to act within those expectations, it can in turn expect other states to acknowledge greater rights and responsibilities in relation to international order. That is, a hegemonic state becomes 'empowered' by the community of states with certain prerogatives and rights.

Alternatively, if a hegemonic state acts outside the bounds of legitimate behaviour associated with its identity as hegemonic leader, then the community of states has the capacity to withdraw recognition of its identity. As a consequence, a hegemon can no longer expect voluntary assistance in the achievement of common goals, but would have to resort to costly dominating behaviours in order to achieve its interests. The potential loss of societal recognition of a hegemon's leadership position thus has the capacity to constrain hegemonic power.

Whilst we have identified the constructivist view of hegemony as a socially recognised leadership role in international society, we have not discussed the expectations of legitimate behaviour which will cause other states to recognise its identity as a hegemonic leader. Precisely what these expectations are depend upon the normative structure of international society at a particular time as role prescriptions evolve through state practice in response to challenges to international order. A number of constructivists have sought to elucidate what 'hegemony' as leadership means in the contemporary period.

Drawing from Gramscian and English School theory,[94] scholars such as Cronin and Reus-Smit argue that subordinate states will follow a hegemonic leader if the basis of the international order it promotes is not purely exploitative but is universal in conception in the sense of being compatible with their interests.[95] Whilst the hegemon is recognised as having a greater interest and prerogatives in terms of maintaining system stability and order, in return subordinate states expect that the hegemon will accept certain limits in their efforts to do so. For Cronin, these limitations include 'that legal (sovereign) equality be maintained...; that the hegemon follow the rules and avoid unilateral acts that may violate them; that its freedom to manoeuvre be limited by its responsibilities;... that it accommodate the secondary powers of major importance' and that it follows procedural limits when acting in the role of hegemon.[96]

To substantiate this approach, in the empirical chapters to come we should expect to find evidence to support the constructivist conceptualisation of hegemony as a leadership role in international society with associated rights and obligations in relation to the maintenance of international order. As such, there should be evidence of the expectations of proper behaviour of the hegemon held by states which cause them to recognise and validate the identity as leader and respond to it appropriately.[97] In the case studies to follow, the norms enshrined in the UN Charter provide a framework for deriving the normative parameters of the role of hegemonic leader in the security realm. It is here that we find the post-Second World War core expectations for proper, rightful and appropriate behaviour between states in general as well as for those states acknowledged to have a leadership role in international society. As Innis Claude argued almost 50 years ago:

> [t]he phenomenal feature of 1945 was not so much that the Great Powers extracted concessions to their strength ... the Charter scheme represented acceptance by the great powers of a framework of constitutional limitations within which their de facto power was to be exercised.[98]

Here he was referring to both the recognition in the Charter of the responsibilities of the permanent five members of the Security Council over systemic matters, but also their responsibility, somewhat safeguarded by majority voting, to use their leadership position for the pursuit of common, rather than parochial, interests.

Whilst the terms of the Charter formally recognise a role prescription for 'leaders' in the security realm, it is the interpretation of these formal prescriptions in state practice which will provide us with the current expectations associated with the role of hegemonic leader. If we wish to understand how hegemonic leadership is constituted in the post-Cold War era, we need to delve deeper into state practice after 1989, a task that we will undertake through the examination of our two case studies.

Central hypotheses, methodology and research design

We are now left with two alternative theoretical conceptualisations of hegemony – hegemony as a relation of dominance and hegemony as a socially constituted leadership role in international society – which take divergent stances on the impact of legitimacy on the relationship between a hegemon and subordinate states, as a source or constraint on hegemonic power, and as a stabilising force for international order. In the case studies to follow, our aim is to evaluate which of these conceptualisations of hegemony provides us with the most compelling explanation of US hegemony in the post-Cold War era. To do so we ask the question: why did states choose to either follow the US or reject its leadership in either crisis? A conceptualisation of hegemony as dominance relationship would put forward material interests as 'causes' of state behaviour, whilst a conceptualisation of hegemony as a leadership rule would look for norms as a 'cause'.

The latter claim raises some methodological complications. It is acknowledged that it is difficult to fit the effects of social facts into a 'scientific' model of explanation and therefore make the claim that legitimacy has 'causal' effects. We say this, because the positivist covering law model of explanation is not easily applied to cases in which norms are a significant factor in the phenomena to be explained, for two reasons. First, unlike the initial conditions in positivist explanations, norms can be thought in limited instances as 'causing' occurrences. As Ruggie has explained:

> [n]orms may 'guide' behaviour, they may 'inspire' behaviour, they may 'rationalise' or 'justify' behaviour, they may express 'mutual expectations' about behaviour, or they may be ignored. But they do not represent a cause in the sense that a bullet through the heart causes death.[99]

Introduction and theoretical framework 19

Thus where norms are involved, it is difficult to come up with general covering laws. The second problem in applying a covering law model of explanation where norms are at issue is that, under the covering law model, even a single counterfactual occurrence places some doubt on the validity of the covering law.[100] Where norms are concerned, however, a single, or even many counterfactual occurrences do not necessarily refute a norm. Whether violations of a norm refute or invalidate it depends primarily upon if the violation is accepted by a large number of states who follow suit through practice.[101]

Whilst we cannot truly speak of legitimacy having true causal effects in the way it is used under scientific models of explanation, constructivists have come up with broadly causal arguments which problematise state identities and interests, and the cultural and institutional environments in which states act.[102] Norms can be said to constrain and enable forms of action by deeming some acts legitimate and not others. Using a rational-choice model, we hypothesise that legitimacy has three causal effects that can be directly applied to US attempts to assert leadership over the international community in both crises. First, legitimacy constrains and enables the choice of certain preferences by deeming some preferences desirable, proper and appropriate and not others. In the case of the use of force, legitimacy constrains and enables the range of goals or interests states seek to achieve through its use. Second, legitimacy constrains and enables the choice of means by which states attain their interests, by deeming some desirable, proper and appropriate, and not others. Third, the ability of a state to hold a socially recognised leadership position within international society is constrained and enabled by shared normative beliefs about legitimate behaviour associated with that role.

Thus, to assess the persuasiveness of our two opposing theoretical conceptualisations, both material and normative hypotheses are put forward to explain the 'causes' of followership or the rejection of US leadership. If hegemony is most aptly defined as a relation of material dominance, then we would expect that the decisions of subordinate states to either accept or reject US leadership are primarily derived from rational calculations about the material costs or benefits that would accrue from doing so. If hegemony is more accurately defined as a socially recognised leadership role, then we would expect to find good evidence that followership or the rejection of US leadership was the result of a normative assessment of whether the practice of leadership by the US conformed to the expectations of legitimate behaviour associated with a leadership role in international society. Here we would also expect that followership or rejection of US leadership was influenced by a normative assessment of whether the vision or plan put forward by the US to resolve the particular threat to international order was legitimate in relation to its goals and means. In other words, it is hypothesised that legitimacy can have 'causal' effects.

The research design of the book reflects the goal of evaluating the two major theoretical approaches to hegemony against the actual practice of hegemony in two case studies. We have chosen two case studies in which the United States sought to take leadership over international society, in the context of the purported threat to international peace and security derived from particular actions taken (or not taken) by the state of Iraq, and which called for the consideration of collective support for the use of force. As we have mentioned earlier, we have chosen to focus on the use of force because theories within the realist tradition claim to provide superior explanations of 'high politics' and it is in this area that the greatest degree of scepticism exists about the efficacy of norms in changing the behaviour of states. Whilst most studies of hegemony focus on the behaviour of the hegemonic state itself, here attention is primarily given to the potential motives for followership among subordinate states. This is necessary because the two alternative conceptualisations of hegemony depend upon the exercise of different forms of power – coercive, reward and legitimate – and distinguishing between these forms can only be done by isolating the motives of the subordinate states rather than those of the hegemon. Further, as Gow and Bellou have argued, it is the 'alters' image' or the 'perceptions and expectations of other states and governments concerning the leader's policies' which 'determines the legitimisation of leadership'.[103] A hegemon's self-perceptions of the legitimacy of its own leadership practices are irrelevant unless shared by the society of states it seeks to lead.

A case-study method has been chosen because the importance of legitimacy to the operation of hegemonic systems can only be substantiated through an in-depth study of actor motivations. To be able to determine whether states were motivated by their normative beliefs, we are faced with the problem that norms are not directly observable.[104] Whilst they may be intangible, they can be observed to the extent that agents seek to justify their actions to their social peers. Thus, a number of constructivist scholars have sought to find evidence of the normative context in which states act through the reasons for action given by decision-makers at key decision points.[105] As Finnemore argues:

> when states justify their interventions, they are drawing on and articulating shared values and expectations held by other decision-makers and other publics in other states. It is literally an attempt to connect one's actions to standards of justice or perhaps more generically, to standards of appropriate and acceptable behaviour.[106]

The justifications used by state representatives for political decisions provide us with evidence of the normative context in which these decisions are made. It is via these justifications that we are able to identify expectations of legitimate behaviour which may have motivated states to reject or accept US leadership in our chosen case studies.

In terms of evidentiary sources for state justifications for action, in both the 1991 Gulf War and the 2003 Iraq War the significance of the threat to international peace and security activated the interest of the general United Nations Membership and the UN Security Council. As such, there is a large volume of statements made by state representatives about their reasons for either supporting or rejecting the US's proposals for the resolution of both crises. Where these statements were insufficient to flesh out the possible normative motivations of states, reliance is placed upon personal memoirs, biographies and autobiographies, as well as news reports.

In relying on the justifications used by state representatives as a means of identifying motivations for action, we are faced with a methodological problem. What of the possibility that there is a gap between a state's public justifications for action and their actual motivations? In discussing this problem, Wheeler draws attention to the work of Quentin Skinner on the constraining role played by language on action. Skinner argues that even if an agent claims to be acting on the basis of a normative principle but is in fact insincere, their room for manoeuvre will be constrained by their public justifications. Action must plausibly be consistent with the normative justifications given for them.[107] However, as Wheeler points out, this does not completely close the gap, particularly in the international context where rules and norms are often delimited imprecisely.[108]

Whilst there is no watertight solution to this methodological problem, we have, through our research design, attempted to determine how wide the gap is between justifications and motivations on a case-by-case basis. Confidence is not placed on the public justifications of states alone as the basis for explanation. That is, because our evidence of normative motivations relies primarily upon the justifications of states for their actions, we have also examined other additional motivating factors – material factors – that could otherwise also plausibly explain followership or rejection of US leadership in each case study. Ultimately, we have sought to evaluate whether notions of legitimacy provide a necessary and sufficient explanation for the decisions of potential follower states.

The research design of the book reflects our aim to evaluate whether hegemony should be conceptualised in terms of material dominance or in terms of a leadership role in international society. To do this we investigate whether 'followership' or lack of followership of the US in the two case studies was substantially motivated by the material interests of states and/or their normative beliefs about legitimate state behaviour and the exercise of leadership in international society. Each case study investigates the motives for followership of the United States, or the rejection of its leadership as the case may be, and is divided into two chapters.

The first chapter of each case study (Chapters 2 and 4) are devoted to investigating the normative motivations for followership. We confine our discussion to examining whether states were motivated to follow the US by a belief in the legitimacy of the 'vision' it put forward for the resolution of the crisis in terms of its goals and means, or failed to follow because of a rejection of this 'vision' on normative grounds. The subset of international norms that proved relevant were those related to the resolution of disputes between states, particularly the norms governing the use of force. Here we also look for evidence of the expectations of legitimate behaviour associated with the role of leader in international society, and whether these expectations further influenced state responses to US assertions of leadership.

The second chapter of each case study (Chapters 3 and 5) are committed to investigating the material motivations for followership or the rejection of US leadership. In these chapters we focus on four states which played an integral part in the original coalition against Iraq in 1990–1991 because of either their military or financial contributions: Germany, Japan, France and the United Kingdom. These states have been chosen because their involvement contributed significantly to the success of the group enterprise as a whole. We return to study the motives of these states in our second case study which provides an opportunity to compare the factors that may have motivated them to either oppose or persist in supporting the leadership of the US 11 years later.

In these chapters three material factors are isolated that may have affected the decision by states to either make a significant contribution to the US-led coalition or to reject participation: oil dependence, shared material threat assessments and alliance dependence. In relation to the first material factor, it is possible that state decisions were influenced by a dependency on oil as a fuel source and the material interest in safeguarding supplies of oil from the Middle East at a reasonable price. Second, we take the material components of Stephen Walt's balance of threat theory, and ask whether states were motivated to follow the US because of a shared threat perception of Iraq, based on its aggregate power, geographic proximity and offensive capabilities – the traditional realist explanations for power balancing behaviour. Walt also argues that threat perceptions are formed on the basis of an assessment of an adversary's perceived intentions. It is argued, however, that perceptions of intent are to a large degree dependent upon an assessment of an adversary's past behaviour and the extent to which it conforms to expectations about legitimate conduct between states in international society. That is, an assessment of 'perceived intent' is more correctly viewed as a normative motivation for action. We have therefore dealt with motivations based on shared perceptions of Iraq's threatening intentions separate to an analysis of material assessments of the Iraqi threat.

Third, we ask whether the decision to follow or reject US leadership was motivated by the presence or absence of a significant alliance dependency upon the US. All states in alliances with more powerful partners face a dilemma when deciding whether to support their stronger ally in a conflict that is not integral to the pursuit of their own national security. Two fears arise: first, the fear that a failure to support the alliance will lead to abandonment in a future conflict which does threaten national security directly; second, the fear of becoming entrapped in or entangled in a costly but ultimately low-priority war. It is likely that a state would follow the US where its fears of abandonment outweighed its fears of entrapment, with the opposite being true where US leadership was rejected.

Finally, in Chapter 6 of the book a comparative analysis of the two case studies is made to determine which motivations, material and normative, are able to best explain the pattern of followership or the rejection of US leadership in both cases. Here, we also assess whether the approach to leadership taken by the two US Administrations of Bush Senior and Junior had a significant impact on the decisions by states to follow the US or to reject US leadership. Our overarching purpose is to use these empirical findings to make an informed assessment of which theoretical conceptualisation of hegemony – as a relation of dominance or as a socially recognised leadership role – provides the most cogent and persuasive explanation of events in both studies. Given the relative ascendancy of material approaches to hegemony in IR scholarship, the book hopes to determine whether a normative approach in fact provides a deeper and more accurate understanding of the operation of hegemonic systems, including the scope and limits of hegemonic power in the post-Cold War era.

In comparing both case studies, we have found that international legitimacy and the material factor of alliance dependence were the most significant motivations for followership of the US or the rejection of US leadership in either case. Whilst alliance dependency proved to be a strong motivating factor for state action for France, Germany, Japan and the UK, it could not however completely explain the breadth and depth of followership in the first case, or the rejection of US leadership in the second. Followership can be directly traced to state beliefs in the legitimacy of the US plan of action or vision for the resolution of the crisis, as well as a belief in the legitimacy of US leadership itself. Essential to the latter was the perception that the United States was acting as leader to achieve the interests of the collective, rather than to exploit the position of leadership for the pursuit of its own interests. Similarly, the rejection of US leadership, particularly in the second case, can in turn be traced to the shared belief among a majority of states that the US vision was illegitimate in terms of its goals and means. Further, states were also shown to be reacting to US behaviour which fell outside the expectations of proper behaviour associated with a 'leadership role' in society. Particularly, states reacted to the perception that US attempts to lead the international community were motivated by a desire to achieve its own self-defined interests rather than common interests of all states. Overall, in terms of our empirical aims, we argue that, without a consideration of the impact of legitimacy on the formation of state interests, an explanation of either case study is substantially incomplete.

In theoretical terms, we will argue that our findings support the view that hegemony in the post-Cold War era should be conceptualised as a leadership role within international society rather than in purely material terms. Such a conceptualisation is able to provide a more complete and persuasive explanation of events in international relations. This conceptualisation draws attention to the role of legitimacy as both a form of power as well as a constraint on power. This is particularly apparent in terms of the willingness of states to share in the burdens of maintaining international order. The ability of the society of states to recognise or to withdraw recognition of the leadership status of a hegemon within international society is itself a form of power which impacts on the costs associated with the maintenance of order as well as its longevity and stability. Thus, whilst the society of states was unable to prevent the United States from achieving regime change in Iraq, it has been able force the US to bear alone the sizeable costs of conducting the war and restoring order and government in Iraq.

2 Legitimacy and hegemony in the Gulf Crisis

The international response to the Iraqi invasion of Kuwait in August 1990 is a historical event that is commonly categorised as an almost ideal case of collective security in action as envisaged under the UN Charter. Here the Security Council was able to come to agreement relatively quickly on both the identification of the invasion as a 'threat to international peace and security' under Article 39 and on the appropriate measures to take to restore it under Articles 41 and 42. For some, the strong international consensus that emerged on these two issues showed that a majority of states held strong beliefs about the legitimacy of core principles enshrined in the Charter, principles which were seen to be obviously breached by the invasion and therefore worthy of defence.

In the Gulf Crisis, the United States also undeniably led the international response to the invasion in diplomatic, financial and military terms. In the Security Council it acted as the clear agenda-setter, initiating and garnering support for key resolutions which applied a series of serious and escalating measures on the Iraqi regime. In military terms, the US displayed an unwavering commitment to the defence of Saudi Arabia, the enforcement of an embargo and the forcible eviction of Iraq by contributing the bulk of the military forces in the coalition, a coalition which in the end included forces from 40 states from all corners of the globe and a wide range of political persuasions.[1] It is also clear from the statements of US leaders that these acts were undertaken with the conscious intent to play an international leadership role. As Secretary of State James Baker argued before Congress, '[w]e remain the one nation that has the necessary political, military and economic instruments at our disposal to catalyze a successful response by the international community.'[2]

This seeming unity of the international community behind the leadership of the United States provides us with a useful case in which to study the attempts by the US to assert hegemonic leadership over the international community and the significance of legitimacy as a consideration by states in largely accepting this aspiration. In our earlier discussion of the theoretical treatment of the concept of hegemony in IR scholarship, we determined that hegemony is usually characterised as either a relationship of dominance or of leadership, with the former being primarily reliant on the exercise of coercive or reward power to keep subordinate states in line, and the latter on the phenomenon on self-enforcement derived from a normative acceptance of the legitimacy of a hegemonic order. In this and the following chapter, our goal is to evaluate which conceptualisation of hegemony is most persuasively supported by the events in the Gulf Crisis.

To do this, the following two chapters ask the question: why did states choose to follow the lead of the United States in the Gulf Crisis of 1990–1991? Some may argue that the unity of the international community behind US leadership did indeed stem from a normative commitment to the UN Charter system, the hierarchical relations enshrined within it and a normative belief in the legitimacy of the US 'vision' for the resolution of the crisis. All of this would support a demonstration of hegemony as a leadership role of international society. On the other hand, others may view the response of the international community as a chance overlap between material and normative interests, with the former being the real and decisive factor in explaining state responses to the crisis. Followership motivated by a fear of coercion or through a rational calculation of material self-interest would in contrast provide evidence of hegemony as a dominance relationship over other states.

In order to obtain an accurate explanation of why states followed the lead of the United States in the Gulf Crisis, we will need to examine the evidence in relation to states' reasons for action. In this chapter we will focus upon the extent to which beliefs about legitimate conduct among states were significant in motivating or driving actions to support the US-led coalition in dealing with the invasion of Kuwait through their political, financial and military support. In the next chapter we will examine in more depth the material interests which may have motivated key states in supporting the US-led coalition through such contributions. Because motives for action are usually mixed between the normative and the material, our standard for success cannot be that legitimacy or material interests alone motivated state action. Rather, our standard is whether an explanation of the course of the Gulf Crisis of 1990–1991 is substantially incomplete or flawed without taking account of the normative beliefs of states with regard to legitimate conduct in international relations.

I hypothesise that a broad spectrum of states were significantly motivated to follow the US because of their belief in the illegitimacy of the Iraqi invasion, and the legitimacy of the solution to the crisis or 'vision' put forward by the United States to reverse it. These beliefs and normative processes are most easily accessible through public statements in which decision-makers seek to give reasons to justify the decisions they have made. Focus is therefore placed on arguments put forward by Members of the Security Council, key regional organisations and states to justify or oppose the important decisions made by the Council throughout the crisis.

The analysis to follow will be divided into four sections, representing the four main decisions taken by the international community in response to the Iraqi invasion of Kuwait. These include the decisions to characterise the situation as a threat to international peace and security, to set the liberation of Kuwait as the only appropriate end goal, to choose economic sanctions in the first instance and, finally, when this was perceived to have failed, to use force as the ultimate means to achieve this goal. Within these four sections, the normative justifications used by states to support their decisions will be analysed to determine the extent to which normative beliefs about legitimate state behaviour affected the actions taken by the parties.

Part 1: defining the situation and goal setting

Within four hours of the Iraqi invasion of Kuwait on the morning of 2 August 1990, the Security Council met at the behest of the governments of Kuwait and the United States to discuss and vote upon the text of a draft resolution.[3] This draft was adopted in full with 13 Members in support and one abstaining. Resolution 660 (1990) determined that there was a 'breach of international peace and security as regards the Iraqi invasion of Kuwait' and acting under Articles 39 and 40 of the Charter, condemned the invasion, demanded that Iraq withdraw all its forces to their 1 August positions 'immediately and unconditionally', and called upon Iraq and Kuwait to begin 'intensive negotiations' for the resolution of their differences, with the support of the League of Arab States.

Reaching consensus in the Security Council

The reaching of consensus in the Security Council on the substance of Resolution 660 came quickly and with little difficulty. Within hours of the invasion, the US Ambassador to the UN, Tom Pickering, had been instructed by his President to draft a resolution condemning the Iraqi invasion and demanding an immediate and unconditional withdrawal. He was also asked to attempt to convene an emergency session of the Security Council. By 12 a.m. on the 2 August (US time) a draft resolution had been constructed by the US, UK and Kuwaiti representatives to the UN. By the start of the emergency meeting of the Council at 5.10 a.m., requested by Kuwait and the US, nine states had agreed to its terms and had put their names to the draft as sponsors.[4] The meeting was to last just under an hour with 13 out of 14 states giving their assent to the draft, with the representative of Yemen abstaining after not being able to obtain instructions from his government.

The US clearly asserted leadership of the international community on the issue of the Iraqi invasion by taking the initiative to draft the resolution which was to become Resolution 660 and spurring the Council to take emergency action. There is no evidence to suggest any disagreements or bargaining among the members on the terms of the resolution. Rather, consensus was reached freely and easily, and as will be seen below, stemmed predominantly from a genuine agreement that Iraq's actions were grossly illegitimate and that the implications were serious enough to warrant the invocation of the Council's Chapter VII powers.

Legitimacy and state justifications for action

The statements made by members of the Security Council prior to the vote on Resolution 660 provide strong evidence that there was almost universal

Legitimacy and hegemony in the Gulf Crisis 27

agreement among them that the invasion needed to be harshly condemned. The attack was described by some Members in vigorous terms, with the US describing it as a 'heinous act ... contrary to the Charter, international law, and all the fully accepted norms of international behaviour',[5] Canada as a 'brutal' form of 'aggression',[6] the UK expressing its 'disgust' that such a thing could happen at that point in history[7] and Finland speaking of the 'gross violation' of the Charter.[8] The strength of the condemnation of Iraq stemmed largely from normative commitments to some of the core principles and rules of the post-Second World War international order.

In justifying their strong condemnation of the Iraqi invasion, all states referred to accepted principles of legitimate behaviour between states which they believed had been breached. Of the 11 states that gave justifications for their position, all directly referred, alone or in combination, to the normative principles that disputes between states should be resolved peacefully, that the threat or use of force between states was not permissible at any time (Article 2(4) of the Charter), and/or that force should not be used aggressively.[9] In addition, Colombia, Malaysia and Yemen also defended the importance of the principle of sovereignty and the rights associated with its protection, namely freedom from outside interference in domestic affairs (Article 2(7) of the Charter), self-determination, and the respect for political independence and territorial integrity.[10] Not one state provided a non-normative justification for their condemnation of the Iraqi invasion, and all states who gave a statement of their reasons did so on the basis that Iraq's actions were illegitimate when assessed against the core standards of appropriate behaviour represented in the UN Charter and International law.

Legitimacy and the broader UN membership

The outcry against the Iraqi invasion beyond the Security Council was just as strong among regional organisations and members of General Assembly, showing a remarkable breadth of normative consensus as well as agreement that the only acceptable solution was Iraq's restoration of Kuwaiti sovereignty. The three regional organisations whose members were directly affected by the invasion, the Gulf Cooperation Council (GCC), the League of Arab States (LAS) and the Organisation of Islamic Conference (OIC), expressed their condemnation of the Iraqi 'aggression' in strong terms, with the LAS and OIC rejecting Iraq's claims to sovereignty over Kuwaiti territory, and the GCC stating that the aggression 'constitute[d] a flagrant violation of the independence and sovereignty of a member of the GCC, the Arab League and UN as well as a blatant violation of all Arab, Islamic and international charters, norms and laws'.[11] The EC also found Iraq's actions illegitimate because it breached 'the UN Charter' and constituted an 'unacceptable means to solve international differences'.[12] All groups justified their response in terms of the illegitimacy of Iraq's actions as assessed by common principles of appropriate behaviour they all shared – the non-use of force to resolve disputes between states, the respect for sovereignty, territorial integrity and non-interference in the internal affairs of states.[13]

To get a broader idea of the views of Member states generally about their assessments of the invasion, an analysis has been made of the speeches of 39 states to the General Assembly in 1990/1991. This group of states includes all those who contributed military or financial support to the multinational coalition which enforced the embargo, defended Kuwait or contributed military and other forces that took part in the Gulf War of 1991 and who made statements in the General Assembly. These states were chosen because, as outward 'followers', their statements will help us determine what motivated them to support the US position. In addition, the statements of Brazil, India and Indonesia were also included to represent the views of states in South America, the sub-continent and Asia, as were the views of the Permanent Members of the Security Council.

The views of this sample of states are represented in Table 2.1, Appendix 1. All of these states endorsed the twin goals of restoring the legitimate Kuwaiti government and the immediate and unconditional Iraqi withdrawal from Kuwaiti territory. The goal of achieving the release of foreign nationals being held against their will in Iraq was expressed by 46 per cent of states in their addresses, showing that this was an important but lesser concern. Whilst the table appears to be weighted towards a normative explanation of state motives for following the US lead, not one state provided a material explanation for their condemnation of the invasion and support for the restoration of Kuwaiti sovereignty.

These goals were viewed as the only legitimate responses for two related reasons. First, 69 per cent of states maintained that Iraq's actions constituted a grave threat to international peace and security precisely because it breached the core principles upon which the post-Second World War order had been built, with more than half the sample states referring to Iraq's failure to respect the principle of sovereignty and the peaceful settlement of disputes. Further, only four out of 40 states failed to specifically cite the illegitimacy of aggression. The invasion was thus seen to be a 'litmus test' for what the United Nations could become,[14] with 41 per cent of the view that a failure to address such grave breaches would gravely undermine the UN collective security system as a whole.

Particularly emotive was the repeated warnings that a failure to act here, in a case of clear aggression, would likely be fatal to the organisation, just as the failure of the League of Nations to address the invasion of Ethiopia had ended the collective security experiment before the Second World War.[15] Poland's predictions were most expressive of this point with its representative stating that the 'United Nations will be unable to have even modest achievements in any of the basic areas of world co-operation if aggression goes unpunished, frontiers are violated and States are annexed'.[16] Further, 28 per cent of states directly supported strong action against Iraq because the security of small states was particularly at risk if the fruits of aggression were allowed to stand.

Conclusion

The support for the US vision for the international response to the invasion appears to be most clearly explained by the logic of appropriateness rather than the logic of expected consequences. In the negotiations within the Security Council over the draft of Resolution 660, there is no evidence to suggest that members of the Security Council or states outside it were motivated to follow the lead of the US because of the application of any threats, coercion or monetary or other incentives, and no evidence that any resistance to the US plan was expressed.

Rather, in their public statements, decision-makers drew from their beliefs about legitimate behaviour between states to justify support for the US proposals. Almost all states in the Council, key regional organisations and a large number of individual states agreed that the Iraqi invasion constituted grossly illegitimate behaviour between states because it breached core rules and principles of international order designed to keep the peace. Consistent with this was the overwhelming view that the goal proposed by the US for the international community, that is the liberation of Kuwait, was the only legitimate solution to the crisis. Thus, from the evidence we have examined here, followership of the US was largely motivated by a belief in the illegitimacy of Iraq's actions on normative grounds, and an endorsement of the US proposed goal for the resolution of the crisis as the only legitimate or proper and appropriate response.

Part 2: deciding on non-military means to achieve the end goal

The lightning response of the Security Council to the invasion decided clearly that the invasion was unjustifiable and illegitimate. The material facts had been categorised and an end goal identified, but the means by which to achieve this goal had yet to be decided. Resolution 660 simply demanded an immediate and unconditional withdrawal of Iraqi forces from Kuwait. With little response from the Iraqi regime being forthcoming, it took a mere four days for the Security Council to debate and decide upon the terms of a further resolution which would impose economic sanctions.

Again, the response of the international community was swift and almost unanimous. This time the draft resolution was sponsored by ten states[17] rather than eight and was accepted without amendment on 6 August 1990 with 13 votes in favour, and two abstentions from Cuba and Yemen. Resolution 661 (1990) required that all states prevent imports to, and exports from, Iraq or Kuwait, the sale or supply of any commodities and products into Kuwait or Iraq (with the exception of medical supplies and foodstuffs), the freezing of Iraqi and Kuwaiti financial and economic resources held overseas, and to stop the provision of funds to the Government of Iraq or any other business undertaking in Kuwait. States were also called upon to take appropriate measures to protect the assets of the 'legitimate' government of Kuwait and to refrain from recognising any regime set up by Iraq.[18]

Reaching consensus

In the days following the invasion, the United States turned its full attention to deciding how the goal of liberating Kuwait would be achieved. As early as the morning of 2 August 1990, the US National Security Council discussed the possibility of using economic sanctions as a tool to reverse the invasion, as well as an economic embargo on Iraqi and Kuwaiti oil supplies. At this meeting President Bush instructed his advisors to seek support for a further Security Council resolution to impose economic sanctions on Iraq.[19] By the end of the day, US officials had already made contact with European allies to seek their support for economic sanctions and asked the USSR, France, Italy and China to stop arms shipments to Iraq.[20] Taking the lead on this issue, President Bush announced on 2 August that he had signed an executive order that morning to freeze Iraqi assets in the US, prohibit transactions with Iraq, freeze Kuwaiti assets[21] and called on other states to do the same. On August 3 a more comprehensive range of economic sanctions was put in place by the US via an executive order of the President.[22]

In the memoirs of the prominent US decision-makers President George Bush, National Security Advisor Brent Scowcroft and Secretary of State James Baker, all three recount the importance placed on gaining support for economic sanctions from as many states as possible to counter the perception that the US was merely pursuing its own particularistic interests, and to ensure that the situation would be viewed as a fight in which Iraq 'confront[ed] the entire civilised world'.[23] Over the next few days President Bush approached longstanding allies to gain support for the imposition of economic sanctions.[24] On 4 August, the members of the EC agreed to impose a comprehensive range of economic sanctions on Iraq, including a ban on arms and oil sales and measures to freeze Iraqi assets and protect those of Kuwait and its citizens.[25] These measures represented the strongest and most decisive punitive action ever taken by the European Community, which contrasted with the indecisive position taken in response to earlier crises such as the US hostage affair in Tehran, or following the Soviet invasion of Afghanistan.[26] Around the same time Japan announced the imposition of a similar range of sanctions, as did the United Kingdom[27] with Margaret Thatcher publicly expressing her support for further Chapter VII measures should Iraq fail to comply with Resolution 660.[28]

Of the other Permanent Members, the USSR needed no persuasion on the issue of the imposition of economic sanctions. On 6 August, both states released a joint statement which reiterated their assessment of the illegitimacy of Iraq's actions in strong terms, detailing the sanctions that they had already put in place – the suspension of arms deliveries by the USSR and the freezing of assets by the US – and called upon 'the rest of the international community to join with us in an international cut-off of all arms supplies to Iraq'.[29] China was also supportive, announcing a ban on arms sales to Iraq on 5 August.[30]

Legitimacy and the Security Council

In the statements provided by Security Council members prior to their vote on the proposed Resolution 661, predominantly normative arguments were used to justify their assent to its terms. Only one state, the United States, mentioned any non-normative justification for the imposition of sanctions: the threat to 'international economic health and stability' should Iraq be allowed to control '30 per cent of the region's oil production.'[31] Apart from this, statements in the Council continued to reflect a belief in the serious illegitimacy of Iraq's actions that now justified an equally serious response to reverse it. Action needed to be taken quickly and decisively to support the credibility of international law in general, of core UN Charter principles, and in turn the credibility of the UN Charter system of enforcement.

The preoccupation of members of the Council with the aggressive use of force by Iraq should be seen in the context of the end of the Cold War, which for many states held the promise of re-activating the stalled post-Second World War order. At this point in time, whilst President Bush had not yet made his famous 'new world order' address, elements of it, such as the reiteration of Winston Churchill's call for a world order in which 'the principles of justice and fair play ... protect the weak against the strong'[32] were foreshadowed here. Thus US representative Mr Pickering noted that this was only the second time in history that the Security Council had imposed wide-ranging economic sanctions on a state, 'reflect[ing] a new world order of international co-operation in the Council and elsewhere'.[33] This was mirrored by comments of the representative of the USSR who declared that the invasion '[went] against the positive international trends and the improvement in international life'.[34]

The shared conception of the situation as one involving the aggressive use of force in turn can be seen to have compelled members of the Council to take serious action to prevent it from occurring in the future. The US emphatically declared that

> by our action today, we will declare for all that we will not countenance the continuation or repetition of this aggression ... Iraq's aggression must be – and will be – stopped, lest Iraq, or others, conclude that its will can prevail.[35]

This sentiment was echoed also by Canada[36] and Zaire.[37] As members of the Security Council, a role or identity imbuing these states with responsibility for the maintenance of international peace and security, such action was normatively expected of them by the rest of the international community. Given that economic sanctions had only been applied against one other state, Southern Rhodesia,[38] in the history of the UN, economic sanctions were considered to have sufficiently onerous consequences, at this stage, which fit the serious 'crime' that had been committed.[39] More significantly, the sanctions regime imposed on Iraq was in fact the 'broadest range of sanctions ever put in place against a State Member' of the United Nations. Whilst it was acknowledged that significant hardship would be placed not only on Iraq but also on its major trading partners, it was believed that these 'sacrifices [were] necessary to maintain ... the integrity of the international system ... safeguard the rule of law and to deter future aggressors'.[40]

Whilst it was agreed that the situation required serious action, the response of the Council was still circumscribed by a normative commitment to the peaceful settlement of the dispute. No one state called for the use of force at this early stage, and two states, Malaysia and the United Kingdom,[41] specified that the draft resolution would not support the use of force, whilst China emphasised the efforts to resolve the crisis by a number of Arab states. Malaysia particularly made clear that its support for the draft was 'predicated on the premise that it will remove the prospect of any unilateral military or quasi-military action in the region by outside Powers'.[42] Thus it was clear that, at this early stage, states believed that serious but peaceful means of obtaining Iraq's compliance with Resolution 660 were the only legitimate means available.

Legitimacy and the General Assembly

The addresses made by states to the 45th Session of the General Assembly provide us with some insight into the level of support given to the choice of economic sanctions as the means to reverse the invasion, as well as the underlying justifications for this. The analysis that follows again draws from the same sample of the addresses of 39 states used in Table 2.1, Appendix 1, but isolates the issue of the choice of means. As shown in Table 2.2, Appendix 1, of the sample, 90 per cent of states expressed their support for economic sanctions and 62 per cent directly justified their support for sanctions on the basis of the principle that disputes between states should be settled by peaceful means. Of these states, the consensus view was that, if at all possible, the international community should attempt to 'put a stop to aggression while avoiding war'.[43] Of particular note for our next chapter, the commitment to the peaceful settlement of the dispute was clearly expressed by both the representatives of Japan and West Germany.[44]

Conclusion

In this episode, there is clear evidence to show that the US sought to lead the international response to the invasion by proposing that sanctions be used to encourage the Iraqis to withdraw. US decision-makers made considerable efforts to gather support for this approach, which were successful prior to the meeting of the Security Council on 6 August with respect to members of the European Union, Japan and the USSR. At the start of the meeting, nine states had joined the US in sponsoring a draft resolution to impose sanctions on Iraq. The statements made by Permanent and non-Permanent Members of the Council reflect a strong consensus view that Iraq's invasion was grossly illegitimate when assessed against the core principles of legitimate conduct between states expressed in international law and the UN Charter. As such, the Iraqi aggression could not be allowed to stand because of the damage that would be done to the credibility of the UN collective security system. As a serious and grave breach of commonly held core principles of international order, serious action was needed to oppose it.

Legitimacy and hegemony in the Gulf Crisis 33

Economic sanctions were agreed to represent such serious action, with sufficiently onerous consequences for the aggressor, whilst also fitting within the principle that disputes between states should be settled by peaceful means. Interestingly, only the United States expressed a material reason for justifying the imposition of sanctions. The analysis undertaken of the statements made at the 45th Session of the General Assembly confirm that a majority of states raised these principles of legitimate behaviour in justifying their support for the imposition of economic sanctions. No state in the sample mentioned any material justification for their support for sanctions. In this episode, using public statements alone as evidence, a strong majority of states followed the US lead in imposing economic sanctions against Iraq because of a belief in the legitimacy of this choice of means in achieving the goal of liberating Kuwait.

Part 3: escalating enforcement – deciding to enforce the embargo

On 25 August 1990, the Security Council met to discuss and vote upon a resolution which would effectively allow for the military enforcement of economic sanctions upon Iraq and occupied Kuwait. The decision by the Security Council to impose economic sanctions on Iraq under Chapter VII activated the duty of all Member States to comply with its terms, but did not provide for the possibility of non-compliance by either Member States or Iraq.[45] Resolution 655 was passed in the context of continued defiance by Iraq of Security Council resolutions and an escalation in its breach of legitimate standards of behaviour.

Since the passing of Resolution 660 and 661, Iraq continued to show a strong disregard for international law by declaring the annexation of Kuwait by Iraq, and taking hostage a large number of Western diplomats and citizens, acts that were again condemned in Resolutions 662 and 664. Of all the resolutions that had been passed so far, the negotiations surrounding the adoption of Resolution 665 were the most contentious. As moves were made to use more serious means of achieving the liberation of Kuwait, differences emerged on whether there needed to be a shift in means from economic sanctions alone, to sanctions backed by force.

On 25 August 1990, seven states submitted the draft of a resolution providing UN Security Council authorisation to the US, UK and any other interested state to enforce economic sanctions on Iraq and Kuwait, including powers to stop and search all inward and outward shipping, and to use force where necessary to detain any ships that refused cargo inspection.[46] The wording of the draft omitted any explicit mention of the use of force but instead called upon states with naval forces in the Gulf to use '*such measures commensurate to the specific circumstances as may be necessary* under the authority of the Security Council to halt all inward and outward maritime shipping' (my emphasis).[47] The resolution was passed with 13 states in favour, with Cuba and Yemen abstaining. In making this decision, beliefs about the legitimacy of the use of force appeared to play a strong role in guiding the eventual outcome.

Reaching consensus in the Security Council on Resolution 665

In the weeks that followed the adoption of Resolution 661, the predictable threat to the effectiveness of the sanctions regime came not from the failure of states to cease trading with Iraq, but from the efforts by Iraq to break the embargo.[48] Despite the lack of explicit provision in Resolution 661 for the enforcement of the sanctions regime, the United States and the UK believed they had authority to do so as an act of collective self-defence stemming from Article 51 of the UN Charter, having received a request from the Emir of Kuwait on 12 August 'to take appropriate steps as necessary to ensure that the UN mandated economic sanctions against Iraq and Kuwait are immediately and effectively implemented'.[49] With this in view, the US and UK announced that their warships operating in the region would intercept ships suspected of violating the sanctions and use 'minimum force' should they refuse to cooperate.[50] This announcement met with almost immediate criticism from France, Canada and the Soviet Union, who argued that no state could implement the sanctions resolution unilaterally.[51]

Rather than persisting with the assertion of a legal right to act under Article 51, President Bush chose to alter course on the advice of Secretary of State James Baker and the US and UK Ambassadors to the UN.[52] Baker argued that it was important to attempt to maintain the strong consensus position against the invasion, particularly in the event that the crisis would require greater investment, acknowledging the strategic importance of a legitimising UN Security Council resolution.[53] The USSR was initially very reluctant to move to a military enforcement of the embargo; however, when it became clear that Iraq was not responsive to last-ditch attempts to negotiate a peaceful withdrawal, Soviet objections were withdrawn.[54]

The US first draft

At this time the US began to sound out its position on a possible further resolution with the other Permanent Members. Its preferred option was for the Security Council to delegate authority to use force to the various states with naval forces in the Gulf, with each retaining operational control over their own forces. The alternative approach preferred by the Soviet Union and China[55] was to utilise the dormant Chapter VII provisions for the making of force agreements with the Security Council,[56] with a state's armed forces placed under the command of the Military Staff Committee.[57] Under this option, the Security Council would have operational command of the ad hoc naval coalition in the Gulf. With mounting evidence of Iraqi attempts to break the embargo, the US and UK saw the need to find a negotiated solution or otherwise risk undermining the credibility of the sanctions regime in the eyes of the Iraqi leadership. The draft resolution finally presented to the Security Council on 25 August contained two concessions to the Soviet and Chinese: a dilution of the language used to authorise the use of force; and an ambiguous reference to an oversight role for the Military Staff Committee.[58]

Concessions on both sides

The Soviet Union's objections to the initial draft were based on two concerns, both principled and pragmatic. First, support for the peaceful resolution of interstate conflicts and the central role of the collective security mechanisms within the UN Charter formed two of the core principles of Gorbachev's 'new thinking'.[59] The Soviet Foreign Ministry statement of 9 August 1990, for example, emphasised both considerations, stating that

> the Soviet Union is against reliance on force and against unilateral decisions. The experience of many, many years convincingly proves that the surest, most sensible line of action in conflict situations is collective efforts and the full use of UN mechanisms.[60]

On a more pragmatic and material level, a greater role for the UN helped to claw back losses in standing and prestige which had accompanied the end of the Cold War and allowed the USSR to take a principal role in influencing the outcome of the crisis without having to make any military deployments.[61] Its insistence on the need to obtain further Security Council approval for the embargo was an example of the desire to influence events by circumscribing moves towards war by the US.[62]

The two concessions the USSR was able to extract from the US both limited the scope of the use of force as well as placing it under greater UN control through the operation of the Military Staff Committee. The substitution of the words 'minimum force' in the draft resolution for the convoluted phrase 'measures commensurate to the specific circumstances as may be necessary' was intended to limit any discretion over the use of force that the ad hoc coalition sought to exert in enforcing the embargo. This desire for greater oversight of the use of force was clear in the correspondence between the Soviet Foreign Minister Eduard Shevardnadze and James Baker, in which it was stated that the USSR did not seek to change the 'substance' of the original resolution, but did wish to 'widen the range of means which can be used *for the purposes of control*'[63] (my emphasis). The further amendment to the draft, consisting of a request that states coordinate their actions via the Military Staff Committee, again demonstrated an attempt to limit and oversee the use of force, to ensure that force was used for the purposes of the collective and to reduce the prospect of conflict escalation.[64] In a later speech to the General Assembly in September 1990, Shevardnadze showed a remarkably serious commitment to the idea of resurrecting the Military Staff Committee by declaring a willingness to execute an agreement to place Soviet forces under the Committee's control.[65]

The Chinese response to the crisis up until this time had many elements of contradiction which some analysts put down to a desire to please too many disparate audiences at the same time.[66] The initial approach of the Chinese was to advocate reliance on the peaceful resolution of the crisis via the diplomacy of the Arab nations and to oppose the intervention of the superpowers. This opposition stemmed from a fear that the conflict may dangerously escalate with the military involvement of the superpowers but, primarily, China sought to exhibit solidarity with states of the Third World.[67] At the same time, however, it also supported the right of Saudi Arabia to appeal for outside help, which would of course involve the intervention of the US and other developed countries.[68]

Prior to voting on Resolution 665, Chinese officials became the subject of intense lobbying from the US and Kuwait to soften their stance on outside military intervention and to support the enforcement of a blockade. The US Assistant Secretary of State Richard Solomon and Kuwaiti Foreign Minister al-Ahmed al-Jabir al-Sabah are reported to have visited Peking in mid-August offering assurance of economic aid, loans and improved bilateral relations. These assurances appeared to be successful, with the Kuwaiti Foreign Minister announcing Premier Li P'eng's agreement to abstain on any vote on the resolution.[69]

In negotiations over the terms of Resolution 665, the Chinese joined with the Soviets in opposing the inclusion of the term 'minimum force' from the US-sponsored draft. The agreed new wording was sufficient to placate the Chinese desire to strictly delineate the parameters of the use of force by the US, and according to the Chinese, was consistent with 'the wishes of many Third World countries'.[70] Whilst it was clear to all members of the Security Council that force had indeed been authorised, the Chinese insisted that the amended resolution did not 'contain the concept of using force'.[71] Again, this statement appears to have been motivated by a desire to position itself as a champion of the Third World in the Security Council, who would ensure that where force was to be used under UN auspices, only community purposes would be served.

Whilst the two concessions made to the Soviet Union and China would appear to be significant on paper, their effect in reality was very limited. While the wording of the draft had been changed to invoke the legal principles of proportionality and necessity, in practice there was still a reasonable degree of latitude allowed to coalition naval forces to enforce the blockade. Similarly, while Resolution 665 took note of the USSR's preference for a resurrection of the Military Staff Committee, the coordination of naval operations through the Committee was in the form of a request rather than a mandatory obligation. In enforcing the blockade in the following months, coalition forces continued to operate using their own operational command structures.[72]

Overall, the United States and United Kingdom were able to obtain authorisation in a form that did not compromise their core objectives. Both sides made concessions – the US and UK in agreeing to some form of UN oversight of their enforcement operations, and the Soviet Union and China agreeing in substance to support the enforcement of Resolution 661. Ultimately all sides were in agreement about the core illegitimacy of the Iraqi invasion, and subsequent actions to annex Kuwait and use Western hostages as bargaining chips. They were also in agreement about the importance of ensuring that peaceful means were given a real chance to work. Finally, the US and UK were able to agree to the broad oversight of their naval forces by the Security Council, understanding that it was important symbolically to show that force would be used strictly to enforce the sanctions on behalf of the international community and, at this point, for nothing more.

Legitimacy and the Security Council

An interesting feature of the debate surrounding the adoption of Resolution 665 was the fact that states who were both for and against it appealed to the same normative prescriptions to justify their positions. The differences between the opposing views stemmed from varying interpretations of how these norms were to apply in a particular case.

There were four overarching normative principles which can be used to categorise the arguments put forward by 13 states supporting the adoption of Resolution 665. First, the original normative reasons for the condemnation of Iraq's invasion of Kuwait remained and, if anything, were bolstered by further acts showing a complete disregard for accepted norms of legitimate behaviour shared by states in the international community. Not only had Iraq failed to withdraw from Kuwait, it had taken even further steps to cement its occupation through the purported official annexation of Kuwait, the brutal suppression of resistance movements and hostage-taking of Western diplomats. These acts served to strengthen the resolve of a majority of states to achieve the liberation of Kuwait as the only legitimate and necessary end goal. As such, it was clear that the present means adopted by the Council had not persuaded Iraq to change course and needed to be reinforced.[73]

Second, strong support was expressed for the peaceful settlement of disputes between states. Resolution 665 expressly bolstered the economic sanctions regime, which for a number of states represented the only effective peaceful means available to compel Iraq to comply with previous resolutions of the Council. It was therefore important to ensure that the intention behind Resolution 661 was not allowed to be thwarted by Iraqi attempts to violate the embargo.[74] In contrast, the two dissenting states, Yemen and Cuba, believed that all peaceful means had not yet been exhausted given that 30 days had not yet elapsed since Resolution 661 had been adopted. In these circumstances, Iraq had not yet been given sufficient time to comply.[75]

Third, Iraq's continued defiance of prior Council resolutions was seen to threaten the authority of the Council, the credibility of the UN and the principle of collective security embodied in its terms. For example, Zaire spoke of the need to act to ensure that Iraq could not 'mock' the Security Council decisions with 'impunity',[76] whilst the United Kingdom stated '[i]f these open acts of defiance succeed, the authority of the Council and of the United Nations itself, will be gravely undermined'.[77] Similar sentiments were expressed by the US and Canada.[78]

Finally, there was also strong support for the prohibition on the use of force contained in the Charter, and concurrently, for a restricted interpretation of the two exceptions to the prohibition: the use of force where the vital security of the state was a stake (self-defence) or to serve the collective interest of all states, the maintenance and restoration of international peace and security (Chapter VII). Debate centred primarily on whether the existing terms of the draft resolution sufficiently guaranteed that force would be used strictly to serve the collective good, rather than for parochial ends. To this end, states were keen to ensure, first, that the scope of the authorisation to use force was clearly delimited, and that mechanisms to ensure the adequate supervision of coalition forces were put in place. In respect to the former, states such as France, Malaysia, the Soviet Union and Finland emphasised that the use of force should be kept to the minimum necessary to carry out the embargo and that support for the resolution did not imply that 'a blanket authorization for the indiscriminate use of force'[79] had been given. For Cuba and Yemen, the two dissenting states, whilst the draft had been amended to include allusions to the legal principles of necessity and proportionality, it still left far too much discretion in the hands of the coalition as to how the interdiction of shipping in the area would in fact take place. No specifications were given as to which actors were authorised to use force, in which theatre of operation, and under what kind of rules of engagement.[80]

On the issue of adequate Security Council oversight of the use of force, both Cuba and Yemen argued that the Security Council was not taking proper responsibility for international peace and security by delegating authority to the broad coalition of maritime forces in the Gulf. For Cuba, there was a serious lack of accountability provisions in the resolution, and should the situation escalate, Cuba asked 'are we in the Security Council also required to take responsibility for possible hostilities that may arise from the acts of forces not under our command?'[81] In essence, these states were convinced that the Security Council was only able to ensure that force was used responsibly and for collective purposes if military forces were to come under the command of the UN through the Military Staff Committee.[82] As we have discussed above (p. 35), while the Soviet Union also supported the involvement of the Military Staff Committee,[83] the final resolution did not make this mandatory. The consensus position was that the Security Council could faithfully exercise its Chapter VII responsibilities by authorising the use of force by states or a group of states, and did not need to have command of these forces directly.[84] The decision to provide a level of discretion on the use of force to the US and the naval coalition in the Gulf may also have been the result of an implicit acknowledgement that only these states had the capacity to actually enforce the embargo.

Conclusion

The negotiations preceding the adoption of Resolution 665 presents a clear example of the US assertion of leadership and a conditional acceptance of this role by a majority of states as long as it was willing to make concessions that signalled that leadership was primarily sought to achieve common interests. Beliefs about legitimate or appropriate and proper behaviour for state in international relations were a strong motivation for most states in agreeing to the 'vision' or plan of action put forward by the US to resolve the crisis. These beliefs provided a set of criteria with which to judge the US-sponsored draft resolution, and the amendments offered as a compromise.

In this episode, beliefs about legitimate or appropriate and proper state behaviour motivated states to follow the US plan in this episode in three ways. First, the end goal of reversing the invasion and restoring Kuwait retained acceptance within the group because of the continued belief in the illegitimacy of the aggressive use of force and the need to defend this principle or risk critical damage to the credibility of the UN Charter system. The support for the use of economic sanctions to achieve Kuwait's liberation also remained unchanged because of the belief that disputes between states should be solved through peaceful means as far as possible. In the context of Iraqi actions to further cement its occupation of Kuwait and mounting efforts to break the sanctions regime, the enforcement of the embargo was agreed to be necessary to make sure peaceful means of resolving the dispute were given every chance to succeed.

From the statements of various members of the Council, we can also conclude that the insistence by some Permanent and non-Permanent Members that a further Security Council resolution be sought, the authorisation of force be strictly limited to what was necessary to achieve an embargo, and the Military Staff Committee should have some oversight role, was based on the belief that, in these circumstances, force should be used only to serve the collective interests of all states – the maintenance of international peace and security through the enforcement of international law. Whilst no one state denied the legitimacy of using force in self-defence, for states to follow the US, reassurance needed to be offered to prove that the US was truly leading the international community to achieve a common goal. Supervision of naval forces in the Gulf by the UN Security Council served this purpose. The US's willingness to compromise its original position and to seek further Council authorisation stemmed from an acknowledgement that, for states to follow its lead, it would need to demonstrate the genuineness of its principled stand.

Part 4: the ultimate enforcement – deciding to use force to achieve the end goal

Probably the most significant issue faced by the Council in the course of the Gulf conflict was whether the sanctions under Article 41 would convince Iraq to relinquish control of Kuwait. After two months, the embargo was proving to be effective in stopping Iraqi attempts to export oil and import technical and military goods. However, whilst few doubted that the Iraqi economy was under serious strain, the Iraqi leadership remained unresponsive to diplomatic approaches from states such as France, the USSR and China, and ultimately was refusing to budge from Kuwaiti soil.

By around mid-October 1990, members of the US leadership team began to lose faith in the efficacy of the sanctions regime.[85] President Bush recalls in his memoirs that whilst his initial opposition to the invasion was formed from a belief that aggression was a 'dangerous strategic threat and an injustice', the hostage-taking practices of the Iraqi leadership and the emergence of harrowing stories of Iraqi atrocities in Kuwait convinced him that the crisis was now also a 'moral crusade'.[86] To amplify the pressure placed on the Hussein regime, a strategy of coercive diplomacy was put in place[87] through the deployment of a further 200,000 troops to the Gulf on 31 October.[88]

The decision was made to go back to the UN for a resolution that would authorise the use of force, but only if the US could be sure that such a resolution would be successful.[89] A draft resolution was prepared which used the phrase 'all necessary means, including military force', a formulation which authorised, rather than mandated, the use of force.[90] No mention was made of the Military Staff Committee or any other terms which would allow for the interference of the Council in the prosecution of the war. An ultimatum was included with the deadline of 1 January 1991 for Iraqi compliance written into the draft. With this in hand, James Baker set off for a trip around the world to meet with the leaders of the Permanent and non-Permanent Members of the Council.

By the end of November the US had received assurances from a majority in the Council for their support of a resolution authorising force. At a meeting of the Council on 29 November, Resolution 678 was passed with 12 states in favour,[91] China abstaining and Yemen and Cuba against. The use of 'all necessary means' by states cooperating with Kuwait was authorised, for the purpose of upholding and implementing prior resolutions of the Council and to 'restore peace and security in the area'. Iraq was given until 15 January to implement these resolutions, 'as a pause of goodwill'.

Reaching consensus

In the diplomatic negotiations which ensued in the month of November, the US received relatively little resistance to its push for the setting of an ultimatum on the use of force. This did not mean, however, that the US did not have to offer incentives to some states for their 'yes' votes. Baker himself wrote of his November trip: 'I met personally with all my Security Council counterparts in an intricate process of cajoling, extracting, threatening, and occasionally buying votes. Such are the politics of diplomacy.'[92]

Among the non-Permanent Members, Canada, Finland, Romania, Zaire, Colombia, Ethiopia and Cote d'Ivoire were solidly in support. Ethiopia and Zaire were said to be supportive of the use of force as a matter of principle because as small states they had reason to be interested in preventing aggression. Of the non-Permanent Members, Zaire and Cote d'Ivoire took this opportunity to attempt to extract some benefit from their support for the resolution. For Zaire, support was influenced also by the promise by Baker that the Administration would attempt to persuade Congress to reverse a decision to cut off military aid. Suffering from a financial crisis, Cote d'Ivoire sought to extract a promise from the Administration to push for debt forgiveness in the G-7. Whilst no guarantees were given on this score, Baker was under no illusions that support for the resolution by Cote d'Ivoire would require a response to this wish list.[93] In some cases veiled threats rather than inducements were made to secure support for the draft resolution. For example, the Malaysian leadership believed that the sanctions regime needed to be given more time, and saw a double standard being applied to Iraq in comparison to US policy on the Israeli–Palestinian problem. From Baker's memoirs it can be deduced that Malaysia's vote was secured after his intimation that a no vote would do serious damage to bilateral relations.[94] Unsurprisingly Cuba remained immune to US overtures, as did Yemen, despite the threat of the cancellation of foreign aid.[95]

Of the Permanent Members, France[96] and the United Kingdom remained in solid support of the US position. UK Prime Minister Thatcher in fact proved to be more hawkish than her US counterpart by persisting in the view that Article 51 provided a sufficient legal basis to act, regardless of whether Security Council authorisation was forthcoming. The USSR and China, however, needed further persuasion. The Chinese proved to be unsupportive of any moves to use force in the crisis and preferred to give economic sanctions more time to act. For some analysts, China's reluctance to vote in favour of the use of force was attributed to the fact that Iraq was one of China's largest markets for the export of goods and labour, accounting for $4.16 billion in arms sales in the 1980s. In addition, China's self-image as the representative of the Third World concerns in the Security Council meant that it needed to avoid the perception of being too quick or willing to accommodate US policy proposals.[97] Support for the draft, however, also provided China with an opportunity to rehabilitate its status and reputation in the West which had taken a plunge following the 1989 Tiananmen Square massacre.[98]

To achieve this end, the Chinese sought to extract a prize visit to China by the US President, as the price for support. For the US, the goal of negotiations was to secure an abstention vote as a minimum, and a 'yes' vote if possible. In a 18 November meeting between the two sides, Secretary of State Baker offered Chinese Foreign Minister Quan Qichen an 'incentive proposal' in which 'the President would see him for a yes vote', whilst an abstaining vote would result in a visit to Beijing by Baker himself.[99] China was discouraged from taking the latter approach with Baker arguing that even an 'abstention' would also be costly to China by drawing criticism from both Congress and the US public which would in turn reduce the Administration's ability to attempt to warm relations between the two countries. By 28 November, the US had effectively capitulated by agreeing to allow Qichen to visit the President in Washington, in return for the lesser prize of an abstention.

The agreement of the Soviet Union to the draft resolution came after some compromise on the timeframe for the ultimatum given to Iraq and the scope of the authorisation on the use of force. Baker had successfully convinced Shevardnadze that economic sanctions alone would not be effective because the Hussein regime was willing to allow its population to suffer. He was also sympathetic to the logistical and economic difficulties faced by the US in keeping its forces in the Gulf indefinitely, and agreed that the resolve of the international community might well falter if the crisis became too protracted.[100] At the same time, the Soviets were reluctant to rush too quickly to war. In a note to the President at the time, Baker wrote, 'Gorbachev's image of the new international order is such that he has a hard time reconciling the fact that we might need to use force in this initial test.'[101] On Soviet insistence, the words 'including force' were removed from the resolution, a change that was accepted but in practice did not alter the fact that the resolution did in fact authorise military action. It also succeeded in extending the ultimatum date from 1 January to 15 January and inserting the idea of a 'pause of goodwill'.

Whilst the views of China and the USSR did pose some obstacles to the use of force by the US-led military coalition, these obstacles were relatively easily overcome. Like the amendments proposed to Resolution 665, the compromises sought on the wording of Resolution 678 did not alter the substance of what was being authorised: permission to use force, by a date in January 1991, with minimal interference by the Security Council on how forces were to be deployed.

Legitimacy and the Security Council

The debate surrounding the adoption of Resolution 678 centred not so much upon the normative principles which marked Iraq's annexation of Kuwait as illegitimate, but in relation to the means by which to defend and uphold these principles. In passing 11 resolutions prior to 678, the members of the Security Council had maintained a unanimous stance, even among those states that had voted against or abstained,[102] that the invasion and annexation of Kuwait was an grossly illegitimate act which needed to be reversed. The aggressive use of force by Iraq cut across all of the core principles of the Charter, making it easily identifiable as grossly illegitimate and worthy of a strong response.[103] However, there was an escalation of rhetoric on the need to take decisive action to bolster the credibility of the collective security system embodied in the United Nations, a system which many states hoped could now operate successfully as part of a New World Order. States such as Malaysia, Colombia, Cote d'Ivoire, Canada and Finland[104] joined with the superpowers in declaring faith in an 'emerging world of civilised behaviour'[105] now that the Cold War was over. In these circumstances the Council needed to deliver the clear message that aggression never pays.[106]

The second question that needed to be addressed by those advocating force was why there was a need to escalate matters at this particular point in time. The principle that disputes should be settled peacefully provided a structural constraint for both advocates and detractors of the use of force. There were two strands to the arguments used by supporters of the resolution. First, Iraq's failure to comply with the 11 resolutions passed on the matter so far showed that it did not intend to comply and that existing means were not proving to be effective.[107] Not only was Iraq continuing to occupy Kuwait, but it had taken active steps to entrench its occupation by crushing Kuwaiti resistance.[108] Numerous states had attempted bilateral talks with the Hussein regime without success. On this view, the peaceful settlement of the dispute was unlikely.

These arguments were rejected by Yemen and Cuba, who believed that the almost land-locked nature of Iraq would eventually cause the sanctions regime to bite.[109] China's preference for peaceful means of enforcement stemmed from both the pragmatic view that, whilst sanctions may take longer to effect their purpose, 'the cost would be lower and the sequelae less serious', particularly in relation to the possible consequences of military action on 'world peace and stability' and the world economy.[110] It chose to abstain rather than to cast a negative vote because, whilst it could not agree on the means chosen to liberate Kuwait, it did support the legitimacy of this end goal.[111]

The majority in the Council who disagreed with this position also contended that waiting for the sanctions regime to work was a luxury that the citizens of Kuwait could no longer afford.[112] In the two days prior to the Council vote, representatives of the Kuwaiti Government had presented detailed evidence of the destruction of assets and gross violations of the human rights of Kuwaiti civilians to the Security Council. Thus, the Iraqi regime had pursued a destructive course in Kuwait that could prove to be irreversible, or reversible only through great personal and economic cost unless the Council acted with greater urgency.[113] This view was held not only by the Permanent members, but by states such as Ethiopia and Malaysia,[114] with the former stating: '[w]e must not ... wait much longer, for justice delayed ... could very well be justice denied'.[115]

With the majority of states in agreement that the breach of core principles by Iraq was grave, that sanctions had proved ineffective and that the need to liberate Kuwait had become urgent, the next logical step was the escalation of pressure on the Hussein regime through the threat or use of force. In the words of Mr Dumas of France:

> [e]verything we have done together so far was intended to make the aggressor see reason, in other words, to bring about a peaceful settlement to the crisis with due respect for law. Since our calls have fallen on deaf ears, we are compelled to resort to a higher level of pressure in the face of the continuing challenge to the international community.[116]

In an attempt to accommodate both a respect for the principle of the peaceful settlement of disputes, and a defence of the credibility and authority of the Council, the final draft of Resolution 678 called for the use of 'all necessary means' with the proviso that Iraq was given until 15 January 1991 to comply. Iraq had been given one final 'pause of goodwill' to show that the international community was attempting to 'go the last mile in search of peace'. In this interim period, many states emphasised that a diplomatic solution should be sought with greater intensity but the onus was placed on Iraq to settle the dispute peacefully.[117]

Ultimately, Resolution 678 represented the first time since the Korean War that the use of force of such possible magnitude had been authorised by the Council (Resolution 665 was considerably more minor and supplementary in its purpose). For the majority of states, while peaceful means should in the first instance be given every chance of success, where this was shown to be ineffective or inappropriate, the gravity of the norm violated required the Security Council to act with commensurate gravity in its response. For the USSR, the Council's stance in resolution 678 was

> based on the clear awareness and belief that shirking its duty now by failing to reverse the aggression would mean even greater hardship and suffering for the world and all nations. Those who have breached the peace should know that 'all necessary means' will indeed inexorably be used against them.[118]

Conclusion

In this episode, a majority of states who accepted the US's 'vision' for the resolution of the conflict did so primarily on the basis of their beliefs about legitimate and proper behaviour of states. Of this group, whilst Zaire and Cote d'Ivoire attempted to gain concessions from the US prior to the vote, their statements also put forward normative-based motivations for the support for the US position, particularly with respect to their opposition to aggression. From the reasons given by states supporting the resolution, most justified their support on the grounds that the peaceful means that had been relied upon so far to achieve the group goal were not proving to be persuasive to the Iraqi regime.

Authorising the use of force, whilst allowing a 'pause of goodwill', combined two aspects of most states' reasoning processes. First, the core principles of appropriate behaviour expressed in the Charter were so important to the common interests of all that they needed to be defended, even through the use of force. Second, the 'pause of goodwill' backed up by the threat of force gave one last chance to the Iraqi regime to end the matter peacefully. Whilst force was ultimately authorised in the resolution, economic sanctions would continue to operate while Iraq was given time to withdraw. From the view of states expressed in the Council, states were motivated to follow the US's vision for the resolution of the conflict in a large part by their belief that this vision was legitimate given its basis in accepted beliefs about legitimate behaviour between states. The goal sought to be achieved for the group still involved a notion of the greater good for all states, or their common interest in supporting the core principles of international order, principles which were designed to prevent war.

Conclusion

In this chapter we have sought to ask the question, can followership of the United States in the Gulf Crisis of 1990–1991 be credibly explained by their beliefs about legitimate conduct in international society? A positive answer to this question would support the hypothesis that US hegemony during this period could be characterised as a leadership role rather than a relation of dominance. After analysing the motivations for followership by the members of the Security Council, and the broader UN membership at four key decision-points in the crisis revealed by the justifications for action used by these states, it can be convincingly or credibly argued that international legitimacy was a key driver of followership in this case.

At each key juncture – in defining the situation, deciding on an appropriate goal, and defining and adjusting the means used to achieve this goal – states were shown to be significantly influenced to follow the US 'vision' for the resolution of the crisis by shared beliefs about legitimate behaviour between states. Legitimacy directly guided states to follow the US lead from the outset on the interpretation of Iraq's occupation and annexation of Kuwait as an illegitimate use of force – a pure case of aggression – which deeply threatened the core principles underwriting the post-Second World War international order. As members of the

Security Council with responsibilities for the safeguarding of international peace and security, it was therefore incumbent upon these states to take action to defend the credibility of the collective security system embodied in the Charter. The core illegitimacy of Iraq's actions and the normative prescriptions associated with membership of the Security Council guided these states to accept the US proposed goal of liberating Kuwait. Of note is the fact that not one state, within or outside the Council, justified their support for the US-advocated goal on the basis of a material interest.

The acceptance by a majority of states of the various US proposals on the appropriate means to liberate Kuwait was also heavily influenced by shared normative beliefs about legitimate state conduct. Support for the imposition of economic sanctions, the enforcement of an embargo on Iraq and Kuwait, and, finally, war were guided by normative commitments to both the peaceful resolution of disputes and to the prohibition on the use of force between states. We observed that the preference for the peaceful settlement of the dispute provided a structural constraint for all parties with strong justifications being required at each decision point before the use of force was in fact authorised. We also observed that the deep commitment of a majority of states to maintaining the core prohibition on the use of force, and concurrently to a strict reading of the exceptions to this prohibition, motivated many to seek amendments to US draft resolutions which tightened the scope of the use of force and ensured stronger oversight of military action by the Council via the involvement of the Military Staff Committee. In both cases these demands were accommodated because senior members of the Administration were aware of the need to demonstrate that the US 'vision' for the resolution of the crisis was one dedicated to achieving the interests of all states – the defence of Charter principles on which international order was predicated – and not primarily to achieve its own interests, particularly given that sacrifices would be asked of the broader community as a whole.[119]

In the final analysis, the evidence gathered from the public statements of the Security Council and a sample of the General Assembly supports the view that a substantial number of states genuinely followed the lead of the United States in their handling of the Gulf Crisis because they believed in the legitimacy of the vision it put forward to resolve it. Whilst there was evidence of some bargaining between the US and members of the Council in particular episodes, most states appeared to follow the US because of their beliefs about the illegitimacy of the invasion, the normative importance of reversing it, and the legitimacy of the means put forward by the US to resolve the crisis. In other words, followership is more persuasively explained via the logic of appropriateness rather than the logic of expected consequences, with hegemony more accurately represented as a leadership role of international society. However, as we have confined our analysis here to the public justifications used by states for their followership of the United States, it is important to also investigate the other possible un-stated material interests at play. In the next chapter we will evaluate whether three particular material factors may have also motivated four states to make large financial or military contributions to the Gulf coalition.

Appendix 2.1

Table 2.1 Support for goals and rationale[120]

State	Goals			Why was the Iraqi invasion illegitimate?				Underlying rationale		
				Breach of international law and UN Charter principles						
	Immediate and unconditional Iraqi withdrawal	Restoration of the legitimate Kuwaiti Government	Release of foreign nationals	Unprovoked aggression	Peaceful settlement of disputes	Respect for sovereignty, territorial integrity, independence of states	Human Rights – protection of civilians – Geneva Conventions and protocols	Aggression threatens international security – must be deterred	Security of all small nations at risk	Failure to reverse the invasion undermines credibility of UN collective security
Argentina	♦									
Australia	♦	♦		♦						♦
Bahrain	♦	♦		♦						♦
Belgium	♦	♦			♦					♦
Brazil	♦	♦	♦	♦						
Canada	♦	♦		♦				♦	♦	
China	♦	♦			♦	♦		♦		
Denmark	♦	♦			♦		♦	♦	♦	
Egypt	♦	♦	♦			♦		♦		
France	♦	♦			♦	♦		♦		♦
Germany	♦	♦	♦		♦		♦	♦		
Greece	♦	♦			♦			♦	♦	
Hungary	♦	♦	♦		♦	♦		♦		
India	♦				♦	♦	♦			
Indonesia	♦	♦			♦	♦				
EU	♦	♦	♦		♦	♦		♦		
Japan	♦	♦	♦		♦			♦	♦	♦
Luxembourg	♦									
Morocco	♦							♦		♦
Netherlands	♦	♦			♦		♦	♦	♦	♦

	New Zealand	Niger	Nigeria	Norway	Oman	Pakistan	Poland	Qatar	Saudi Arabia	Senegal	Sierra Leone	Singapore	Spain	Sweden	Syria	Turkey	UAE	UK	USSR
	♦		♦	♦	♦	♦	♦	♦	♦	♦	♦	♦	♦	♦	♦	♦	♦	♦	♦
	♦		♦	♦	♦	♦	♦	♦	♦	♦	♦	♦	♦	♦				♦	♦
	♦		♦		♦			♦				♦			♦			♦	♦
	♦		♦	♦			♦	♦	♦	♦	♦	♦	♦	♦	♦	♦	♦	♦	♦
	♦			♦	♦		♦	♦	♦	♦				♦				♦	♦
	♦		♦		♦	♦	♦	♦	♦				♦				♦	♦	♦
					♦						♦								
	♦		♦	♦	♦		♦	♦	♦			♦	♦				♦	♦	♦
	♦		♦		♦		♦						♦			♦	♦	♦	♦
			♦		♦	♦	♦		♦									♦	

Table 2.2 Support for means and normative justification[121]

State	Support for economic sanctions	Justification: peaceful settlement of disputes between states
Argentina	♦	
Australia	♦	♦
Bahrain	♦	
Belgium	♦	♦
Brazil	♦	♦
Canada	♦	
China	♦	♦
Denmark	♦	♦
Egypt	♦	♦
EU	♦	♦
France	♦	♦
Germany	♦	♦
Greece	♦	
Hungary	♦	
India	♦	♦
Indonesia	♦	♦
Japan	♦	♦
Luxembourg	♦	
Morocco		♦
Netherlands	♦	♦
New Zealand		♦
Niger	♦	♦
Nigeria	♦	♦
Norway	♦	♦
Oman	♦	
Pakistan	♦	♦
Poland	♦	
Qatar	♦	
Saudi Arabia	♦	♦
Senegal	♦	
Sierra Leone	♦	♦
Singapore	♦	
Spain	♦	♦
Sweden	♦	
Syria	♦	
Turkey	♦	♦
UAE[122]		
UK		
USA		
USSR	♦	♦

3 Material factors and followership in the Gulf Crisis

In Chapter 2 we found that legitimacy played a significant role in motivating a broad collection of states to follow the US lead in responding to the Iraqi invasion of Kuwait. These findings support a conceptualisation of hegemony as a leadership role in international society, constituted and regulated by shared normative beliefs about legitimate behaviour. Normative beliefs, however, may not have been the only driver of followership in this case. For those who view hegemony as a dominance relationship, followership is likely to derive from the material interests of subordinate states: to avoid the threat of punishment or to acquire positive benefits that accrue from cooperation. In this chapter, our task is to look for evidence supporting the conceptualisation of hegemony as a dominance relationship by asking the question – what material interests might states have been pursuing in following the lead of the United States and how significant were they as motivating factors?

In answering this question we have chosen to focus on four states that played an integral part in the coalition through either their military or financial contributions: Germany and Japan as major financial contributors, and France and the United Kingdom as major military contributors. These states have been chosen because their involvement contributed significantly to the success of the group enterprise as a whole, and their large contributions to the coalition provide an objective indicator of the success of US leadership. As Germany, Japan, the United Kingdom and France were the major non-Arab states which supported the coalition, closer study of their involvement is most likely to provide us with a stronger assessment of whether the US was a true 'leader' in the crisis in the true sense of the word.

There were a number of Arab states which made major contributions to the Gulf coalition in military and financial terms. These states have been excluded from the analysis because of the intense threat these states were under from further military action by the Iraqi regime and their immense security dependence on the United States. Given the heightened proximate threat these states faced from the Iraqi regime, it would have been difficult to differentiate between and evaluate their likely motivations for followership of the anti-Iraq coalition.

Material motivations for followership

In this chapter we have chosen to focus on a limited number of external variables that may have affected the decision by states to make significant contributions to the coalition. That is, we have largely excluded domestic considerations from the equation, as doing so is beyond the scope of the present project. Adapting the research design used by Bennett, Lepgold and Unger in their study of burden-sharing in the Gulf War,[1] we focus on three material motivations which may explain the contributions made to the coalition: oil dependence and interests in oil price stability, the balance of threat, and alliance dependence.

First, we focus on economic motives based on the effect of Iraq's invasion on Middle Eastern oil. States may have contributed to the Gulf coalition to ensure access to oil from the Gulf at a reasonable price. Whilst states could continue to access supplies of oil on the open market, regardless of whether Iraq retained control of Kuwait, states may have taken the view that the potential existed for Iraq to withdraw oil supplies under its control and to intimidate other OPEC states into following suit to raise the world oil price.[2] The persuasiveness of this motive for followership depends upon a state's level of dependence upon oil as a fuel source, and its dependence on oil sourced from the Gulf itself.

On a broader level, states may have been motivated to join the coalition to secure the stability of oil markets generally, as a rise in oil prices would have had a significant impact on a number of states' economies. The non-Arab states that did contribute to the coalition shared a common interest in maintaining international economic stability, and states with a larger fraction of their economies dependent upon trade would value stability even more highly.[3] In addition to oil-related motives, where relevant we focus on economic motives based on direct trade between Iraq and the state involved. Where an important trade relationship can be shown this serves to bolster the other explanations put forward.

Second, we focus on what is known within the literature on intra-alliance behaviour as the Alliance Security Dilemma.[4] This describes the dual fears faced by states within alliances of being either abandoned by one's ally in a specific conflict or entrapped into participating in a conflict in which their own interests are less affected than those of their ally.[5] The dilemma faced by states within alliances is that 'the risks of abandonment and entrapment tend to vary inversely: reducing one tends to increase the other'.[6] For instance, a strategy of strong support for one's ally may in fact encourage the latter to be overconfident in its dealings with a common adversary which may then lead to entrapment in a conflict in which one's own interests are not greatly affected. In the case of the Gulf Crisis, we anticipate that a follower state may have been motivated to participate in the anti-Iraq coalition because their fears of abandonment outweighed their fears of entrapment.[7]

Evidence to support the case for alliance dependence with respect to the four states chosen would include the absence of alternative alliance partners to the United States, statements made by decision-makers alluding to alliance responsibilities, as well as evidence of attempts by the United States as the dominant partner in these alliances to 'raise the costs of non-cooperation'.[8] Examples of the latter could include the threat of withdrawal of relatively irreplaceable economic or military benefits from the state concerned, or more subtle diplomatic pressure evidenced by a correlation between contributions made and requests to do so by US decision-makers.[9]

Our third material motivation for followership relates again to the reasons for intra-alliance cohesion. Here we focus upon shared threat perception as a motive for followership, adjusting Stephen Walt's balance of threat hypothesis for the task. Walt argues that states seek allies not simply to balance against rising power but to balance against threats, with relative power being one factor in an assessment of threat. For Walt, whether a state is viewed as a threat depends upon a calculation of its aggregate power, geographic proximity, offensive capabilities and perceived intentions.[10] In this chapter we assess whether states were motivated to follow US leadership against Iraq because of their assessment that Iraq posed a threat to national security.

However, given that our focus is on material motivations for followership, in this chapter we consider only the first three indicators of threat – aggregate power, geographic proximity and offensive capabilities. The last indicator, an assessment of perceived intentions, cannot be said to be a purely 'material' indicator of threat as it derives from an interpretation of a state's past actions based upon normative expectations of legitimate behaviour.[11] Whether Iraq's invasion of Kuwait constituted 'aggression', which for most states provided evidence of its future aggressive intentions, depended upon a normative judgement of Iraq's behaviour based on expectations of proper behaviour for a state within international society.[12] This question is dealt with in Chapter 2.

Burden-sharing in the Gulf Crisis

The United States' contribution to the Gulf coalition in financial and military terms clearly dwarfs that of any other nation. In financial terms, the United States bore a major share of the cost of conducting military operations against the Iraqi regime. In May of 1992, the US General Accounting Office estimated that the cost of conducting Operation Desert Shield and Operation Desert Storm to be more than $120 billion, which included $50 billion for all costs related to the support of 540,000 military personnel as well as around $10 billion for other costs including the forgiveness of debt of $7 billion to Egypt.[13] Whilst the financial burden of operations against Iraq was clearly heavy, the US received sizeable financial contributions in cash and in-kind from its allies to put towards defraying these costs.

It is difficult to give a completely accurate account of the sharing of the military and financial burdens within the coalition given that we do not know the individual costs incurred by each state in the coalition. However, we do have accurate figures on the financial contributions made by members of the coalition directly to the United States to defray its own costs (see Table 3.1). By May 1992, the Department of Defense reported that it had received $48,729 billion in foreign contributions, which included $5,575 billion in in-kind contributions, with Saudi Arabia, Kuwait, Japan, Germany, the United Arab Emirates and

Korea making the largest contributions to US costs, going by the amounts actually received rather than pledged (see Table 3.1).[14] Thus, of the $120 billion expended by the US on military action in the Gulf, approximately 40 per cent of these costs were directly reimbursed to it by other states.

In terms of military contributions to the Gulf coalition, the United States' contribution once again dwarfs that of any other state. However, the breadth of the coalition did serve to dispel the view that the conflict was between the US and Iraq rather than between the international community and Iraq, with 36 states, including the US, taking part in the military coalition.[15]

It is difficult to obtain exact figures on the contributions made by states involved, and within the literature comparative figures vary to some degree. As can be seen in Table 3.2, the United States made the largest contribution in terms of personnel and hardware, with 350,000 troops or 70 per cent of the coalition's forces. However, there were significant deployments made by Gulf states as well as the United Kingdom and France. Other than the United States, states providing the largest number of ground troops were Saudi Arabia with 40,000, Egypt with 36,000, the UK with 28,000. Elsewhere, estimates of the total number of troops deployed in the Gulf War come to 742,000, with 534,000 coming from the United States (71 per cent), 59,360 from the UK and France, and 148,000 from the Arab and GCC states.[16] France and the United Kingdom also played a strong role in the naval embargo of Iraq and Kuwait as well as naval operations during the war (see Figure 3.2).

Thus, in financial and military terms, the United States bore 60 per cent of the financial costs of prosecuting the war, while its military contributed approxi-

Table 3.1 Contributions pledged in 1990 and 1991 to the United States to offset US costs, commitments and receipts through to May 1992 (US$ millions)

	Commitments			Receipts			Future receipts
	1990	1991	Total	Cash	In-kind	Total	
GCC States	6,845	30,088	36,933	27,812	4,131	31,943	9,176
Saudi Arabia	3,339	13,500	16,839	10,052	3,876	13,928	4,960
Kuwait	2,506	13,500	16,006	13,890	37	13,927	4,199
UAE	1,000	3,088	4,088	3,870	218	4,088	17
Germany	1,072	5,500	6,572	5,772	782	6,554	18
Japan	1,680	8,332	10,012	9,416	571	9,987	142
Korea	80	275	355	150	69	219	136
Other*	3	23	26	4	22	26	0
Total	9,680	44,218	53,898	39,050	5,575	48,729	9,471

Source: United States General Accounting Office, 'Report to the Congress: Operations Desert Shield/Storm – Foreign Government and Individual Contributions to the Department of Defense', GAO/NSAID 92–144, May 1992, table 1.1 titled 'Foreign Government Pledges and Contributions to the United States (as of September 30, 1991)', p. 10.

Note
*Includes Italy, Oman, Qatar, Bahrain, Denmark and Luxembourg.

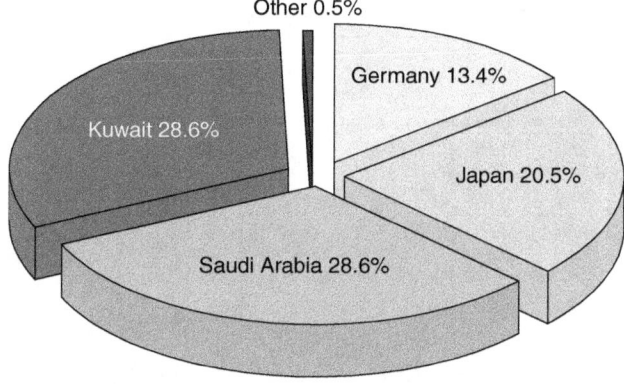

Figure 3.1 Financial contributions to the Gulf War.[17]

mately 70 per cent to the coalition's war-fighting capabilities. However, the significance of the level of burden-sharing by other states, even if less than equitable, should not be understated given that the level of forces contributed in some cases represented a significant portion of a state's standing army. The question of interest for our thesis is why four states – Japan, Germany, France and the United Kingdom – chose to follow the US to war against Iraq, and in all cases contributed significant financial or military resources to the coalition's efforts. We will now turn to discussion of the individual cases.

West Germany

The invasion of Kuwait came at an extremely inopportune time for the leadership and public of West Germany. Absorbed by the costs of and negotiations

Table 3.2 Operation Desert Storm – comparative totals

Coalition forces	Ground troops	Tanks	Tactical aircraft
US	350,000	2,000	1,400
UK	28,000	160	90
France	12,000	130	40
Saudi Arabia	40,000	500	180
Free Kuwait	7,000	60	20
Other GCC	8,000	24	80
Egypt	36,000	400	Nil
Syria	19,000	250	Nil
Canada	Nil	Nil	26
Italy	Nil	Nil	8
Total	500,000	3,520	1,844

Source: Edward Foster and Dr Rosemary Hollis, *War in the Gulf: Sovereignty, Oil and Security*, Whitehall Paper 8, Whitehall, London: Royal United Services Institute for Defence Studies 1992, p. 174.

54 *Material factors and followership*

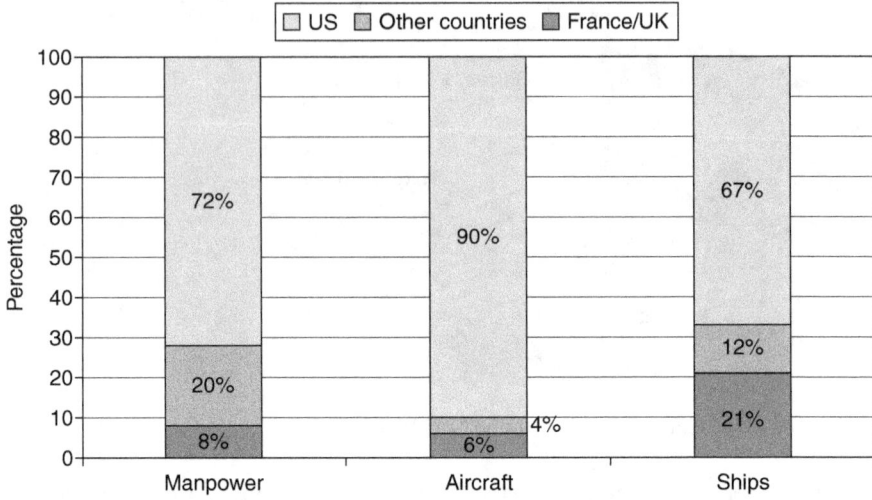

Figure 3.2 Military contributions to the Gulf War.[18]

over the re-unification of the two Germanys and the inaugural all-German elections in December 1990, it was unsurprising that the West German Government's response to the crisis was less than proactive. Yet Bonn managed to make a substantial financial contribution to the coalition effort.

The German contribution to the Gulf coalition came primarily in the form of financial aid to states either affected by the embargo or those with military forces in the Gulf. In terms of its financial contribution, going by the 1991 calculations of the German Finance Ministry, Germany contributed a total of DM17.2 billion (US$11.4 billion) to the coalition, with DM10.3 billion (US$6.67 billion) of this amount going to the United States.[19] This represented 13.4 per cent of the total financial costs of Operation Desert Storm (see Figure 3.1). The bulk of the remainder went to Turkey, the UK, France and Israel to defray their military costs,[20] while approximately DM1.7 billion was allocated for non-military aid to Turkey, Egypt and Jordan, the three states which were most affected by mandatory economic sanctions.[21]

Whilst there was general agreement across the political spectrum that the West German constitution precluded military involvement in war fighting in the Gulf, the historical significance of the military deployments made to support conflict operations should not be underrated. Not since the Second World War had such a large German deployment been sent abroad into areas of conflict.[22] Minesweepers were sent to the Mediterranean for post-conflict operations, 18 Alphajets and 270 troops were sent to Turkey to defend its border, whilst Israel was given a battery of Patriot missiles to counter Iraq's use of Scud missiles.[23] In addition to this, West Germany played a valuable role in providing logistical and transport support for the deployment of US, UK, Canadian and other Gulf forces and equipment to the Gulf.[24]

Explaining Germany's contributions

The oil factor

At the time of the crisis, the German economy was relatively highly dependent upon oil as an energy source, with oil accounting for approximately 37 per cent of all energy use.[25] In terms of the sources of this supply, Germany imported all of its oil, with a relatively small 14 per cent coming from the Gulf (mainly Iran and Saudi Arabia).[26] Given Germany's complete dependence upon imported oil supplies, the German economy was highly sensitive to volatility in the world oil price and, therefore, German decision-makers should have been motivated to join the coalition on this basis.

However, fears about the West German economy's vulnerability to a significant rise in the world oil price were not used by the Government as justification for involvement in the coalition.[27] In the immediate term, the German Economics Ministry did not in fact envisage a significant decline in economic growth, even if world oil prices were to rise should Iraq choose to withhold oil supplies from the market.[28] This confidence may have been based upon a perception that the reduction in oil dependence from 53.1 per cent of energy needs in 1970 to 36.8 per cent in 1990 provided a significant buffer against inflation and lower economic growth.[29] In light of this direct evidence, whilst German decision-makers should have been motivated by the oil factor, they were not in fact highly motivated by it, and appeared to believe that if prices did rise, the economy was able to absorb the increase without too much disruption.

Alliance dependence

As we have detailed above, West German support for the coalition against Iraq under US leadership was strong in terms of its financial contributions. However, over the course of the crisis it can clearly be seen that the timing of these contributions strongly coincided with the application of direct pressure by the US, and at times by other NATO members. It is argued that, on this basis, alliance dependence was likely to be a strong motivation for followership in this case.

In the initial phase of the crisis, the West German government was quick to give political support to the United States but slow in providing significant military and financial aid to the coalition forces in the Gulf. West Germany was among the first states to condemn the invasion as an illegitimate act of aggression, suspending the sale of arms to Iraq, freezing Kuwaiti and Iraqi assets and imposing economic sanctions along with its EC counterparts.[30] In terms of military support, the US request to use German territory as a logistical base for Operation Desert Shield and to transfer US forces stationed in Germany was granted immediately.[31] However, a more serious US request for military forces made by Secretary of Defence Cheney on 20 August 1990 was rebuffed by the governing coalition[32] on the grounds that the German Constitution, or Basic Law, only allowed military participation in regional collective security defence, i.e. defensive action within the NATO area.[33]

With a growing budget deficit and indications that the US economy was slipping into recession, the Bush Administration came under considerable Congressional pressure to spread the burdens of Operation Desert Shield.[34] Several members of the Senate Foreign Relations Committee were 'disturbed by what they perceive[d] as a grudging attitude among allies such as West Germany and Japan, nations more heavily dependent on Persian Gulf oil than the United States, about helping the Administration'.[35] In West Germany's case, the reluctance to take an active military role in the coalition caused considerable resentment in the House of Representatives, with Germany being perceived to be ungrateful for the protection it had received from the NATO alliance over the course of the Cold War.[36] If military participation was off the table, then strong financial contributions were expected in substitute. Newspaper reports, quoting sources close to the Pentagon, estimated that the US was looking for a contribution of about DM1 billion for a joint aid fund and a monthly sum of about DM62 million allocated to support military operations from Germany,[37] sums that were much larger than the DM200 million Bonn had pledged up to that point.

With this background of Congressional unrest, both President Bush and Secretary of State Baker made separate but well-timed moves to use America's support for re-unification and its role as a security guarantor as leverage to pressure the West German government to increase contributions to the coalition effort.[38] On around 13 September, just prior to the US Senate's deliberations over the '2-Plus-4' treaty, Chancellor Kohl received a letter from President Bush asking West Germany to assume a 'fair share' of the costs of the military build-up.[39] Secretary of State Baker went one further by reminding Kohl directly of the US's support for reunification.[40] These requests for greater burden-sharing were also timed with the announcement that the US was deliberating over possible cuts in troop numbers in Europe to less than 195,000, a figure previously agreed between the US and the Soviet Union[41] that had now 'been overtaken by events'.[42]

These attempts to pressure the West Germans to follow the US position in greater material terms appeared to be directly rewarded. In a meeting with Secretary Baker on 15 September, Chancellor Kohl agreed to provide additional assistance worth more than US$2 billion, half of which was allocated towards financial and logistical aid to the military coalition, with the rest to be directed towards economic support for states most disrupted by the crisis, namely Turkey, Israel, Egypt, Jordan and Syria.[43] German ships were also to be used to transport Egyptian troops and tanks to the Gulf.[44]

As the likelihood of war intensified in the following months, the German government was again forced to respond to demands by the US and other NATO partners to increase its level of burden-sharing. Recognition of the need to meet the expectations of alliance partners came in the form of two key decisions. On 2 January, the West German government announced that 18 Alpha-jets and 200 soldiers would be deployed to Erhac, Turkey, in response to the decision by the NATO Defense Planning Committee to prepare for a possible attack on Turkey by Iraq.[45] Despite their own reservations about the deployment, the governing coalition made considerable efforts to overcome the opposition of other political parties who believed that the Turkish government was misusing the crisis in order to pursue some kind of 'pan-Turkish ambition'[46] in the region. Second, on 29 January, Chancellor Kohl committed an additional US$5.5 billion to the US and US$3 billion to other members of the coalition.[47]

The fear of abandonment was plainly on the mind of Chancellor Kohl and his colleagues in the parliamentary debates over the rightfulness of the war which preceded these announcements. Here the governing coalition made its strongest case yet for German participation, citing legitimacy-based arguments – the enforcement of international law, the failure of peaceful means to avoid conflict, to combat aggression and to support an international order based on Western values – as well as the desire to show loyalty and gratitude to the US as its major ally.[48] In Scott Erb's words, the government made

> [c]onstant appeals to people's memories of the Berlin airlift, postwar care packages, US support for Germany against communism and the importance of NATO to Germany ... in an effort to claim that Germany owed it to the United States not to betray that friendship in a time of crisis.[49]

These sentiments were echoed by Foreign Minister Hans-Dietrich Genscher in an interview given in early February 1991. Here he explained his country's foreign policy rationale as involving the historical moral responsibility for the defence of Israel, and the affirmation and demonstration of its 'unrestricted solidarity with the allies' to ensure that 'no one has reason to doubt Germany's reliability in the [NATO] alliance',[50] sentiments that were repeated in his later memoirs.[51]

The importance placed on maintaining the alliance by Genscher and his coalition colleagues is highly plausible given the dependence by Germany on US support for re-unification; particularly as the external aspects of the 2-Plus-4 Treaty had not yet been concluded. Neither the WEU nor the CSCE provided a substitute for NATO as a mechanism to balance against the residual forces of the Soviet Union. At the same time, given that German forces were integrated within NATO force structures, NATO provided reassurance to Germany's European neighbours 'that there would be no critical mass of forces under German control positioned in the centre of Europe'.[52] NATO thus served a dual purpose for the West Germans, to deter as well as reassure.

Whilst the alliance dependence as a motive for followership in this case is strongly supported by the evidence, the reactive nature of the German response can be partly explained by the fact that the needs of unification necessarily took precedence over foreign policy. This included apprehensions about the costs of rehabilitating the East and a reluctance to therefore assume financial burdens elsewhere, but also anxieties about military involvement in the coalition and the impact this might have on continued support for unification by the Soviet Union. As Genscher later explained in his memoirs, German participation had to come in a form that would 'in no way supply the forces that opposed Mikhail

Gorbachev's policy in regard to Germany with valid arguments',[53] namely, the fear of the Soviets (and others) that a united Germany would once again threaten the European continent.[54] Chequebook diplomacy, rather than full military participation in the coalition, was a method of demonstrating the new united Germany's anti-militarism, and posed the least risk of jeopardising the withdrawal of Soviet forces from German territory, and therefore unification.[55]

The balance of threat

Using the balance of threat hypothesis, materially defined, it is unlikely that the West German followership was motivated by a perception that Iraq posed a significant threat to its national security. Iraq certainly possessed a strong military capability, possessing the fourth-largest army in the world, with an active regular strength of over 800,000 personnel in early 1990.[56] This army was certainly well equipped;[57] however, Iraq did not possess sufficient ballistic missile capabilities to threaten Germany directly. Military intelligence estimates reported that Iraq possessed approximately 1,000 modified Scud missiles, including the al Hussein and the al Hirajah (previously named the al Abbas), with maximum ranges of 600 and 800 kilometres respectively, putting them within reach of regional states, but not states in Western Europe.[58] Further, as we have discussed above (p. 55), the threat posed by Iraq to oil interests was not viewed as significant by the West German Government. Thus, it is unlikely that Germany was motivated to follow the US to combat a perceived material threat emanating from Iraq.

What we do find evidence of is the perception among the German leadership that Iraq posed a normative threat to international order and Western values. In justifying Germany's participation in the coalition, the Kohl Government likened Saddam Hussein to Adolf Hitler and viewed military action as necessary to prevent future aggression by demonstrating the West's willingness to defend 'freedom, law and justice'.[59] This evidence, however, provides support for followership based on normative, rather than material, motives.

Japan

Over the course of the Gulf Crisis, the Japanese government made substantial pledges of financial and in-kind contributions (medical and logistical aid)[60] to the United States and other coalition partners, in support of Operation Desert Storm and Operation Desert Shield and to those states hardest hit by the enforcement of economic sanctions, Turkey, Egypt and Jordan.[61] These commitments came in three instalments from late August 1990 to late January 1991 (represented in Table 3.3), with the final total being valued at US$13 billion, the third-highest financial contribution made by any coalition member.

Japan made a minor military contribution to the Gulf coalition, which involved permission for the use of existing US bases to support operations in the Gulf as well as the deployment of four minesweepers and supporting personnel in April of 1991. The Japanese government, led by President Kaifu, did attempt

Table 3.3 Japanese contributions to the anti-Saddam coalition (US$)

Military contributions	Costs unknown
Permission to use existing US bases in Japan	
Deployment of minesweepers to the Gulf, April 1991	
Financial contributions	
Pledged in 1990	
Grants and loans to Egypt, Jordan and Turkey	$2 billion
Cash grant to the United States	$0.961 billion
In-kind assistance to the United States: construction and engineering support, vehicles, electronic data processing, telephone services, medical equipment and transportation	$0.637 billion
Pledged in 1991	
Cash grant to the United States	$8.332 billion
Cash grants to other coalition partners	$0.668 billion
Total	$12.598 billion

Source: Hearing Before the Committee on Ways and Means, House of Representatives 102nd Congress, 'Foreign Contributions to the Costs of the Persian Gulf War', US GPO, 102–65, pp. 37–38.

to send military forces to join the coalition in logistical support roles which required the passing of legislation in the Japanese parliament to authorise the deployment. As will be discussed below (p. 62), the government was ultimately unable to gain support for the bill for constitutional reasons, and was forced to withdraw it in November of 1990.

Explaining Japan's contributions

Oil dependence

With the second-largest economy in the world and a total dependence on imports for its oil needs, Japan would be placed in the category of states with a significant interest in ensuring access to important sources of oil in the Gulf and the stability of the oil market. At this time, Japan was dependent on the Middle East for 60 per cent of its oil imports[62] (10 per cent of which was sourced from Iraq and Kuwait), compared to 12 per cent for the United States, and oil represented just over half of overall Japanese energy consumption.[63] As a trading state, higher oil prices would have created the risk of higher inflation and a resulting reduction in economic growth.[64] Given Japan's dependence on Middle Eastern oil, and the risk posed by higher oil prices on its economy, one would have assumed that Japan had a strong interest in maintaining the balance of power in the Gulf region by reversing and containing Saddam Hussein's ambitions. This was a common perception among some members of the US Congress who therefore expected Japan to react similarly to other Western states.[65]

Contrary to these expectations, government officials and members of the business elite took the view that the Japanese economy was well-insulated from the effects of oil price instability because of a number of peremptory measures taken after the oil price shocks of the 1970s. First, the Japanese policy of oil stockpiling provided the economy with a strong 142-day reserve of oil supplies as of August 1990, a level of forward stocks that was the highest in the industrialised world.[66] It was reported that, at the time of the invasion, the Japanese government believed that developments in the Gulf would have little effect on the economy because of these forward reserves.[67]

Second, it was believed that any disruption to oil supplies would have a minimal effect on economic growth because of the success of a consistent and successful policy of promoting energy efficiency. As a result of energy-efficiency measures, the Japanese economy in 1990 produced 'twice the output for the same energy input as in 1973', with 1988 figures showing that energy requirements as a share of GDP had reduced from 0.39 to 0.27.[68] Third, whilst all of Japan's oil needs were imported, it had consciously endeavoured to reduce oil dependence by diversifying into other forms of energy supply, particularly coal, liquefied petroleum gas and nuclear energy. From 1980 to 1990, the percentage of imported energy supplies taken up by oil fell from 80 per cent to 55 per cent,[69] with one-fourth of its electricity needs supplied by nuclear power.[70]

Apart from the perceived effect of policies to reduce the Japanese economy's oil dependence, many of Japan's business elite were not alarmed by the prospect of disrupted oil supplies from the Middle East for other reasons. It was argued that it was not important whether Saddam Hussein or the Kuwaiti Emir controlled Kuwaiti oil fields, because either would want to sell oil on the world market.[71] Others argued that as long as an increase in the price of oil affected all industrial economies equally, then Japan's economic competitiveness would be maintained.[72]

In summary, the oil factor does not provide a convincing explanation for Japan's significant contribution to the coalition against the Iraqi invasion. Whilst economically it would be logical to assume that Japan had a strong interest in maintaining the stability and sources of its oil supplies, an energy source to which it was heavily dependent, the actual perceptions of key decision-makers were just the opposite. Policies designed to reduce the effects of an oil shock on the Japanese economy were seen to have worked, such that decision-makers were confident that the Japanese economy could ride out the storm. We need to look elsewhere for a more convincing explanation for the significant Japanese contribution.

Alliance dependence

At the time of the Gulf Crisis, Japan remained highly dependent upon its alliance with the United States for national security. Whilst the main rationale for the alliance had faded with the unravelling of the Soviet Union, a number of factors remained to ensure that the security alliance with the US remained highly valued by Japan. First, whilst the Soviet threat had clearly diminished, Japan lacked alternative alliance partners in the region to combat the perceived new emerging threats from an increasingly self-confident China and volatile North Korean regime.[73] Second, the nuclear umbrella provided by the US alliance gave protection against these threats and additionally allowed Japan to avoid producing its own home-grown nuclear capacity. This was important not only from a cost perspective, but also avoided the real risk that a regional arms race would be ignited.[74] Apart from this, Japan would remain dependent on the US alliance so long as it remained restrained by its restrictive constitution, which barred the use of force for purposes other than in self-defence. This legal commitment to anti-militarism had become entrenched in Japanese society following defeat in the Second World War and, on these grounds alone, it was unlikely that Japan would be able to develop a sufficient offensive military capacity that would obviate the need for close US–Japanese security cooperation.[75]

These factors objectively support the assessment that, at the time of the Gulf Crisis, Japan remained highly dependent upon its alliance with the US, and therefore had material interests in making significant contributions to the coalition. Over the course of the crisis, the strong correlation between Japanese aid and the application of direct political pressure by the Bush Administration and Congress[76] suggests that a fear of abandonment was in fact a significant motivation for Japanese followership.

Japanese financial contributions were made in three instalments, each preceded by some form of arm-twisting or veiled or overt threats designed to play on Japanese anxieties about abandonment by the US. The first announcement of a contribution of US$1 billion on 29 August 1990 was made in response to a direct request from President Bush on 14 August to help those Gulf states with deep trade relations with Iraq and Kuwait that would be most severely affected by the sanctions regime.[77] However, the aid package was viewed by the Americans as token and self-serving as financial assistance was offered in the form of low-interest loans which could only be used on projects for which Japanese companies could tender.[78] With the growing realisation of the severity of the recession within the US, and the perception that the budget deficit was reaching unmanageable levels,[79] US expectations of greater burden-sharing by Japan would not prove to be deflected by this initial package.

On 30 August, President Bush named Japan, West Germany, Kuwait, Saudi Arabia, the UAE and South Korea as states whose burden-sharing had been inadequate, given their interests in the 'free flow of oil' and 'a stake in international order'.[80] Within Congress, Japan and Germany were targeted as states that had failed to meet their alliance obligations. As a warning to Japan, on 13 September the House passed a motion by 370 to 53 to amend a defence authorisation bill to require the withdrawal of 5,000 American troops a year from Japan unless it paid the full cost of the US military presence there.[81] To alleviate what had become a crisis in alliance relations, the Japanese Cabinet made the announcement of its second instalment of financial aid of US$3 billion the following day.[82] The US kept up this pressure, right up to the start of hostilities, and managed to extract a further US$9 billion from Tokyo, which was almost double the amount that had originally been offered.[83]

Apart from placing strong pressure on Japan to contribute financially to the coalition, the Administration also intimated that a military contribution was expected. In mid-August, Bush made the request that Japan send minesweepers and oil-supply ships to the Gulf, a request which Japan attempted to avoid through the offer of financial aid. After a meeting with Bush at the end of September 1990, Prime Minister Kaifu made the announcement that his government would send its Self Defence Forces to the Gulf. Details of the conversation between the two statesmen are not known. However, at around the same time, US Ambassador to Japan, Michael Armacost, stated publicly his country's expectation that Japan would make a significant contribution given its economic strength, oil dependence and desire to take a greater leadership role in the UN.[84] Armacost undiplomatically warned Japan that it was unlikely to become a Permanent Member of the UN Security Council if it failed to send a military contingent to Iraq.[85]

It was under this sustained US pressure to make a human contribution to the coalition that the government of President Kaifu introduced a United Nations Peace Corps Bill into the Japanese Parliament. This bill sought to create a special corps comprised of members of the SDF and civilians who would take non-military roles in military operations sanctioned by the UN and would only be allowed to use force in self-defence. The bill generated a great deal of public debate because it challenged the existing agreed interpretation of Article 9 of Japan's pacifistic post-war constitution which renounced the use of force 'as a means of settling international disputes'.[86] In 1989, all major political parties had agreed that the constitution allowed the use of Japan's self-defence forces only in the defence of Japanese territory.[87] Under this agreement the deployment of Japanese forces to foreign theatres, such as the Gulf, would have been unconstitutional. In the parliamentary debates that ensued, Kaifu argued that the deployment was indispensable in maintaining good relations with the US by illustrating that Japan was willing to act as a great power.[88] Ultimately, the bill failed to gain the required support because of a lack of political consensus, even within government ranks, about whether it was constitutional to send Japanese forces overseas, even in defensive roles.[89]

Whilst the attempt to send troops to the Gulf failed, it still says much about the Japanese government's willingness to please its major ally. The divisive constitutional debate which followed came at much political cost to the government and required a significant amount of political capital to be expended against a pacifistic public and parliamentary opposition. Both groups were not prepared to meet the expectation that Japan would cast aside the Yoshida doctrine by playing a larger political and military role in the world, rather than simply an economic one.[90] The eventual deployment of minesweepers to the Gulf in April of 1991 served to at least symbolically demonstrate to the United States that Japan was a committed ally.[91]

The balance of threat

If we consider the three material elements of Stephen Walt's balance of threat criteria, Japan should have judged Iraq to be a low security threat. Whilst its relative aggregate power was regionally significant, Iraq is not geographically proximate to Japan and lacked offensive military capabilities sufficient to directly threaten Japanese territory. As we have argued above (pp. 59–60), the threat posed to oil supplies was not regarded by decision-makers as significant. As such, the balance of threat does not provide a convincing explanation of Japanese followership of the US in this case.

France

France emerged from the conclusion of the Gulf Crisis as the second-largest military contributor to the coalition of all the European countries. From the outset of the crisis, France made a decisive military commitment on 9 August, deploying the aircraft-carrier *Clemencau* to the Saudi Arabian military base of Yanbu, in support of the UN economic embargo of Kuwait and Iraq.[92] By 29 August 1990, it was reported that nine French ships were in the Gulf or en route, manned by a force of 3,500 personnel, whilst one company of paratroopers (109 men) had been ordered to Abu Dhabi in the United Arab Emirates.[93]

The decision to join the coalition forces in defence of Saudi Arabia was spurred by an attack on the French Embassy in Kuwait on 14 September by Iraqi forces. In the incident the Embassy was ransacked and the military attaché and three French citizens were briefly taken prisoner. The following day, President Mitterrand announced that 4,200 soldiers and sixteen combat aircraft were to be sent to Saudi Arabia as part of *Operation Daguet*.[94] In a move that signalled a hardening of the French position against Iraq, France requested the Security Council to consider passing a resolution to tighten the embargo.[95]

By the start of hostilities in January 1991, the French military contribution consisted of between 10,000–12,000 troops, 150 light and heavy tanks, 130 combat and transport helicopters, 54 aircraft (elsewhere 76 combat aircraft[96]) and a dozen warships.[97] In addition, permission was granted for US B-52 bombers to fly over French airspace, 'the use of airport facilities for the refuelling of KC-135 cargo planes, and the provision of transport vehicles for US troop movements in Saudi Arabia'.[98] French aircraft participated in the first air strikes on Iraq, whilst in the ground battle, its forces performed the valuable task of outflanking the Iraqi forces to the West, blocking the retreat to Baghdad of the Iraqi republican guard.[99]

Explaining France's contribution

Oil dependence and other economic motives

In terms of oil dependence, using 1989 figures, France was noticeably dependent on oil as a source of energy, with 43 per cent of energy supplies derived from crude oil.[100] Further, France was dependent on Middle Eastern suppliers for 45 per cent of its oil needs, with Saudi Arabia supplying 18.7 per cent and Iraq 8.1 per cent.[101] In objective terms, France should have been highly motivated to follow the US in the Gulf Crisis to ensure stable oil supplies at reasonable prices.

However, there is little direct evidence to support the view that oil dependence was in fact a significant motivating factor for French decision-makers.

Rather, there were a number of factors that caused the French government to have confidence in the ability of the economy to weather the consequences of oil supply fluctuations due to the embargo of Iraq and Kuwait, or of war. First, since the oil shocks of the 1970s, France had aggressively sought to reduce its dependence on oil by developing a greater nuclear energy capacity.[102] By 1990 France's 50 nuclear reactors were able to satisfy all of the country's electricity needs and it had become the largest nuclear energy exporter in the EC.[103] Second, France had successfully reduced its dependence on Middle Eastern sources of oil since the oil shocks of the 1970s from 74 per cent to 45 per cent of all oil imports,[104] with supplies from the North Sea fields and Africa making up the difference.[105] Finally, Grunberg suggests that French decision-makers were confident that their strong ties to Arab states would ensure that oil supplies could be obtained bilaterally at reasonable prices, regardless of the spot price for oil. She quotes Saddam Hussein's half-brother Barzan el Tikriti as saying: 'What are the French doing in this business? We have always sold them all the oil they wanted, at the price they wanted. Let alone the arms that we have been buying from them ...'[106] In short, despite France's oil dependence on the Middle East, there is little evidence that this played a significant part in policy calculations.

In relation to other economic interests, France was actually disadvantaged by joining the anti-Iraq coalition. During the 1980–1988 Iran–Iraq War, France became Iraq's second-largest supplier of arms, behind the Soviet Union,[107] supplying it with an estimated 17 billion dollars' worth of weaponry. At the conclusion of the Iran–Iraq War, French companies were rewarded for their country's support of Iraq with important construction and electronics contracts. By July 1990, Iraq was in debt to France by US$4–4.5 billion, and in July 1990, the two countries had reached an agreement on rescheduling part of Iraq's debt, an agreement that was made redundant by Iraq's invasion. By joining the coalition, France effectively went against its material interests by risking the recovery of the significant debt owed to it by Iraq.[108]

Alliance dependence

The question of whether France was motivated to participate in the coalition because of its dependency upon its alliance with the United States is more difficult to answer than the cases that we have examined thus far. When examining the approach to the crisis taken by the French Government, three major goals of policy can be identified: the preservation of French independence and influence; the defence of international law and order; and demonstration of French reliability as an ally of the United States.[109] The sometimes contradictory behaviour of the French leadership during the crisis can be explained by the difficult attempt to maintain French independence whilst also seeking to express alliance solidarity. The desire to defend international law and order could be achieved without contradicting these other goals of policy.

Since De Gaulle, French foreign policy has consistently sought to advance and maintain the ability to influence events in international affairs, commensurate with its self-perception as a great power.[110] This desire to influence was expressed through policies to maintain France's ability to act independently in world affairs, through the maintenance of an independent nuclear capability, the construction of a European political entity in which France would hold a leadership role, and through the preservation of close economic and political relations with former colonies in North Africa, the Middle East and black Africa.[111] To pursue this objective, France sought to distinguish itself from the Gulf coalition by insisting on a separate and independent role for its forces, and undertook a number of pre-war diplomatic initiatives to minimise any damage that might have been inflicted on relationships with former colonies through its participation in the coalition.

Over the course of the crisis, significant diplomatic resources were devoted to maintaining its influence over former colonies in the Arab world, particularly those that had not directly opposed the invasion. Given the pro-Iraqi stance taken by the Tunisian and Algerian governments, French decision-makers had strong incentives to at least be seen to advocate a peaceful solution to the conflict, if at all possible.[112] In August 1990, Mitterrand sent 12 emissaries to 24 countries[113] to stress that France sought a diplomatic solution to the crisis and that its participation in the coalition was directed towards Iraq alone, rather than against the Arab world in general.[114] This line was pursued by President Mitterrand in an address to the UN General Assembly in September 1990 where he suggested that Iraq's verbal acceptance of the Security Council's resolutions would be enough to avoid war. Whilst this policy was without doubt constructed with the Arab audience in mind, eventually, under pressure from the Bush Administration, the French were forced to return to the hardline coalition position.[115]

The final diplomatic attempt to preserve French influence in the Arab world consisted of a last-minute peace initiative to the Iraqis on 14 January, without the knowledge of its allies, after the failure of separate talks between the US, EC and Iraq in early January 1990. Mitterrand's initiative was not welcomed by Washington or London as it offered the guarantee of an international peace conference on the Middle East in exchange for a withdrawal from Kuwait, a stance which was seen to be encouraging a diversionary link between the invasion and the Palestinian–Israeli conflict. Whilst the French initiative was rebuffed by the Iraqis, it provided a concrete demonstration of French sympathy for the Arab interests which was hoped would prevent the weakening of its position in the region after the hostilities were over.[116]

To a more superficial extent, France also attempted to maintain an independent position in the use of its armed forces within the coalition. While France sent naval forces to the Gulf in August of 1990, it specifically declined to join US and UK forces in defence of Saudi Arabia, stating that the deployment would independently support the UN economic embargo.[117] Whilst this position was eventually abandoned, as part of the coalition, France insisted that its forces be given a distinct and separate mission. It was for this reason that French forces were tasked with the defence of the western flank of the coalition forces.[118]

Whilst the French policy consistently sought to at least appear to be independent of the US position, in the final analysis alliance solidarity was put ahead of independence, with French forces playing a strong role in the prosecution of the war under the operational command of the United States. The significance of the latter decision should not be understated as it represented a significant departure from the historical stance towards independence from the superpowers begun by De Gaulle.[119] Whilst Mitterrand clearly felt the need to 'express solidarity with its allies when the chips were down',[120] the question then remains as to why the alliance continued to be of value to France now that the Cold War had ended.

The most reasonable explanation for this stems from what Hoffman termed the revival of the 'German question'.[121] The great fear of the French government was that a newly united Germany might choose neutrality over membership of NATO, raising the prospect of a 'loose Germany on the deck of Europe'.[122] The French sought to avoid German neutrality, with Foreign Minister Dumas stating in March 1990 that 'trans-Atlantic ties and the American presence in Europe must continue to be recognised as key elements in the future stability of our continent'.[123] Maintaining the NATO alliance thus aided the political containment of Germany.

Apart from anxieties about a united Germany, the United States, through NATO, continued to provide the only real protection against future threats emanating from the USSR, even if this threat had diminished.[124] Whilst France's somewhat contradictory plan for the long term was the enhancement of its independence through the development of a European security structure to rival NATO,[125] at the time of the crisis, the Western European Union had yet to develop any serious capacity for common defence.[126] This left NATO and the US alliance as the most viable alliance option for the French for some time.[127] Thus, whilst France's interest in preventing its future abandonment was less pronounced than in the case of Japan and Germany, it still represented at least a motivation of medium-level significance.

The balance of threat

Taking the material elements of the balance of threat hypothesis into account, it is unlikely that French followership was substantially motivated by a perception that Iraq posed a strong threat to its national security. Whilst Iraq had a strong conventional military force, as discussed above (p. 58), it was not believed to have the delivery capabilities to reach the French mainland.[128] The lack of geographic proximity and sufficient offensive capabilities is significant here. Finally, as we have already discussed at length above, the threat to French economic interests in oil supplies was not regarded as serious by decision-makers. Thus, the balance of threat hypothesis, materially defined, cannot provide an explanation for French followership of the US.

The United Kingdom

The United Kingdom provided both a strong political and military contribution to the Gulf coalition. In political terms, the British held a resolute and consistent line against the Iraqi invasion, with Prime Minister Thatcher unambiguously supporting and advocating the exertion of maximum pressure on the Iraqi regime (see Chapter 2).

The UK contribution

In military terms, by the start of hostilities the UK's naval, air and ground forces made up the third-largest contingent in the coalition after the sizeable forces of the United States and Saudi Arabia.[129] Very early in the crisis, the UK Government committed itself militarily to the collective defence of Saudi Arabia and the enforcement of the economic embargo against Iraq and Kuwait at the request of Saudi King Fahd. Between late August and early September 1990, the UK Navy added seven warships to its permanent flotilla in the Gulf. These forces were supported by three squadrons of Tornado F3 air-defence and ground-attack aircraft, and a squadron of Jaguar fighter bombers that had been sent to Saudi Arabia, Bahrain and Oman. A small contingent of around 2,200 soldiers was deployed to defend the airfields in Saudi Arabia, Bahrain and Oman.[130]

Additional land and air forces were sent to the gulf on 14 September 1990 for the purpose of defending Saudi Arabia, preventing further aggression by Iraq against other Gulf states and to implement the UNSC mandated embargo.[131] This consisted of an armoured brigade of 6,000 troops, 120 tanks and an additional squadron of Tornado GR1 and air-defence aircraft. As the Security Council began to negotiate over whether the use of force would be authorised, the UK Government sought to ratchet up the pressure on Iraq by establishing a 'credible

Table 3.4 The UK contribution to the Gulf coalition[132]

Contribution	Estimated cost
Naval forces 11 frigates and destroyers, two submarines, ten mine countermeasure ships, three patrol craft, three naval helicopter squadrons and a Royal Marine detachment	£2,500,000
Air forces 51–60 Tornado GR1 and GR1A strike/attack craft, 18 Tornado F3 Defence fighters, 12 Jaguar GR1A attack craft, 12 Buccaneer S2B maritime strike aircraft, 15 C-130 transports, nine VC10 tankers, eight Victor K2 tankers, one Tristar KC1 and one HS125 transports, three Nimrod MR2 maritime reconnaissance aircraft and six phantom FGR2s.	
Ground forces Total of approximately 42,100 personnel – 30,000 army, 7,000 RAF, 5,000 navy and 100 civil servants 176 main battle tanks	

offensive military option' that would encourage Saddam Hussein to see that there was no option but to withdraw.[133] For this purpose, an additional armoured brigade and two minesweeping vessels were deployed to Saudi Arabia, bringing the total number of UK forces to 30,000 personnel.[134]

By the start of hostilities in January 1991, some 40,000-to-45,000 British troops were committed to Operation Granby, taking a major supporting role in the fighting in all phases of the military attack. The relatively large British contingent of ground forces played a strong part in the ground offensive which began on 25 February. The preceding month, RAF aircraft took part in the operations to establish air superiority,[135] whilst UK Naval forces played a major role in gaining control of the Northern Gulf and neutralising the threat to coalition vessels and important port facilities in Saudi Arabia from missile attack. In all, 26 UK ships were deployed in the area during the conflict, with minesweepers tasked with enabling the coalition's amphibious forces to invade through Kuwait and US battle ships to bombard the shore.[136]

Whilst it is difficult to come to a monetary estimate of the risk to life associated with participation in war, the total financial cost of Operation Granby was estimated at £2,434 billion.[137] However, the United Kingdom was able to recover around £2,049 billion of this from the most affected Gulf states including Kuwait, Saudi Arabia and the UAE, with significant additional funds coming from states such as Germany and Japan.[138]

Explaining the UK contribution

Oil dependence

As a net exporter of oil, UK followership cannot be explained by oil dependence. With the discovery of oil in the North Sea, the United Kingdom moved from being a net oil importer of petroleum prior to 1980, to a net oil exporter[139] with the UK's oil trade surplus reaching £2 billion in 1990.[140] The public justifications for UK followership also support the view that oil dependency did not factor highly as a motivation. In the words of Foreign Minister Douglas Hurd, 'It is not a question of who should rule Iraq ... It is not a matter of the price of oil or access to oil. If that were the issue, everyone would have settled with Saddam Hussein long ago ...'[141] Rather, whilst the invasion did not directly threaten UK oil supplies, it did result in the more diffuse threat to 'world economic stability' that would result if Saddam Hussein were to control 20 per cent of world oil supplies, based on the assumption that oil would become a political weapon in his hands.[142] As a trading state, the United Kingdom would have had some interest in ensuring the continued supply of oil at reasonable prices as the health of its trading partners' economies depended on it.

However, the reasoning process used by UK decision-makers on this point cannot be said to be derived from the United Kingdom's material interests alone. The assumption that Saddam Hussein would use his control of the combined Kuwaiti and Iraqi oil fields to advance his regional hegemonic ambitions was based on a normative judgement of the illegitimacy of aggression in international society. The fact that Saudi Arabia had control of more than 20 per cent of the world's oil supplies was not seen as a threat to the region or to the world economy because Saudi Arabia acted within the bounds of legitimate conduct between states. In contrast, Iraq's serious illegitimate behaviour marked it out as a pariah among states, a state whose intentions were assessed to be aggressive. Saddam Hussein's past aggressive actions were interpreted to predict his future intentions: to attain regional hegemony militarily and economically through the control of oil resources. For the British, this course of action would threaten the world economy and the stability of the region. In this sense, it is the normative framework within which UK policy was formed, rather than an oil price stability argument, that is most persuasive in any explanation of the motivations behind the United Kingdom's involvement in the coalition. That is, both the British material interest in maintaining oil supplies and/or oil price stability provide weak explanations for UK followership in this case.

Alliance dependence

Like the German and Japanese cases we have already examined, UK followership in the Gulf Crisis can be tied to a fear of being abandoned by the United States in the post-Cold War environment. However, there is no clear evidence that followership was extracted from the UK through the imposition of overt political pressure by the Bush Administration. Throughout the crisis the UK shared identically the justifications and reasoning used by the US for its response to the invasion, and in some instances, both Margaret Thatcher and John Major used similar reasoning to their US counterparts to justify UK actions to counter the invasion of Kuwait. For both leaders, the Iraqi invasion had to be reversed to deter aggression, uphold the rule of law, to protect the vulnerable position of small states, ensure the credibility of the UN and to safeguard world security, oil supplies and economic stability.[143] There is no evidence of the US having to pressure anyone within the government to make these arguments, and little evidence of pressure being applied in relation to military contributions. Rather, on some issues, such as the use of Article 51 to justify the enforcement of the embargo and the use of force to liberate Kuwait, Margaret Thatcher took a stronger line than the US, arguing that UN authority was unnecessary.[144] Thatcher was closely involved in the continuing debates among Bush's advisors during the crisis, whilst the military, intelligence-gathering and diplomatic efforts of the two countries were closely meshed.[145]

Whilst there was no overt pressure applied to encourage the British to make a military contribution, a number of factors suggest that followership was highly motivated by a fear that the end of the Cold War would lead to the US abandoning its commitment to European security, and thus a weakening of the Atlantic partnership.[146] The fear of abandonment was fuelled by two anxieties of the British leadership about the continued usefulness of the UK in the eyes of the new Bush Administration. First, whilst Thatcher had successfully reinvigorated the 'special relationship' between the US and UK during the Reagan years, at the time Thatcher believed that President Bush sought to distinguish himself from his predecessor by downplaying the importance of the UK over other European states.[147] Second, Thatcher also believed that a re-unified Germany was perceived by the Bush Administration as being the more natural European partner, rather than the United Kingdom, given its strategic position and economic power.[148] This fear was confirmed in 1989 with President Bush referring to the US/German relationship as a 'partnership in leadership'.[149]

On the other hand, the continued usefulness of the US alliance from the British perspective was not in doubt. With Thatcher taking the line of accepting greater European monetary union, but not political or defence union, the US remained the United Kingdom's most important ally. Whilst Prime Minister Major was more receptive to closer integration of the European Community, the belief in the value of the special relationship with the United States continued.[150] The United Kingdom sought to ensure that NATO continued to have a central role in European security with the United States serving to 'broker and contain the post-Cold War "re-nationalisation" of Europe',[151] i.e. the risk of a more assertive united Germany.[152] With this in mind, the UK consistently opposed the strengthening of the WEU as a substitute for NATO, but rather insisted that it act as the 'European pillar of the Atlantic Alliance'.[153]

For these reasons, the Gulf conflict provided the UK with an opportunity to avert abandonment by demonstrating to the US the benefits of a strong alliance with a state that did not shy away from sharing the burdens of international leadership. Margaret Thatcher demonstrated her strong political loyalty to the US by chastising her NATO allies for failing to make a significant contribution to the coalition's efforts in the Gulf and essentially taking a free-ride at the United States' expense:

> [w]e cannot expect the United States to go on bearing major military defence burdens worldwide, acting in effect as the world's policeman, if it does not get a positive and swift response from its allies when the crunch comes – particularly when fundamental principles as well as their direct interests are just as much at stake.[154]

Foreign Secretary Douglas Hurd also made statements connecting the British response to its 'place in the world' and to US expectations of UK support.[155] In the end, the high level of UK followership during the crisis succeeded in assuaging the fear that the special relationship was in decline, with President Bush expressing his country's 'respect and affection' towards the United Kingdom, which was 'deep' and 'profound' and 'if anything stronger than it's ever been'.[156]

The balance of threat

The threat posed by Iraqi military capabilities to UK national security was weak if we use the three material criteria utilised by Walt's balance of threat hypothesis: aggregate power, offensive capabilities and geographic proximity. As we have suggested above (p. 58), Iraq possessed a credible conventional military capability. In addition it possessed a proven chemical weapons capability and a nuclear programme believed to be five-to-ten years away from producing a nuclear weapon.[157] Developments in April 1990 made Iraq's nuclear and ballistic missile ambitions clear with UK Customs seizing a shipment of nuclear capacitors and components for a 'super-gun' bound for Iraq, reported to have a range capable of hitting targets in Iran and Israel.[158] However, whilst Iraq possessed a ballistic missile capacity which was troubling its regional adversaries,[159] it still lacked the ability to reach the UK and was therefore unlikely to be considered a serious direct threat to national security. The more diffuse threat to UK interests in maintaining the stability of oil prices has been dealt with above.

Conclusion

In the 1990–1991 Gulf Crisis, the United States found strong military or financial support for its opposition to the Iraqi regime from the four states we have chosen to focus upon in this chapter. Our purpose has been to examine the decision-making processes in each state during the crisis to determine whether followership of the United States was motivated by three particular external material motivations: oil dependence and oil price stability, alliance dependence, and material assessments of the Iraqi threat. Evidence of significant material motivations for followership provide support for a conceptualisation of hegemony as a dominance relationship in which order is maintained by either the application of threats or coercion, or the provision of incentives or benefits to

Table 3.5 Oil dependency and followership

State	Sensitivity to world oil price stability/ dependence on oil		Persuasiveness of explanation
	In fact	Perception of impact	
Germany	High	Low	Low
Japan	High	Low	Low
France	High	Low	Low
United Kingdom	Nil	N/A	Low

Table 3.6 Alliance dependence and followership

State	Fear of abandonment	Fear of entrapment	Persuasiveness
Germany	High	Low	High
Japan	High	Low	High
France	Medium–High	Medium	Medium
United Kingdom	High	Low	High

Table 3.7 The balance of threat and followership

State	Aggregate power	Offensive capabilities	Geographic proximity	Persuasiveness
Germany	Credible	Insufficient	Not proximate	Low
Japan	Credible	Insufficient	Not proximate	Low
France	Credible	Insufficient	Not proximate	Low
United Kingdom	Credible	Insufficient	Not proximate	Low

subordinate states. After closer analysis of each case study, we have found that the only persuasive material motivation for followership for all states was a significant alliance dependence upon the United States.

In terms of our other two external material motivations, neither oil dependency and the interest in maintaining oil price stability nor the balance of threat hypothesis were able to provide persuasive explanations of followership in any case. Whilst Japan, West Germany and France were highly dependent upon oil for their energy needs, no clear evidence was found to support the view that followership was actually motivated by material interests in maintaining low world oil prices or access to oil from the Middle Eastern. Japan and France had for some time embarked on an energy diversification strategy away from oil, increasing confidence among decision-makers that any increase in the oil price as a result of the invasion would be absorbed without significant economic disruption. Whilst still highly oil dependent, West German leaders were in fact convinced that higher oil prices would be absorbed by the economy without major effects on economic growth. As a net oil exporter, the United Kingdom was not at all concerned with securing supplies from the Middle East. Whilst members of the government did express concern about the threat to world oil prices should Saddam Hussein keep control of the Kuwaiti oil fields, we have argued that UK concerns can only be understood within a normative framework which marked the Hussein regime as a threat, and it is this framework which more clearly motivated followership in this case.

Under the balance of threat hypothesis, states which shared the US assessment that Iraq posed a threat to national security would be likely to ally, or in this case 'follow', the US in any confrontation with Iraq. However, in all the cases examined, the Iraqi threat to national security was judged to be low, based on three material indicators of threat – aggregate power, offensive capabilities and geographic proximity. For all states, whilst Iraq did possess credible military forces and a proven chemical weapons capacity, it was not geographically proximate to any of these states and lacked the offensive capability to reach their territorial boundaries with its weapons arsenal. Thus, under the balance of threat hypothesis, defined in material terms, Japan, Germany, France and the UK should have rejected US leadership, rather than provide strong followership.

In contrast, alliance dependency can persuasively explain followership by all states. All states remained dependent on the US to varying degrees for their security, and in all cases the fear of abandonment overcame any fears of entrapment. In the case of Germany, alliance dependence provided the most convincing motivation for the strong financial contribution made to the coalition effort to reverse the Iraqi invasion. Germany's response to the crisis was highly reactive to direct pressure placed by the Bush Administration to share in the burdens of opposing the Iraqi invasion. Members of the Bush Administration openly reminded the German Government of the US's past military support during the Cold War as well as political support in the cause of German re-unification. The Kohl Government appeared to recognise the importance of participation for maintaining the strength of the alliance, particularly the need to sustain US support for unification given that the external aspects of the 2-Plus-4 treaty had not yet been concluded. Apart from this, existing European security structures could not provide a substitute for NATO, which performed the dual function of balancing against the Soviet Union whilst also reassuring European neighbours that a reunified Germany remained restrained within alliance. Both Chancellor Kohl and Foreign Minister Genscher publicly demonstrated their fear of abandonment by acknowledging the need to participate in the coalition to demonstrate Germany's loyalty, gratitude and reliability within the NATO alliance.

Japan's contribution to the coalition was also clearly related to its security alliance with the United States. At the time of the crisis, the Japanese Government continued to highly value the US alliance because of the constraints imposed on offensive military action by its pacifistic constitution, the advantages accruing from the US nuclear umbrella, the rise of regional threats such as North Korea and China, and the absence of alternative regional security institutions. During the course of the crisis, there was strong evidence that members of the Bush Administration and other US representatives communicated the expectation that Japan should play a role in international affairs commensurate with its economic power, and that the alliance would be damaged if it did not. The passing of a defence bill by US Congress threatening the withdrawal of 5,000 US troops a year from Japanese bases unless Japan bore the full cost of the US military presence there provided a blunt message on the consequences for Japan if it failed to make a significant contribution to the coalition. The timing and size of Japanese contributions, correlated directly with the application of such political pressure, suggested that Japanese followership was strongly motivated by the desire to prevent abandonment by its major military ally.

In the case of France, alliance dependence again provided the most persuasive explanation for followership of the US. However, in the French case political leaders grappled more clearly with the fear of becoming entrapped in a conflict which was of greater importance to US interests than its own, and which in fact undermined its interest in preserving a sphere of influence over former Islamic colonies in North Africa and the Middle East. We found ample evidence of French assertions of independence from the US in terms of the use of its military forces and through numerous attempts to broker a peaceful outcome. This was argued to have been driven by an interest in preserving its influence over a number of Arab ex-colonies in North Africa that opposed the use of force against Iraq. However, from the evidence it appears that the fear of abandonment ultimately outweighed the fear of entrapment, particularly given the continued value of the NATO alliance in institutionally containing the possible ambitions of a united Germany and as a continued balancing force against the military might of the USSR.

74 *Material factors and followership*

Finally, in the British case, of the three material factors that may have influenced it to follow the US we must conclude that alliance dependence again proved to be the most persuasive. The British enthusiastically joined the coalition without prompting, and appeared to independently come to the same view on the illegitimacy of Iraq's actions, and the goals and methods that should be pursued in response. Whilst this in itself was a significant factor in the British response, the size of the contribution and the absence of free-riding behaviour can also be explained as a response to its alliance dependence on the United States. UK decision-makers were concerned to prevent abandonment by the US, with NATO being seen to stabilise relations within Europe and stem the risk of a more assertive united Germany. The UK also feared that its usefulness to the US was at risk with a united Germany being seen as a more natural European partner. The potential weakening of the alliance was of particular concern because the Conservative government did not appear comfortable with greater European political cooperation, let alone military cooperation, making the US its only major military ally. The Gulf Crisis enabled the British to nurture and protect the 'special relationship' between the two allies through demonstrations of loyalty in the hope that this would give it greater influence over the policies of its stronger partner and to encourage the US to continue to play a strong role in European security. Alliance dependency across the four cases thus provides the only significant material explanation for followership of the US during the Gulf Crisis, providing some support for a conceptualisation of hegemony as a dominance relationship.

Appendix 3.1

Table 3.8 Countries participating in the military coalition

Argentina	Oman
Australia	Pakistan
Bahrain	Philippines
Bangladesh	Poland
Belgium	Qatar
Canada	Romania
Czechoslovakia	Saudi Arabia
Denmark	Senegal
Egypt	Saudi Arabia
France	Senegal
Greece	Sierra Leone
Hungary	Singapore
Italy	Spain
Kuwait	South Korea
Morocco	Sweden
Netherlands	Syria
New Zealand	United Arab Emirates
Niger	United Kingdom
Norway	United States

Source: Susan Rosegrant and Michael Watkins, *The Gulf Crisis: Building a Coalition for War*, Boston: Harvard University Press 1994.

4 Legitimacy and hegemony in the Iraq Crisis

The two cases of the Gulf Crisis and the Iraq Crisis provide us with a study of contrasts with respect to US standing as a leader of international society. Whilst the first case demonstrated widespread followership among a broad spectrum of states, the second was marked by a revolt against US leadership aspirations by foes and friends alike. In the Iraq Crisis, the US showed a very belated commitment to lead the community to disarm Iraq in September 2002, after many months in which a unilateral right to act was asserted in both domestic and international forums. When it did seek the support of the international community, it was able to obtain only partial support for its vision for the solution to the Iraq problem. Consensus in the Security Council was achieved in relation to the goal sought – that is, the goal of ensuring that Iraq was disarmed of any nuclear, chemical or biological weapons capabilities (weapons of mass destruction or 'WMD') it may have retained after 1991, or re-established after 1998. However, the US vision on the means to be used to secure Iraqi disarmament was decisively rejected, with the US being unable to convince a majority of states in the Council that the Iraqi threat was so grave as to require the abandonment of the inspections process in favour of the use of force. Whilst the US was able to convince a small number of states to join in the forceful removal of the Hussein regime, the depth of this coalition was exposed by the paucity of real burden-sharing in all respects in both waging war and reconstructing Iraq.

As such, the Iraq Crisis provides us with a valuable case study of both the assertion of hegemonic leadership by the US, and the failure to recognise this role by the majority of the international community. In this chapter we focus on the question of whether normative beliefs about legitimate behaviour guided decisions by states to reject US leadership. Here we are again seeking to test the explanatory value of a conceptualisation of hegemony as a socially constituted and regulated leadership role within international society. In the following chapter we will test the veracity of the competing conceptualisation of hegemony as a dominance relationship, by looking for material motivations for followership or the rejection of US leadership. Our overarching goal is to assess which approach offers the most persuasive explanation of the Iraq Crisis.

This chapter will look for evidence of hegemony as a relation of leadership by investigating whether there is a substantial link between the normative beliefs of states and the rejection of US leadership in the Iraq Crisis. We hypothesise that a majority of states rejected the US vision for the resolution of the Iraq problem because of their normative commitments to the core prohibition on the use of force and to the peaceful settlement of disputes reflected in the UN Charter. We also hypothesise that US leadership was rejected in this case because the US's behaviour did not conform to the expectations of proper behaviour associated with the role of hegemonic leadership. Essential to this role of leadership is the expectation that a hegemon seeks leadership primarily to achieve the common interest of all states, rather than to achieve its own parochial interests. To find evidence of normative beliefs, attention is again given to the arguments put forward by members of the Security Council and the broader UN membership to justify the important decisions made by the Council throughout the crisis. Because motives for action are notoriously mixed, our standard for success here is whether an explanation of the Iraq Crisis is substantially deficient without taking account of the normative beliefs of states with regard to legitimate conduct in international relations.

The following chapter will be divided into two sections representing the important decision-points during the crisis as dealt with by the Security Council. First, we will examine the lead up to the unanimous decision to pass Resolution 1441. Here the contested issue was whether the situation should be framed as one that threatened international peace and security, an issue that necessarily involved a normative assessment of Iraqi behaviour. Second, we will examine the debates over what means would be used to disarm Iraq. Focus is given to the meetings of the Council convened after presentation of the first and second reports of the inspectors of the IAEA and UNMOVIC. The issue of contention here was whether to escalate the means used to enforce Iraqi disarmament from a robust inspections process to the threat and use of force.

The chapter will conclude that there is strong evidence to suggest that US leadership was rejected on normative grounds. Whilst the US was able to gain support for the view that potential Iraqi re-armament posed a threat to international peace and security, it was unable to gain support for its choice of means to achieve disarmament. Here internationally accepted norms about the legitimate use of force and the peaceful settlement of disputes guided a majority of states to reject the US position. The unilateralist approach taken by the US to resolve the Iraq problem also undermined the persuasiveness of its vision, by fuelling distrust of its motives in seeking leadership. States ultimately declined to recognise US assertions of leadership of the international community because they had little confidence that leadership was sought for the right reasons, i.e. to achieve the common good. Subordinate states did not subsequently feel obligated to assist the US in its goal of disarming Iraq through forcible regime change.

Part 1 – defining the situation and deciding on goals and means

Following Iraq's comprehensive defeat in the 1991 Gulf War, the UN Security Council sought to ensure that Iraq should never again be allowed to threaten regional and international security. To achieve this goal a range of disarmament obligations were imposed on Iraq as a condition of cease-fire set out in UN Security Council Resolution (UNSCR) 687 of 3 April 1991, with compliance linked to the lifting of economic sanctions. Under this resolution, Iraq was obligated to reveal and destroy all its ballistic missiles with a range greater than 150 kilometres, all chemical, biological and nuclear stockpiles, and to renounce any intention to acquire and produce such weapons. In the period between 1991 and 1998, both the UN Special Commission ('UNSCOM') and the International Atomic Energy Agency ('IAEA') made good progress on Iraqi disarmament, with the help of defectors, despite the Iraqi regime's determined efforts to conceal and deny the extent of its programmes.[1]

However, by 1997 the regime began to systematically block the access of UNSCOM inspectors to suspected weapons sites, and by late February 1998 Kofi Annan had given in to Iraqi demands that restrictions be placed on inspections of Presidential palaces, including the requirement that advance notice be given of the inspectors' arrival.[2] Within the Security Council it became clear that only the United States and United Kingdom considered the containment of Iraq to be a high priority,[3] whilst Russia, China and France had lowered their assessment of the Iraqi threat and had begun to question humanitarian cost of the sanctions regime on Iraqi civilians. The situation reached crisis point in October 2002 with further acts of non-cooperation with the inspections teams by Iraq. By mid-December 2002, UNSCOM had been forced to withdraw all inspection teams because of Iraqi obstruction. This was immediately followed by retaliatory air strikes by the US and UK on around 100 suspected WMD sites, without the authorisation of the Security Council as part of Operation Desert Fox.[4]

This show of force, however, was not sufficient to convince the Hussein regime to allow the inspections teams back in. In the continuing absence of consensus in the Council, Iraq succeeded in breaking free of the inspections process. By late 2002, Iraq had gone without international monitoring and control of its possible WMD capabilities for four years, and within the Security Council momentum had further shifted towards an easing of the sanctions regime. This situation would have continued if not for a change in policy by the Bush Administration after the terrorist attacks of September 11, 2001.

US threat perception and the case against Iraq

The September 11, 2001 terrorist attacks on New York and Washington had a profound effect on the threat perceptions of the US Government. The attacks demonstrated to the Administration that, despite the US's overwhelming military power, as an open society it remained vulnerable to terrorist attacks by groups that had proven to be both determined and capable.[5] By November 2001, the threat posed by these groups had become magnified with intelligence gathered from Afghanistan revealing connections between Pakistani nuclear scientists and al-Qaeda members, together with designs for the making of a crude radiological weapon or 'dirty bomb'.[6] Whilst there was no direct evidence linking Iraq to the September 11, 2001 terrorist attacks, the release of the Bush Administration's first *National Security Strategy*[7] ('*NSS*') in September 2002 made it clear that the possibility of an alliance between 'rouge states' and transnational terrorist groups was seen to pose the core threat to US national security.

In his speech to the General Assembly in September 2002, President Bush identified Iraq as the epitome of a rogue state, as defined by the *NSS*,[8] citing the Hussein regime's past history of aggression against Kuwait and Iran, the use of chemical weapons against segments of the Iraqi population, and failure to comply with the Security Council's resolutions demanding WMD disarmament going back to the 1991 Gulf War.[9] In essence, rogue states like Iraq threatened international peace and security because of their aggressive behaviour, disregard for the basic principles of international order and dogged pursuit of WMD. It was therefore considered imperative to prevent them from successfully acquiring WMD, as the options available to the international community to contain such 'aggressive designs' would then become severely curtailed.[10] Whilst these arguments had been raised before, what was unique about US threat perceptions here was the belief that any rogue state in possession of WMD would have a compelling incentive to share this technology with international terrorist groups who shared a common enmity of the United States.[11] This multiplied the threat to national security posed by both groups.

Given the lack of interest shown by the Security Council in containing Iraq at this time, the US needed to make a convincing case that the very possibility of an alliance between terrorist groups and Iraq formed a serious threat to international peace and security requiring urgent collective action. As a rogue state with a history of illegitimate behaviour, it was arguably not irrational to believe in the likelihood that Iraq and al-Qaeda would join forces against a common enemy. This nexus, unproven but anticipated, was the cornerstone of the US's argument that the Iraqi threat needed to be confronted with urgency.

Apart from tackling the threat perceptions of other states, the US also sought to transform strategic thinking on the appropriate means to deal with these new threats. In particular, it was argued the Cold War strategy of deterrence would not work against either group because they both lacked a fear of overwhelming retaliation that was the essence of mutually assured destruction. Rogue states were undeterrable because their leaders placed little value on the lives of their own populations and tenaciously pursued WMD because these weapons provided the key to a number of strategic objectives: to achieve regional hegemony, prevent outside intervention and to provide a counterweight to US's superior conventional capabilities. The policy of deterrence was also argued to be ineffective in preventing international terrorist groups from seeking to acquire and use weapons of mass destruction. These groups actively sought to produce spectacular human casualties, were indifferent to their own self-preservation and, as non-state actors, had no home base that could be targeted for retaliation.[12] Therefore, a new proactive strategy was needed to prevent rogue states and their terrorist clients from obtaining WMD. The centrepiece of this new proactive strategy was the Administration's declaration of its intention to 'act alone if necessary, to exercise our right of self-defence by acting pre-emptively'.[13]

The doctrine of pre-emption

The doctrine of pre-emption as declared by the *NSS* asserts a unilateral right to use force in self-defence in much wider circumstances than envisaged under existing international law. Article 51 of the UN Charter recognises the 'inherent right' of an individual state to use force in its own defence only after it has suffered an 'armed attack'. Among international lawyers there has been considerable debate over whether the UN Charter codified international law on self-defence up until 1945, with those in favour of this view arguing that Article 51 therefore prohibited the use of force in self-defence before a state actually became the victim of an armed attack.[14]

Since the time of the Cuban Missile Crisis, long before September 11, 2001, this restrictive interpretation of Article 51 has been criticised on the grounds that it fails to take account of changes in the practice and technology associated with modern warfare, particularly the advent of nuclear weapons and improved delivery systems. It was argued that to expect a state to wait until it had suffered the consequences of a catastrophic attack, whether by conventional or nuclear weaponry, was an irrational and unrealistic expectation[15] that would require states to 'assume the posture of sitting ducks' when faced with 'complete obliteration'.[16] Further, the many advancements in technology used for intelligence gathering and reconnaissance could be used to guard against abusive practices.[17] In these circumstances, it was argued that states should be allowed to use force in self-defence if there was clear evidence to show that an attack was imminently about to occur.

Supporters of this pragmatic approach look for justification in the terms of Article 51, reading the term 'inherent' as an explicit recognition of the continued operation of customary international law on the use of force in self-defence, particularly of the principles of necessity and proportionality elucidated in *The Caroline* incident. On this view, the use of force in self-defence would be acceptable under international law where the necessity of its exercise was 'instant, overwhelming, and leaving no choice of means, and no moment for deliberation', and where the specific act of self-defence was limited in terms of its 'intensity and magnitude to what was reasonably necessary' to achieve the object of repelling the threat of attack.[18] Thus, it is contended that the use of force in self-defence is acceptable under customary international law where an attack is imminently about to occur, as supported by clear objective evidence, and where other peaceful means of response were unavailable or ineffective – also known as the doctrine of anticipatory self-defence.[19]

Whilst the arguments made by eminent jurists are certainly relevant to any discussion of the legality of anticipatory self-defence, post-1945 state practice and *opinio juris* does not evidence strong support for it within the society of states. In terms of *opinio juris*, prior to September 11, 2001, only Israel, Iraq, Japan, the US and Canada had overtly advocated the acceptance of a right to anticipatory self-defence and, of these states, only Israel and Iraq have actually asserted the right in practice.[20] More commonly, states have instead justified their use of force as an act of self-defence in response to an armed attack, however far-fetched might be the circumstances. Israel, for example, did not justify the use of force against Egypt, Jordan and Syria in 1967 under this doctrine, but instead argued that acts to prevent the use of the Straits of Tiran by Israeli vessels constituted an armed attack.[21]

Of note is Israel's destruction of the Iraqi Osiraq nuclear reactor in 1981 on the basis of an explicit claim to act in anticipatory self-defence which was conclusively rejected by a majority of states. Here the Israeli Government destroyed the Iraqi nuclear reactor prior to it becoming operational or 'hot' based on the judgement that the reactor was not built merely for the purpose of energy production, but to manufacture nuclear weapons.[22] From Israel's perspective, given the numerous statements made by members of the Hussein regime of the intent to 'support the liquidation of the racist Zionist entity', any nuclear weapons produced by Iraq would inevitably be used against it, at an unknown future time.[23] From this perspective, the requirement of imminence had been satisfied as there was a necessity of self-defence, instant and overwhelming, given that the reactor could only be destroyed prior to it becoming 'hot'.

These arguments for the use of anticipatory self-defence were rejected by the Security Council and were instead marked as acts of aggression within UN Security Council Resolution 487 (1981) and also by a resolution of the General Assembly.[24] Of the 38 states that gave their views on the matter in the Security Council, only six were prepared to accept the doctrine of anticipatory self-defence.[25] Even then, none of these states believed Israel had satisfied the test of imminence, i.e. that there was evidence of an imminent attack by Iraq. Rather, Israel was in fact arguing that self-defence could be used in circumstances which fit the definition of preventive war, i.e. where an enemy attack 'while not imminent, is inevitable, and that to delay would involve greater risk'.[26] Among the consistent objections raised was the possibility that an acceptance of a right to anticipatory self-defence would be open to abuse, particularly by powerful states.[27] For many states, there was little distinction between anticipatory self-defence and aggression, and absolutely no distinction between aggression and preventive war.

It is against this background that the invocation by the Bush Administration of a right of pre-emptive self-defence must be understood. This doctrine sought to broaden the scope of self-defence beyond the already shaky boundaries set by anticipatory self-defence to effectively encompass preventive war. In the *NSS*, the US argues that the concept of imminent threat of attack must be adapted 'to the capabilities and objectives of today's adversaries': rogue states and international terrorists. Of particular importance is the contention that the standard of imminence under the Caroline principles is modelled on an outdated view of warfare between states. Traditionally, evidence of an impending attack would be clearly visible, through the 'mobilisation of armies, navies, and air forces preparing to attack'.[28] In contrast, America's new enemies, well aware of the clear imbalance of military power, would logically employ asymmetrical tactics of war such as terrorist attacks using 'weapons that can be easily concealed, delivered covertly, and used without warning', and potentially in the form of WMD.[29] In these circumstances, the potential target of such an attack would not easily be able to make a determination about whether an attack was imminent. Thus, where the means of attack are covert and concealed, and the consequences of inaction are potentially catastrophic, the US maintains that it has no choice but to act where an attack is not necessarily imminent, but highly likely to occur in the near future.

This attempt to stretch the bounds of self-defence posed a distinct challenge to the core principles of the post-Second World War order encapsulated in the UN Charter. The Charter was constructed by states in an effort to avert the repeat of a worldwide conflict through the imposition of 'serious and sweeping self-limitations of their sovereign prerogatives in the form of the mutual obligation to refrain from using or threatening force'.[30] On a broader level, the essence of collective security, reflected in the Charter, is the prevention of the aggressive use of force through the prospect of collective punishment of the aggressor. All uses of force between states are considered aggressive under the Charter unless it is used in self-defence after an armed attack has occurred or to defend the common interest in international peace and security under Chapter VII. Together with respect for the principles of sovereignty, non-intervention and the peaceful settlement of disputes, these restrictions on the use of force were designed to ensure that force would no longer be used as a normal instrument of foreign policy.

None of these core principles of the Charter have gone without some re-interpretation in the years since 1945 and particularly in the post-Cold War era. Whilst it was recognised that the reciprocal recognition of state sovereignty reduced the likelihood of conflict between states, in the 1990s the Security Council recognised that the major threats to international order derived not from conflicts between states but from disorder within them.[31] Previously unthinkable circumstances were considered 'threats' to international peace and security requiring international intervention such as humanitarian human rights violations in Iraq, Somalia, Rwanda, Bosnia and Kosovo,[32] the restoration of democratic government in Haiti, and the extradition of terrorist suspects in Libya. This practice has served to weaken the idea that sovereignty is absolute and replace it with the idea of conditional or responsible sovereignty.[33] The supportive response of the international community to US military action against Afghanistan extended the idea of conditional sovereignty to allow the use of force in self-defence in clear cases of state sponsorship of terrorism, where an armed attack had already occurred.

The doctrine of pre-emption asserted in the *NSS* can be interpreted as an attempt to further expand the idea of conditional sovereignty to 'rogue states' who pursue WMD. In September 2002, Richard Haas, the Director of Policy Planning for the US Department of State, asserted that '[w]hen certain regimes with a history of aggression and support for terrorism pursue weapons of mass destruction, thereby endangering the international community, they jeopardise their sovereign immunity from intervention including anticipatory action to destroy this developing capability'.[34]

Whilst state practice in relation to Afghanistan (and Libya) showed an acceptance by the international community that state sponsorship of terrorism is illegitimate, this did not evidence a general acceptance of a right to take pre-emptive action against 'rogue states', unless it could be shown that an attack had already occurred or was clearly and imminently about to occur, based on sound intelligence. In making the case for the pre-emptive use of force against 'rogue' states such as Iraq, the suspicion that a WMD capacity was being pursued, or had been acquired, was argued by the US to pose a threat worthy of the use of force. The intention to use such weapons at some future time was drawn by inference from the very nature or identity of the regime itself.

Whilst this was a cause for concern in itself, the greatest challenge posed by the *NSS* was its assertion of an *individual* right to pre-emption against rogue states intent on acquiring WMD in a form that was expressed in expansive terms. Individual states would have wide discretion to decide that the use of force was required to pre-empt the threat of future attack, with no guidelines being provided for what form of proof would be adequate to sustain this assessment.[35] In these circumstances the *NSS* did not provide clear criteria for distinguishing between pre-emption and the aggressive use of force, potentially fuelling a dangerous escalation in regional conflicts where long-standing adversaries might be tempted exploit a temporary first-strike advantage.[36] The possibility that the doctrine was open to abuse by powerful states meant that force could once again become an instrument of foreign policy, rather than a last resort as envisaged by the Charter.

Unilateralism and the Bush Administration

The *NSS* and the position of the Bush Administration on Iraq must also be understood in relation to the challenge posed to multilateral controls on the use of force under the Charter. In his September 2002 speech to the General Assembly, President Bush took the line that a failure to act by the members of the Security Council would signify the abrogation of their special responsibilities to protect international stability, the common interest of all states. The lack of will to enforce its decisions would directly undermine the underlying rationale of collective security and in these circumstances it was argued the US had no choice but to act unilaterally to fill the breach.

This justification had been used on two previous occasions by the United States, to justify the use of force against Iraq in Operation Desert Fox as well as

NATO action against Serbia in the Kosovo conflict. In the case of Operation Desert Fox, it was undisputed that Iraq had materially breached the terms of the cease-fire agreement contained in Resolution 687, a fact that had been formally recognised by a number of resolutions demanding full cooperation with the inspections process. The US and UK argued that the original mandate to use force against Iraq in 1990 under Resolution 678 had been revived as a result of Iraq's material breach, thereby removing the need for a further Security Council resolution to authorise Operation Desert Fox. Whilst this argument was legally inventive, it was rejected by a strong majority of the Council who were of the view that the 'will' of the Council was not designed to be interpreted by individual states.[37]

In the case of Kosovo, a number of NATO states used a similar argument to justify the use of force against Serbian positions without authorisation by a specific Council resolution. Here, NATO states argued that military action was undertaken to enforce the 'will' of the international community as expressed in Resolution 1199 (1998) which identified the humanitarian situation and the displacement of refugees as a threat to international peace and security. Whilst this justification was considered to be unlawful under the terms of the Charter, the action was perceived to have 'moral' rather than legal legitimacy because a strong majority of the Council had in fact supported it and had been thwarted by the threatened use of the veto by Russia. The legitimacy of the unauthorised use of force by NATO mainly hinged on the fact that it sought to prevent a grave humanitarian catastrophe from occurring and was conducted by a collective organisation rather than an individual state, which at least inserted some procedural safeguards against abuse.[38] The use of force against Iraq in 2003 did not ultimately fulfil these criteria.

The second argument used by the US to justify the unilateral disarmament of Iraq was the right to pre-emptive self-defence.[39] Whilst the word 'pre-emption' was not used within the Security Council, the Administration asserted the right to defend itself against a future, rather than imminent, threat. Clear and reliable evidence was not provided to prove that Iraq had in fact reconstituted its WMD programmes or had formed an alliance with al-Qaeda or other like-minded groups. These threat perceptions were based on inferences drawn from Iraq's past illegitimate behaviour. Both justifications for unilateral military action effectively usurped the central role of the Council to determine what action to take where a threat to peace and security emerged, thereby removing the multilateral controls over the use of force which restrained its use for parochial ends.

An unanticipated by-product of US unilateralism was the detrimental effect this had on the credibility of its belated assertion of a right to act as a leader of the international community on this issue. Since November 2001, the Administration had been building its case against Iraq and, by January 2002, had already asserted its willingness to act unilaterally to prevent 'rogue' states from acquiring WMD. In threatening unilateral action if the international community did not follow its lead on this score, the Administration showed its unwillingness to compromise and to take the views and interests of other states into consideration.

This was in direct contrast to the inclusive leadership style of the first Bush Administration in the Gulf Crisis of 1990–1991. Here the Administration was declaring its unilateral right to decide the legitimate goals of the collective and the means by which to achieve them.

Aside from a dictatorial leadership style, the fact that the US was prepared to act unilaterally to change the Iraqi regime, and believed in its right to do so, caused some to question its real motives in seeking the support of the international community at this stage. If the Administration was so confident in the legitimacy of its cause, and the need for regime change, then it need not have sought the involvement of the Security Council. This was indeed the view of Vice President Cheney who publicly stated in August 2002 that 'a return of inspectors would provide no assurance whatsoever of [Saddam Hussein's] compliance with UN resolutions. On the contrary, there is a great danger that it would provide false comfort that Saddam was somehow back in his box.'[40] If the Administration had little confidence that inspections would succeed in disarming Iraq, then what purpose was served by going to the UN?

There were of course real instrumental benefits for the US should the Security Council have endorsed the use of force against Iraq via a Council resolution. The legitimacy accorded by the Security Council would allow other states to obtain support domestically for their involvement in any action against Iraq and give the US the right to expect a level of burden-sharing among the broader UN membership. This obvious pragmatic motivation gave many states cause to doubt US arguments about the seriousness of the Iraqi threat and the urgent need to disarm it. The question was whether the US was truly seeking to lead the community to achieve the common interest in stability or to achieve its own parochial interests.

The substance of the case put forward against Iraq, the assertion of revolutionary doctrines on the use of force, and the uncompromising leadership style of the Bush Administration, together became important elements in the decisions of states to follow or reject the leadership of the US throughout the crisis. In the following sections we turn our attention to the role of international legitimacy in motivating states to accept or reject the vision put forward by the Administration to ameliorate the Iraqi threat, as well as to recognise its status and identity as a leader of the international community.

Negotiations over Resolution 1441

From early October to 8 November, the members of the Security Council undertook protracted negotiations to agree on a new draft resolution. In all, three drafts were presented to the Council by the US and UK on 2 October, 25 October and 5 November, and one draft was presented jointly by Russia and France on 23 October.[41] The changes made to these draft resolutions reflect the opposing positions within the Council, particularly among the Permanent Members, and the compromises they were eventually willing to make. There were two major differences between the positions presented to the Council by the UK and US and the counter-position presented by France and Russia.

First, the draft resolutions reflected divergent assessments of the level of threat Iraq posed to international peace and security, and displayed differing levels of urgency on the issue of Iraq's disarmament. The US and UK drafts sought a clear statement of all Iraq's prior violations of its disarmament obligations and the setting of unambiguous benchmarks by which the Security Council could judge the adequacy of Iraq's compliance. By contrast, the draft presented by France and Russia omitted many of the listed breaches of prior Security Council resolutions and did not define what would constitute a serious failure by Iraq to comply with its disarmament obligations. On this point the French and Russians conceded the need to define what constituted a material breach of the new resolution, with the final draft specifying two criteria for failure: the making of false statements or omissions in its declaration of its WMD programmes and facilities;[42] and the failure to cooperate 'immediately, unconditionally, and actively with UNMOVIC and the IAEA'.[43]

The second major difference between the drafts by the US/UK and by France/Russia was their view on whether the use of force should be authorised should Iraq fail to comply with the new resolution. The US and UK sought direct authorisation for the use of force, whilst the Russian and French draft of 23 October conspicuously did not, but rather envisaged a two-stage process in which a further resolution would be required to authorise the use of force. The first resolution would set out the conditions and criteria for a resumption of inspections and would threaten 'serious consequences' should Iraq be reported by the inspectors as having breached its conditions. If Iraq was found to have breached its obligations, then a second meeting of the Council would be called to decide whether the use of force should be authorised in response. The two-stage process put a brake on the use of force by requiring that the Council meet again to decide whether a change in means was necessary. Whilst, on the face of it, the US agreed to compromise by accepting the Russian and French two-stage approach, in practice the US delegation believed that the authorisation of force would be a mere formality. In the months to come, this belief proved to be mistaken.

Legitimacy and Resolution 1441 – the Security Council

The final draft resolution which was accepted unanimously by the Security Council on 7 November 2002 showed a partial acceptance of the US vision for the solution to the Iraqi problem. The US was able to engender support for the goal of disarming Iraq by successfully framing the situation as one involving a threat to the common interests of all states, the stability of international order. For member states, shared norms about legitimate behaviour for states in general, and states with the responsibilities attached to the role of a Security Council member, played a primary role in justifying both the acceptance of the situation as a threat, and the re-establishment of an inspections process as the means to ameliorate it. In other words, the decision-making process used by state representatives showed that they acted under a logic of appropriateness.[44]

To follow the US vision for the solution to the Iraq problem required the members of the Security Council to agree that the potential for Iraq to be armed with WMD was a danger to international peace and security (see Table 4.1). On this point, all 15 states agreed with the US, uniting behind the goal of disarming Iraq of its WMD capabilities. In the preamble to the terms of the resolution, a strong list of Security Council resolutions that Iraq had failed to obey was reproduced, which in themselves evidenced the non-recognition by Iraq of the legitimate standards of behaviour expected of states. Iraq had failed to comply with resolutions requiring the dismantling of its WMD programmes, the destruction of stockpiles, the cessation of support for terrorist organisations, an end to repression of its civilian population, a return of Kuwaiti and other prisoners of war, and a return of property seized by Iraq during the Gulf War. This past illegitimate behaviour identified Iraq as an aggressive and revisionist state, and as such its possible possession of WMD was agreed to pose a threat to international peace and security.

What also convinced a number of states to agree with the US frame of the situation was the belief that Iraq's defiance of Security Council resolutions was itself a threat to international peace and security. Seven states justified their support for the resolution on the grounds that a failure to do so would undermine the credibility of collective security under the UN Charter. As had been argued in the first Gulf War, a failure to defend the principles of the Charter would undermine the ability of the Council to deter other states from defying its determinations in the future.

Once states within the Council had accepted that the situation was one in which a threat to the common interest was at stake, their role as defenders of the common interest required them to act. In terms of the logic of appropriateness, the answer to the question – what situation is this? – led to the questions – who am I and what is appropriate behaviour for an actor with my identity in this situation?[45] Seven states referred to their obligation as members of the Council to take action where international peace and security was threatened, whilst 11 states specifically declared their belief that the Security Council was the only legitimate body with authority to decide the appropriate response to threats to international peace and security. Similarly, many of these states referred approvingly to the call by Kofi Annan for the Security Council to 'face its responsibilities' if 'Iraq's defiance continues'.[46]

Whilst the US vision for the solution to the Iraq problem was accepted as legitimate in terms of its goals, its preferred means of achieving this goal were rebuffed on normative grounds. As can be seen in Table 4.1, 11 out of 15 states justified their support for disarmament through an enhanced inspection regime (and a rejection of the authorisation of force) on the basis of two normative beliefs: that the settlement of disputes between states should be achieved peacefully, and/or that force should be used only as a last resort. Given their common expectations of legitimate behaviour for states in international society, it was inappropriate to authorise the use of force at this stage, before all peaceful means had been exhausted.

In keeping with this normative prescription, some states appeared to be motivated by a desire to prevent war being seen as inevitable, given US declarations of the intent to act unilaterally if the Council did not. Support for the two-step process was justified on this basis. For example, the French delegate stated that all his country's 'diplomatic efforts' up to that point had been 'directed towards giving peace a chance',[47] whilst the Russian delegate asserted that the most important aspect of Resolution 1441 was the deflection of the 'direct threat of war' and the enhanced prospects of a 'political diplomatic settlement'.[48] Even the two states most eager to affect Iraqi disarmament, the US and the UK, officially supported the peaceful settlement of the dispute.[49]

Whilst the rejection of the US push for a single resolution was motivated by a normative commitment to the peaceful settlement of disputes, there is evidence to suggest that it was also motivated by a desire to defend the role of the Security Council as the body with the legitimate right to decide on appropriate measures to defend international order. In their speeches to the Council, a number of states were clearly reacting against the US's two justifications for the unilateral disarmament of Iraq: the enforcement of previous Security Council resolutions; and the doctrine of pre-emptive self-defence.[50] Both justifications for unilateral action threatened to usurp the rights and responsibilities of the Security Council on matters of international peace and security, as well as setting a precedent for the use of force without multilateral controls on the goals to be pursued by it.

In the Council, only the UK expressed the view that the unilateral enforcement of the Security Council's resolutions was a legitimate course of action, and none positively supported the right to pre-emptive self-defence. A total of 11 states made direct reference to their support for the central role of the Security Council in matters of international peace and security, and implicitly expressed their disapproval of the Bush Administration's assertion of the right to take a unilateralist course within this domain. Of note was the statement by France that the 'main and constant objective of France' in the negotiations over Resolution 1441 was to ensure that it 'strengthens the role and authority of the Security Council' which was 'reflected in our request that a two-stage approach be established ... ensuring that the Security Council would maintain control of the process at each stage'.[51] Russia warned against 'yielding to the temptation of unilateral interpretation of the resolution's provisions',[52] and China expressed its hope that the resolution would 'contribute to preserving the authority of the Council' which bore the 'primary responsibility for the maintenance of international peace and security – a responsibility ... entrusted to it by the Charter'.[53]

Underlying these sentiments was the desire to ensure that, if force was to be used to achieve Iraqi disarmament, it would be a decision made by the Security Council as a safeguard against the use of force for parochial rather than collective interests. Whilst no member state directly voiced their doubts about US motives and their apprehensions about the doctrine of pre-emption, an unnamed French diplomat explained that French support for the two-stage process was designed to ensure that multilateral controls were maintained over the use of force by the Council to prevent any nation from doing 'what it wants, where it wants'.[54] This is consistent with the views expressed by Jacques Chirac in September 2002, in which he stated that the general acceptance of a right of pre-emptive self-defence would be 'extraordinarily dangerous' and would have 'tragic consequences'. In Chirac's view, the decision to take preventive action 'must be taken by the international community, which today is represented by the United Nations Security Council'.[55] Apart from these French concerns, the two-stage process was also reported to assuage the concerns of non-Permanent Members, including Cameroon, Guinea, Mauritius and Mexico, that the US had its own interests in regime change, and that it was only involving the UN to legitimise this course of action.[56]

Part 2 – changing the means?

The passing of Resolution 1441 (2002) by a unanimous vote in the Security Council was a moment of great success for the US leadership during the Iraq Crisis. Whilst it had compromised on the issues of setting a deadline for Iraqi compliance, and on the direct authorisation for the use of force, the decision to give Iraq 'one final opportunity' to comply with the Security Council's demands to disarm gave rise to the expectation by the US and its followers that force would be authorised by the Council if Iraq was found to be in breach of its obligations. The US vision on the goal of Iraqi disarmament had been successfully accepted as legitimate by a strong majority of the Council. However, over the coming months, support for the US vision on the choice of means to ensure Iraqi disarmament began to falter, ultimately leading to the rejection of US leadership on the issue by a majority of states. In the next section, we will attempt to examine whether the rejection of US leadership on the use of force against Iraq was significantly motivated by beliefs about legitimate behaviour between states.

Assessments of Iraqi compliance

The initial all-important assessment of Iraq's compliance with the terms of Resolution 1441 came on 27 January 2003, with the presentation of the first inspectors' reports by the UN Monitoring, Verification and Inspection Commission ('UNMOVIC'), the body that replaced UNSCOM, and the IAEA to the Security Council. Resolution 1441 required Iraq to comply with two main obligations in order to avoid the threat of war.[57] First, Iraq was obligated to provide the international community with a full declaration of its WMD weapons programmes and stockpiles within 30 days.[58] Iraq would be considered in 'material breach' of its obligations if the inspectors were to find that 'false statements or omissions' had been made in this declaration.[59] Second, Iraq was required to demonstrate an intention to disarm by assisting the inspectors to verify the accuracy of its declaration. This required two things: first, 'immediate, unimpeded, unconditional, and unrestricted access' to sites, information, personnel etc.; and, second, immediate, unconditional and active cooperation with the inspectors.[60] A failure to comply with either of these obligations constituted a 'material breach' of Resolution 1441 triggering 'serious consequences' under its terms.

In their first reports to the Council, the Directors of both UNMOVIC and the IAEA were unable to attest to Iraq's full compliance with its obligations under

Resolution 1441. Whilst the IAEA could not fault the accuracy of Iraq's declaration in relation to nuclear issues without conducting further inspections,[61] Iraq's cooperation with the IAEA's inspection teams was criticised as lacking both proactivity and transparency.[62] That is, in the IAEA's assessment, Iraq had cooperated 'immediately' and 'unconditionally' but not 'actively' as Resolution 1441 required,[63] with the verification of Iraq's nuclear status only possible if there was 'sustained proactive cooperation by Iraq'.[64]

The head of UNMOVIC, Hans Blix, was even more harshly critical of Iraq's compliance with the terms of Resolution 1441. In his view, Iraq's declaration failed to include any information in its 12,000-page dossier which clarified the 'many open disarmament issues' listed in the last UNSCOM report of January 1999, including the failure to provide evidence to verify Iraq's claim to have destroyed all stocks of anthrax and chemical bombs.[65] On the key issue of cooperation, Blix harshly criticised Iraq for cooperating on process, that is, on access to sites of interest, but not on substance.[66] Even in relation to process, however, Blix reported to the Council that Iraq was obstructing UNMOVIC's use of U-2 spy planes for aerial imagery and surveillance during inspections. Overall, Blix was highly critical of the level of cooperation he had received from Iraq and stated clearly that he did not believe that Iraq had come to a 'genuine acceptance – not even today – of the disarmament which was demanded of it …'[67] In his view, Resolution 1441 had shifted the onus on Iraq to show its willingness to disarm by showing complete openness to scrutiny and complete cooperation with efforts to verify its declaration.[68]

Reaction to the reports

Whilst neither the IAEA nor UNMOVIC explicitly determined that Iraq was in 'material breach' of Resolution 1441, both had been critical of its level of compliance, thereby providing considerable ammunition from which to draw such a finding. This was the view of the United States, followed by the United Kingdom and Spain, who all argued that Iraq should now face the 'serious consequences' contemplated under Resolution 1441.[69] However, at least 11 other members of the Council were unprepared to follow the US vision to disarm Iraq through the use of force and instead called for the inspectors to be given more time.[70]

The unwillingness to follow the US lead on the choice of means stemmed in part from a reluctance to authorise the use of force on the basis of inferences drawn from Iraq's lack of full and active compliance. That is, the pre-emptive use of force against Iraq at this stage was not widely supported. Rather, both the French and Russians called for the US to present convincing proof that Iraq was actively deceiving the inspectors.[71] In doing so, both states effectively reversed the onus of proof from Iraq to the US, a burden that was not intended under the terms of Resolution 1441, as had been strongly argued in Blix's 27 January report. However, given the strong objections to the use of force by key states, the US made the political decision to lay bare its intelligence in order to prove that Iraq was in fact actively deceiving the inspectors, which would thereby ameliorate the concerns associated with the pre-emptive use of force.

However, this attempt to provide direct proof of Iraq's guilt ultimately failed to convince the majority of the Council that Iraq was actively concealing WMD stockpiles or a reconstituted weapons programme, or both. On 5 February 2003, US Secretary of State Colin Powell used intercepted telephone conversations and satellite images showing movements of vehicles and temporary buildings around suspected chemical weapons and ballistic missile production facilities as proof that Iraq was actively deceiving the inspectors. Emphasis was placed on the existence of mobile biological-weapons production facilities that could be easily concealed and difficult to differentiate from legitimate civilian infrastructure.[72] The reliance on satellite imagery without sufficient human intelligence to explain them meant that much of Powell's evidence held only circumstantial value.

On the issue of Iraq's links with al-Qaeda, Powell presented evidence that an al-Qaeda associate, Abu Musab Zarqawi, was operating a terrorist-training camp in north-eastern Kurdish Iraq, as well as a 'cell' in Baghdad which coordinated the network's activities.[73] However, Powell could not provide reliable evidence to prove that the Iraqi Government was aware of the group's activities, let alone operated, controlled or sponsored it.[74] In the days to come, Hans Blix refuted a number of US claims, including the existence of alleged 'mobile laboratories' used to move biological weapons. The US was therefore unable to reveal a 'smoking gun' in the form of conclusive proof of deception or links to al-Qaeda sufficient to shift opinions within and outside the Council about the necessity of the use of force.

Without this 'smoking gun', the United States was ultimately unable to attract sufficient support for its 'vision' to disarm Iraq through the use of force. The US, the UK and Spain put forward two draft resolutions which gave Iraq until 17 March to show the Council that it would provide 'full, unconditional, immediate and active cooperation', with the implied threat being that military action would follow after this date if it could not.[75] Opposing this course was an alternative plan put forward by France, Russia and Germany, and endorsed by China,[76] which called for a peaceful solution to the crisis via a strengthened inspections process.[77] Under this plan the inspectors would be given a further 120 days to verify Iraq's compliance, at which time a final report would be given to the Council on their progress. When it became clear that a majority of the Council did not support the US-sponsored drafts, and that both the French and Russians would cast a veto over any resolution authorising the use of force,[78] the decision was made by the US, UK and Spain that a 'coalition of the willing' would invade Iraq, without a second resolution.[79]

Legitimacy and the choice between inspections and war

In the key February to March 2003 period of the crisis, the US vision for the achievement of Iraqi disarmament was decisively rejected by a majority of the Council on two normative grounds: first, that peaceful options for the settlement of the dispute had not yet been exhausted; and, second, that the acceptance of the US vision would imply the acceptance of pre-emptive or preventive war, a doctrine which threatened to undermine the core prohibition on the use of force and the norms associated with state sovereignty contained in the Charter. On the first issue,

Legitimacy and hegemony in the Iraq Crisis 91

all states shared the view that, in the first instance, the international community should attempt to disarm Iraq via peaceful means, i.e. through an enhanced inspection process. However, there was a clear divergence of views over whether all peaceful means had been exhausted. From the US and UK's point of view, the failure of the Iraqi regime to provide the inspectors with complete and active cooperation showed that it did not genuinely accept the demand to disarm.[80] In these circumstances, without the application of extreme levels of external diplomatic and military pressure, Iraq would once again re-activate its WMD programmes and thereby become an actual, rather than potential, threat to international peace and security.[81]

In addition, the US and its supporters believed that the inspections process could not be relied upon to verify and enforce Iraqi disarmament without Iraq's full and active cooperation. Even if more time and resources were devoted to this effort, given the vast size of Iraq's territory, the inspectors would never have sufficient resources or the human intelligence to 'conceivably sniff out the weapons and documentation relating to them without the help of the Iraqi authorities'.[82] For UK Prime Minister Tony Blair, the French/German/Russian plan was 'absurd' because of its reliance on the good faith of the Iraqi government.[83] Whilst the lack of proactive cooperation by the regime was less of an impediment to verification of its nuclear and ballistic missile capabilities,[84] the same could not be said for chemical and biological weapons because the facilities and components used in their manufacture could also be used for legitimate industrial purposes.[85]

On this reasoning, all peaceful means to disarm Iraq had been exhausted and the gravity and urgency of the threat meant that there was no choice other than the use of force. As had been argued by the US in September, in a situation where international peace and security was clearly at stake, it was only rightful, proper and appropriate that the Council act to enforce its decisions, or else 'the credibility of the Council and its ability to deal with all the critical challenges we face will suffer'[86] and would 'encourage ... those possessing weapons of mass destruction who feel that they can systematically violate international law with impunity'.[87]

Both aspects of the US vision of the Iraq problem were rejected by a majority of states in the Council. Whilst 13 members of the Council were in agreement that Iraq's level of cooperation thus far had been inadequate, a strong majority of 11 states believed that peaceful means had not been exhausted and the legitimate course of action to take was to allow the inspections process to continue. Seven states, including Germany, China, Russia and France, thought that Iraqi cooperation had shown improvement, with five of these states also viewing the inspectors' progress on disarmament as promising. In these circumstances, a majority of eight states gave their explicit or implicit endorsement of the French/German/Russian position which would have allowed inspections to continue for at least another three months (Table 4.2).

In terms of the general UN membership, the US vision for Iraqi disarmament received only minor support. Of the 53 states who gave their individual views on the matter at a series of open meetings of the Security Council, 69 per cent agreed that the inspectors needed to be given more time, with 67 per cent justifying their stance on the belief that all peaceful means had not yet been exhausted. Whilst a large number expressed dissatisfaction with the level of cooperation shown by Iraq, 31 per cent believed that Iraq was showing greater active cooperation and 33 per cent believed that the inspectors were making progress on disarmament (Table 4.3). On 11 March, this position was endorsed by the 115 members of the Non-Aligned Movement, the Organisation of African States and the Arab League.[88] Not surprisingly, of the 42 states that gave their views at an open meeting of the Security Council held on 26 March (see Table 4.6), the use of force by the coalition was viewed to be illegitimate because the peaceful settlement of the dispute had been possible (43 per cent of states), and that the coalition had defied the will and authority of the Security Council over matters of international peace and security (36 per cent of states). The 116 members of the NAM, which included all 22 members of the League of Arab states, unreservedly denounced the use of force as an 'illegitimate act of aggression'.[89]

In a broader sense, the failure of the US to convince a majority of states in the Council to abandon the inspections regime can also be seen as a failure on the part of the US to convince other states to share its threat perceptions, as well as its assessment that the only legitimate means to extinguish the Iraqi threat required the pre-emptive use of force. On the issue of threat perceptions, the US and its allies had been unable to persuade a majority of the Council that Iraq was in fact concealing a reconstituted WMD programme from the inspectors, and had formed linkages to international terrorists.[90] Without acceptance of the nexus between al-Qaeda and Iraq, the case for the urgent abandonment of the inspections process considerably dissipated.

Further, without the sharing of threat perceptions on the gravity and urgency of the Iraqi threat, the potential costs of war significantly outweighed the benefits. Concerns were raised about the likely humanitarian costs of war as well as the unpredictable and serious consequences for regional and international stability.[91] The French and Germans argued that the use force against Iraq could undermine the solidarity of the coalition against terrorism, particularly among Arab and Muslim countries where, in the court of public opinion, the Iraqi regime was being unfairly singled out for special attention among the 'rogue' states.[92] For Germany, the situation in Afghanistan was a more serious threat than that emanating from the Iraqi regime and a war in Iraq would risk undermining the success of the nation-building project only just begun in that country.[93]

The rejection of US leadership on this issue must also be seen as a rejection of the US case for pre-emption in the case of Iraq. As we have discussed above (pp. 79–82), pre-emption, whether exercised in self-defence or collectively, describes the use of force against a state on the grounds of a possible future attack, rather than one in which the timing and scope of the attack is known and capable of being anticipated. Throughout the crisis, France, Russia and Germany clearly rejected the use of force in the absence of direct proof of Iraq's possession of WMD and its links to terrorist groups, a position which disputed the legitimacy of the pre-emptive use of force. In opposing the initial push for the 'automatic' use of force under Resolution 1441, the majority of states in the Council effectively refused to countenance the use of force against Iraq without direct proof, from disinterested sources, that it had in fact taken steps to reconstitute its weapons programmes in the previous four years. It was the task of the inspectors to directly verify the status of Iraq's weapons programmes.[94] Even after the critical UNMOVIC and IAEA reports were delivered, the calls by France, Russia and Germany for the US to provide direct proof of Iraq's possession of WMD and its links to al-Qaeda again demonstrated a reluctance to authorise force on the basis of inferred intentions based on the lack of active Iraqi cooperation in combination with its past track record of illegitimate behaviour. What will never be known is whether these states would have been supportive of the use of force had persuasive evidence emerged that Iraq had reconstituted its WMD programmes and had formed an alliance with al-Qaeda. Action on this basis would still have fallen within the category of the pre-emptive use of force, without further evidence that an imminent attack with such weapons was about to occur.

In addition to a lack of belief in the legitimacy of the doctrine of pre-emption, a number of states could also be seen to have rejected US leadership because of their beliefs about the goals which could legitimately be pursued through the use of force, particularly whether war should be used to achieve democratic regime change. Whilst the Iraqi threat was expressed by the United States mainly in terms of the possession of WMD, links to terrorism and challenge to the authority of the Council, by February 2002 the general character of the regime was added to the list of its threatening features. On 26 February, President Bush stated that 'a new regime in Iraq would serve as a dramatic and inspiring example of freedom for other nations in the region'.[95] This reference to 'freedom' reflected the argument that terrorism stemmed not from poverty but from 'profound frustration and despair with the comprehensive decline in the Muslim world relative to other major civilisations'.[96] The solution was to spread democracy to the Middle East, starting with regime change in Iraq, which would have a ripple effect throughout the region. No doubt, the existence of a democratic ally in such a volatile and important economic region for the US was certainly advantageous economically and strategically outside of its effects on the 'war on terror'.

The legitimacy of the use of force for this purpose was, however, a step too far for many states. For France, the use of force to achieve regime change on human rights grounds alone would set a dangerous precedent, which would be extremely threatening to international stability given the large number of regimes which routinely impinged on the human rights of their citizens.[97] Similarly, Russia condemned the war on Iraq to effect democratic regime change as an action which '[ran] totally counter to the fundamental principles contained in the Charter of the United Nations'.[98] The strongest rejection of the US vision in these terms came from the 115-member NAM. At the 11 March meeting of the Council, the representative for the NAM, Malaysia, charged that the 'use of force to bring democracy to a state', or to 'improve human rights in any country' was inherently contradictory to the Charter.[99] In another, more blunt passage, Malaysia stated that 'it would be abusive to obtain the legitimacy of unilateral purpose under the pretext of a multilateral cause'.[100] Clearly, the goal of democratic regime change was not viewed as a collective interest of all states, but a parochial interest of the US and its allies alone.

More broadly, the carving out of an exception to the prohibition on the use of force to allow democratic regime change posed far too great a challenge to the sovereignty principle for a large number of states. As we have discussed above (p. 81), whilst there has been a growing acceptance of the view that the internal governance of a state can constitute a threat to international peace and security, at least among Western states, this has largely been limited to cases of widespread and serious violations of human rights and/or humanitarian crises which have spilled over territorial borders. A widening of this exception to the sovereignty norm to include intervention on the basis of the non-liberal character of a state was agreed to pose an unwanted challenge to the fundamental basis of international order. The large number of illiberal states within the NAM had an immediate self-interest in opposing the idea of conditional sovereignty, whilst all small states feared the acceptance of such practices given their greater vulnerability to intervention by a hegemon equipped with both the material power and supporting ideology to change the world in its image.

Conclusion

In this chapter we have endeavoured to investigate the extent to which normative beliefs about legitimate behaviour motivated states to reject the leadership of the United States in the 2002–2003 Iraq Crisis. Based on the public statements made by members of the Security Council, regional organisations and individual states, we have argued that the rejection of US leadership during the crisis was based on the fact that the vision it put forward to extinguish the Iraqi threat was considered to be illegitimate with respect to its ultimate end of regime means and goal change. Further, we have also argued that states declined to recognise the identity of the United States as a hegemonic leader because of a lack of trust in its motives for leadership and uncompromising leadership style. Both the substance of the US vision and the style of leadership displayed during the crisis caused states to question whether the US was seeking to lead the international community in pursuit of the common interest or in pursuit of its own parochial goals.

In the early phase of the diplomatic process, beliefs about legitimate or appropriate and rightful behaviour between states can be seen to have strongly guided Council members in their negotiations over Resolution 1441. First, the acceptance of the goal of disarming Iraq was largely based on state beliefs about the illegitimacy of Iraq's past behaviour, which made the possibility of its possession of WMD a threat to international peace and security. Second, the need for the Council to take active steps towards meeting this goal was based on shared beliefs about the normative responsibilities associated with the leadership role undertaken by members of the Security Council. A majority agreed that the failure of the Security Council to enforce its own decisions, which had been consistently flouted by the regime, itself constituted a threat to the credibility of the UN as a system of collective security. Third, the normative belief that force should be used to settle disputes between states only as a last resort was shown to have guided the decision to support the use of a renewed inspections regime as the method of securing Iraq's disarmament in the first instance, and subsequently to resist US preferences for the authorisation of the use of force.

The evidence supports the conclusion that states were reluctant to follow US preferences for forcible regime change in Iraq because they questioned whether the United States was genuinely seeking to lead the international community to defend the common interests of states, an expectation of legitimate behaviour associated with the role of leader within international society. The fact that the US had loudly proclaimed its view that regime change in Iraq was in its own national interests, sufficient to justify the unilateral use of force, caused states to doubt whether it was genuinely committed to the peaceful disarmament of Iraq, or merely sought the legitimising effects that would accrue from the support of the Council. A consistent theme in the post-vote statements on Resolution 1441 was the defence of the central and authoritative role of the Security Council over matters of international peace and security. In other words, a majority of states asserted that the definition of what was the 'common interest' would be made by the Security Council, not by the United States alone.

In the early months of 2003, in the debates over the possible use of force against Iraq, the ultimate rejection of US leadership was influenced by beliefs about legitimate state behaviour in four respects. First, the lack of support for the use of force was again guided by the entrenched norm that force should only be used as a last resort. Given that a majority of states believed that Iraq's level of cooperation had improved and that the inspectors were making progress, the authorisation of the use of force at this stage was seen as illegitimate in the circumstances.

Second, US leadership was rejected because it was based on the acceptance of the doctrine of pre-emptive self-defence; a doctrine which a majority of states believed would dangerously undermine the sovereignty norm and the prohibition on the use of force as core foundations of international order. The refusal of states such as Russia, China, France and Germany to authorise the use of force without explicit proof that Iraq was concealing a reconstituted WMD programme or an alliance with terrorist groups represented a rejection of the pre-emptive use of force against Iraq. These states did not accept the US's case for war which was based on inferences drawn from Iraq's lack of proactive cooperation with the inspectors, its past aggressive behaviour and likely shared interest in forming an alliance with another enemy of the United States. In their view, it was the task of the inspectors to provide direct proof of these assertions.

Third, we found that the US push for the use of force was rejected because of state beliefs about the goals to which force could be legitimately applied. In particular, states were wary of the US push to use force to achieve regime change in Iraq in circumstances where most believed Iraqi disarmament could be achieved through inspections and future monitoring, i.e. via a containment strategy. The argument raised by the US that the installation of a democratic government in Iraq would contribute to the war on terror was found to have little support. A number of states denounced the use of force to effect democratic regime change on the grounds that it threatened the sovereignty norm, the cornerstone of international stability. The argument that the non-liberal character of a state posed a threat to international peace and security was especially worrying to small and developing nations for whom sovereignty provided protection from outside intervention. Even for larger states, such as France and Russia, this approach was unacceptable because it would considerably increase the instability of international relations by widening the range of circumstances in which force could legitimately be used.

Finally, the rejection of US leadership on this issue can be seen to have been motivated by the belief that the US was not acting within the bounds of the role prescription associated with hegemonic leadership. Core to the recognition of its right to lead was the belief that a hegemon should be primarily motivated to lead by a desire to pursue the common interests of the collective. The suspicions of states that the US was not genuinely motivated by the common interest in Iraqi disarmament but by a desire to achieve regime change in pursuit of its own interests was confirmed by the uncompromising attitude taken to the use of force. Because the majority of states did not share the US's heightened threat perceptions in relation to al-Qaeda and Iraq, regime change was not seen to be in the best interests of the collective. For a variety of states the costs of war, including its effects on regional stability, the solidarity of the coalition against terrorism and the post-conflict governance of Iraq, outweighed the benefit of ensuring Iraq's disarmament. This was particularly the case given that most states believed that Iraqi disarmament and containment was still achievable through the inspections process. Thus, the uncompromising attitude of the Bush Administration towards the use of force caused many states to withdraw recognition of its status as a hegemonic leader. The actual use of force by the US in defiance of world opinion merely confirmed to many that the US was in fact acting in its own interests and only sought the involvement of the Security Council in order to legitimise these pre-determined goals and to spread the military and financial burdens of regime change onto the international community.

In conclusion, from an analysis of the justifications used by states for their decisions during the crisis, we can argue that there is substantial evidence to support the view that the rejection of US leadership in the Iraq Crisis stemmed both from the inability of the US to persuade a majority of states that its vision for the solution to the Iraqi problem was legitimate under the accepted norms of international society. State beliefs about appropriate behaviour of a state in the role of a hegemonic leader could also be argued to have played a strong role in motivating states to reject US leadership in this case. The assertion by the US of its right to pre-emptive self-defence against Iraq, to unilaterally interpret the 'will' of the international community, together with its uncompromising drive towards the use of force, undermined its credibility to lead international society.

Appendix 4.1

Table 4.1 Resolution 1441 – goals, means and justifications – views of the Security Council

State	UNSC role: UNSC has primary authority over IPS – only legitimate body to decide goals and means	Goal: disarmament of Iraq	Justification for goals		Means: enhanced inspection	Justification for means		Use of force: expectation that the SC would authorise the use of force if Iraq materially breached the terms of resolution 1441
			Iraq threat to IPS			Peaceful settlement of disputes	Use of force as last resort	
			Past aggression	Credibility and authority of the UN challenged if Council does not enforce its own resolutions				
USA	◆	◆	◆	◆	◆			◆
UK	◆	◆	◆	◆	◆			◆
France	◆	◆		◆	◆	◆		
Mexico	◆	◆		◆	◆	◆		
Ireland	◆	◆		◆	◆		◆	◆
Russia	◆	◆			◆	◆	◆	◆
Bulgaria	◆	◆			◆		◆	
Syria	◆	◆			◆	◆		
Norway	◆	◆			◆	◆		
Singapore	◆	◆		◆	◆			
Colombia	◆			◆	◆			
Cameroon	◆	◆			◆	◆		
Guinea	◆	◆			◆	◆		
Mauritius	◆	◆			◆			
China	◆	◆			◆	◆		

Source: Statements by Members of the Security Council after the unanimous vote for resolution 1441(2002), 4644th Meeting of the Security Council, 7 November, UN Document S/PV.4644.

Table 4.2 Summary of views of members of the Security Council – 7 March 2003

State	Cooperation			Disarmament		Means		Proposals	
	Prior cooperation inadequate	Cooperation has improved – shows promise	Cooperation unlikely to improve	Promising progress on disarmament by inspectors	Progress on disarmament insufficient/limited	Peaceful means not exhausted – continue inspections	Peaceful means failed – set deadline for use of force	Support for enhanced inspections – French/Russian/German position	Support for short deadline for use of force
Angola	◆								
Bulgaria	◆	◆							◆
Cameroon	◆				◆	◆		◆[101]	
Chile		◆			◆	◆		◆[102]	
China		◆		◆		◆		◆	
France	◆	◆		◆		◆		◆	
Germany	◆	◆		◆		◆		◆[103]	
Guinea	◆					◆		◆[104]	
Mexico	◆					◆			
Pakistan	◆			◆		◆			
Russia		◆		◆	◆	◆			
Spain			◆		◆		◆		◆
Syria		◆				◆			
UK	◆		◆		◆		◆		◆
USA			◆		◆		◆		◆

Source: Statements made at the 4714th Meeting of the Security Council, 7 March 2003, UN Document S/PV. 4714, p. 28.

Table 4.3 Views of the wider membership – states against the use of force – 11–12 March 2003

State	Supports principle that peaceful means should be exhausted first before the authorisation of force	Support further inspections – more time	Iraq needs to show more proactive and substantive cooperation with inspectors	Inspectors making progress on disarmament	Iraq now showing greater active cooperation	Iraq has shown complete and full cooperation	Inspectors should list key disarmament tasks	Deadline for end to inspections should be set
Non-Aligned Movement (116 states)	◆	◆	◆					
League of Arab States	◆	◆		◆	◆			
Organisation of Islamic Conference	◆	◆				◆	◆	
EU (15 states plus 10 accession countries plus Bulgaria, Romania and Turkey)	◆	◆	◆					◆[105]
Algeria	◆	◆			◆			
Argentina	◆	◆		◆	◆		◆	◆
Belarus	◆	◆						

continued

Table 4.3 continued

State	Supports principle that peaceful means should be exhausted first before the authorisation of force	Support further inspections – more time	Iraq needs to show more proactive and substantive cooperation with inspectors	Inspectors making progress on disarmament	Iraq now showing greater active cooperation	Iraq has shown complete and full cooperation	Inspectors should list key disarmament tasks	Deadline for end to inspections should be set
Bolivia	♦							
Brazil	♦	♦						
Canada[106]		♦	♦					♦
Cuba	♦	♦				♦		
Egypt	♦	♦		♦	♦			
Ethiopia	♦	♦	♦					
Iceland		♦	♦					
India	♦	♦		♦	♦			
Indonesia[107]	♦	♦			♦			
Iran		♦	♦		♦			
Kuwait	♦	♦	♦					
Lao PDR		♦		♦	♦			
Lebanon	♦	♦		♦	♦			
Libya		♦		♦	♦			
Malawi		♦	♦	♦	♦			
Morocco	♦	♦	♦	♦				
New Zealand	♦	♦			♦		♦	
Nicaragua	♦	♦						
Nigeria	♦							

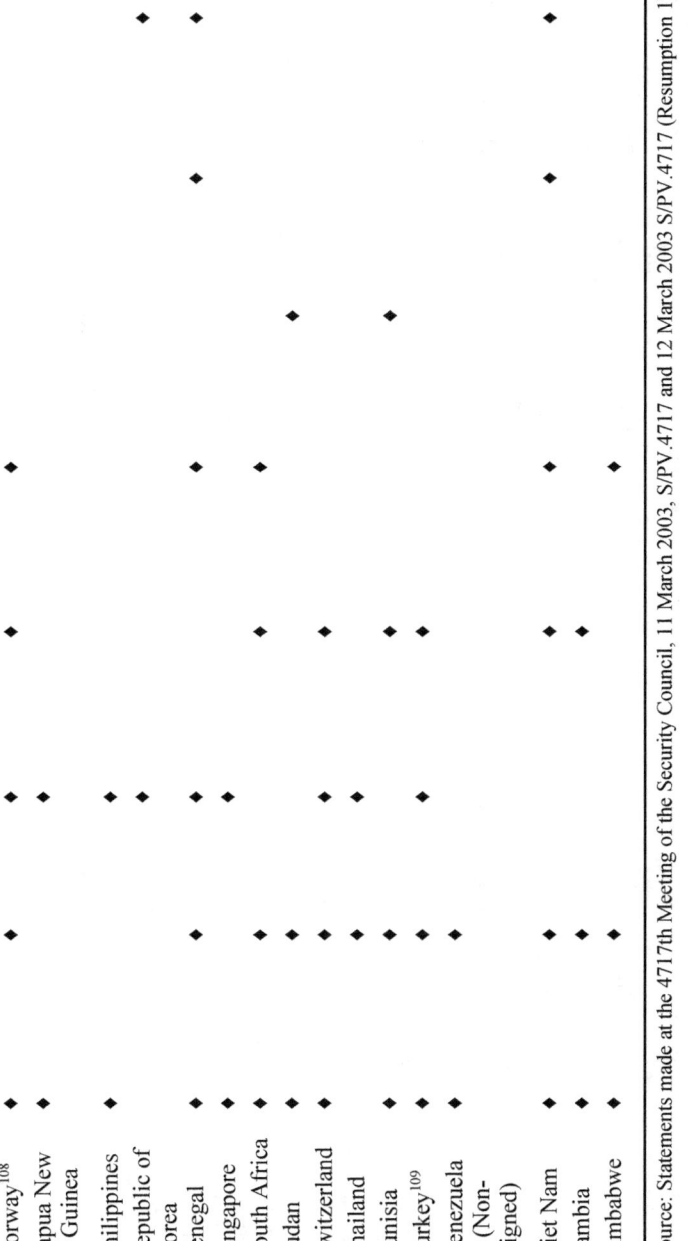

Source: Statements made at the 4717th Meeting of the Security Council, 11 March 2003, S/PV.4717 and 12 March 2003 S/PV.4717 (Resumption 1).

Table 4.4 Views of the wider UN membership – states in support of the use of force

State	Inspections are futile to achieve disarmament without full Iraqi cooperation	Support for the use of force (setting of deadline for end of inspections and use of force)	Weapons inspections have failed – Iraq in breach of Resolution 1441		Security Council must live up to its obligations to maintain international peace and security	
			Lack of immediate, unconditional, and active cooperation	Substantial amounts of WMD unaccounted for	Failure to enforce its decisions undermines credibility of UN	Real threat of proliferation to terrorist groups
Albania	♦					
Australia	♦	♦		♦	♦	♦
Bolivia			♦			♦
Colombia		♦	♦		♦	
Dominican Republic		♦	♦			
El Salvador[110]					♦	
Georgia		♦	♦	♦	♦	
Iceland[111]			♦		♦	
Japan	♦	♦	♦		♦	
Latvia	♦	♦	♦		♦	
Macedonia		♦	♦	♦	♦	
Peru		♦	♦	♦	♦	

Source: Statements made at the 4717th Meeting of the Security Council, 11 March 2003, S/PV.4717

Table 4.5 Views of the Security Council on the legitimacy of the use of force, 26–27 March 2003

State	Legitimacy of the use of force			Illegitimacy of the use of force			
	Peaceful means exhausted	Lack of enforcement undermined SC credibility	Multilateral – enforcement of Security Council decisions	Peaceful means not yet exhausted	Security Council has primary responsibility for IPS – force unauthorised by the SC	Use of force not for collective purposes	Misuse of power
Mexico	♦			♦	♦		
Angola	♦			♦			
Pakistan				♦			
United Kingdom		♦	♦				
Cameroon			♦	♦			
USA	♦		♦				
Russia				♦		♦	♦
China				♦	♦		
France				♦	♦		
Spain	♦			♦			
Chile	♦						
Bulgaria	♦						
Syria				♦	♦	♦	♦
Germany				♦	♦		
Guinea				♦	♦		

Source: Statements of Members of the Security Council, 4726th Meeting of the Security Council, 26–27 March 2003, S/PV.4726 (Resumption 1).

Table 4.6 Views on the use of force expressed at the open meeting of the Security Council on 26 March 2003

State	Illegitimacy of the use of force					Legitimacy of the use of force		
	SC has primary responsibility for IPS – must have authorisation	Use of force for parochial motives	Aggressive use of force	Illegitimate interference with Iraq's sovereignty, territorial integrity, political independence	Peaceful means not yet exhausted – war as last resort	Peaceful means exhausted	Failure to enforce decisions of the SC undermines its credibility	Enforcing decisions of the Security Council
Algeria	◆							
Malaysia	◆		◆	◆	◆			
Egypt	◆		◆	◆	◆			
Yemen	◆		◆	◆	◆			
Kuwait						◆		◆
Libya	◆	◆	◆					
Indonesia	◆				◆			
South Africa	◆			◆	◆			
Cuba	◆	◆	◆	◆	◆			
New Zealand					◆			
India	◆				◆			
Poland						◆	◆	◆
Palestine								
Costa Rica								
Timor Leste								
Honduras								
Dominican Republic						◆		
Uganda						◆		
Sri Lanka							◆	

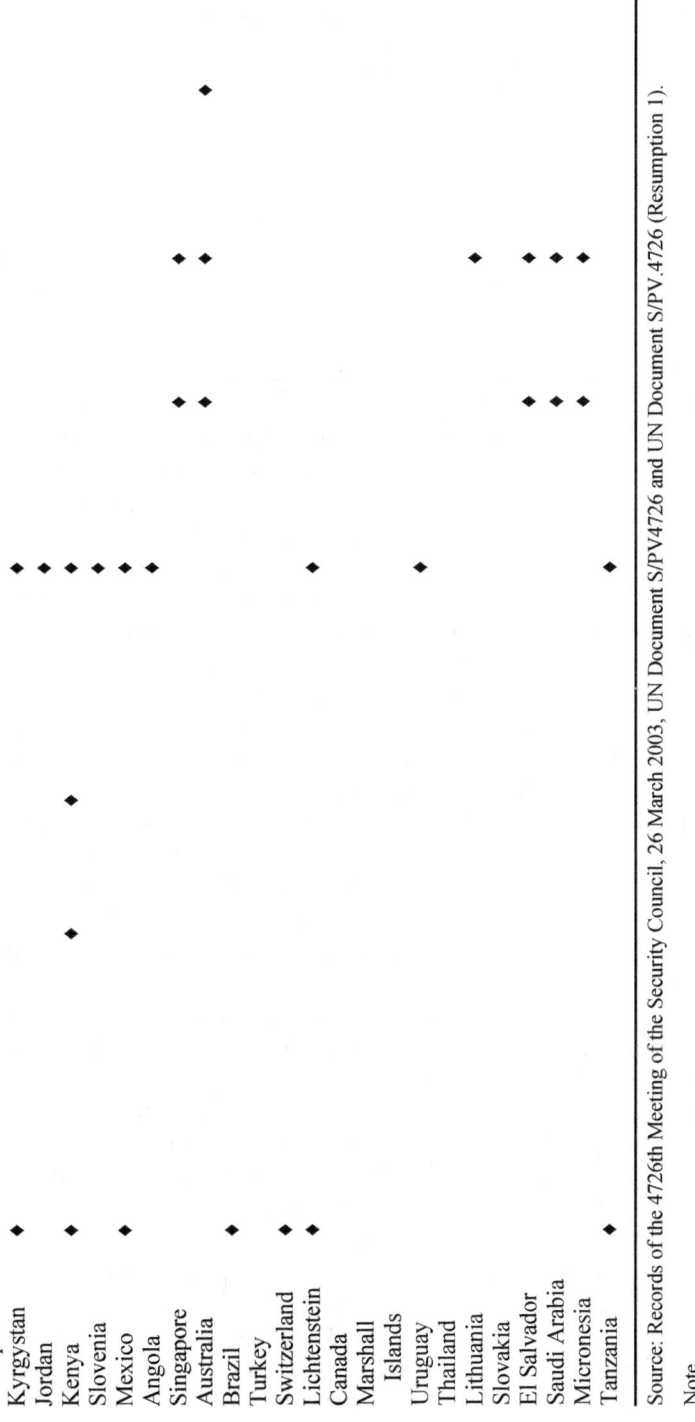

Source: Records of the 4726th Meeting of the Security Council, 26 March 2003, UN Document S/PV4726 and UN Document S/PV.4726 (Resumption 1).

Note
Some states did not give their views on the legitimacy or illegitimacy of the use of force by the coalition but instead focused on the need for the United Nations to become involved to assist the people of Iraq with humanitarian aid. In the table above, these states have no views recorded.

5 Material factors and followership in the Iraq Crisis

Whilst the Iraqi invasion of Kuwait in August of 1990 spurred the international community to unite behind US leadership, as the previous chapter has shown there was a high level of opposition to the US vision for Iraq's disarmament 12 years later. Here the US attempted to assert a leadership role over international society but found little political support among the members of the Security Council and the broader UN membership for the forcible disarmament of Iraq. The interesting question here is why did states largely reject US leadership during the Iraq Crisis? In the previous chapter we examined whether the rejection of US leadership was guided by normative beliefs about legitimate state behaviour. Here we found that questions of international legitimacy did in fact play a strong role in the decision to follow or reject US leadership. As such, the evidence did support a conceptualisation of hegemony as a leadership role in international society. However, could there be another, more compelling, explanation of followership? In this chapter our goal is to test whether the opposing conceptualisation of hegemony, as a relation of dominance, can provide an equally persuasive or better explanation of followership or the rejection of US leadership in the Iraq Crisis. Evidence supportive of a view of hegemony as a dominance relationship would include examples of followership motivated by US threats or coercion, or as a result of a rational calculation that considerable material benefits could be accrued.

The chapter to follow examines the decision-making processes of the same four states that played an integral financial or military role in the coalition against Iraq during the 1990–1991 Gulf Crisis. The Iraq Crisis 12 years later brought about a split in positions among these states, with the United Kingdom and Japan choosing to follow the US lead and France and Germany choosing to reject it. The question we ask in this chapter is whether this pattern of behaviour is related to material motives for action. We have again chosen to focus on three material factors – oil dependence, alliance dependence and the balance of threat hypothesis – that may have affected the decision by states to either make a significant contribution to the coalition or to reject participation altogether. Domestic considerations have been largely excluded from consideration, except in cases where the evidence suggests that domestic opinion strongly impacted on the decisions of governments or political parties.

The first factor analysed is the impact of oil dependence on the decision to oppose or support regime change in Iraq. The impact of oil dependence in 2002–2003 is less obvious than in the Gulf Crisis of 1990–1991. Here there was no immediate threat to supplies of oil from the Gulf region, whether the regime remained intact or was removed from power. Whilst oil-dependent states with existing oil contracts with the Hussein regime may have had an interest in opposing regime change in Iraq, the likelihood of this motivation being a strong one would depend on the quantities of oil being imported. Those countries with good relations with the Hussein regime may also have had an interest in sustaining the regime in the hope of obtaining contracts for the development of Iraqi oil fields in the event that economic sanctions were removed at a future time. Similarly, it has been suggested that states that did not have connections with the Hussein regime might have had a material interest in supporting regime change and contributing to the post-war reconstruction of Iraq in the hope of obtaining contracts to develop Iraqi oil fields by a new Iraqi government. However, given that both hypotheses are highly speculative in nature, clear evidence that decision-makers actually acted on such motivations needs to be found.

Second, we focus on the existence of alliance dependence between the four chosen states and the United States. Smaller states face an alliance security dilemma when they decide to follow or reject the leadership of a larger alliance partner. The dilemma arises as a result of the two contradictory forces in play. Where a state chooses not to support a stronger ally in a particular case, they face the risk of being abandoned by their partner in a future conflict of importance to that state's security. However, where a state chooses to support their stronger ally, they then risk becoming entrapped in a conflict which is less integral to their own interests but of primary importance to their alliance partner.[1]

In the case of the Iraq Crisis, we anticipate that states should have made contributions to the coalition where the fear of abandonment outweighed the fear of entrapment. We would also expect to see that in such cases the US was able to raise the costs of non-cooperation; that is, to act to engender a fear of abandonment within the decision-making processes of its alliance partners. Evidence of such behaviour would include the application of direct pressure by the United States to withdraw economic or military benefits from the state concerned, or more subtle diplomatic pressure demonstrated by a correlation between contributions made and requests to do so by US decision-makers.[2] For those alliance partners that rejected US leadership, we would expect to find evidence that the fear of entrapment outweighed any fear of abandonment despite such tactics.

Third, we focus on whether followership or the rejection of leadership was motivated by threat assessments of the Iraqi regime using a modified version of Stephen Walt's balance of threat hypothesis. As we have argued in Chapter 4, Walt's threat criteria can be divided into material and normative components. In this chapter we use three elements of Walt's balance of threat hypothesis as the basis of a material assessment of the Iraqi threat: aggregate power, offensive capabilities and geographic proximity.[3] In terms of intra-alliance behaviour, we can hypothesise that states are driven to cooperate, and in our case to 'follow', because of a shared assessment of an external threat based on these three criteria, with the opposite true of the decision to reject US leadership.[4]

The fourth element put forward by Walt – 'perceived intentions' – is not a purely material factor as it requires the introduction of normative beliefs into the assessment of security threats.[5] In this case, the important question was whether Iraq continued to have 'aggressive intentions' towards its neighbours, or the intent to disrupt the status quo in more general terms. In the case of Iraq, the assessment of its aggressive intentions involved a normative judgement about Iraq's past behaviour and a prediction of its future intentions based on this. As such, the acceptance or rejection of the US view that Iraq was a rogue state whose potential re-armament with WMD posed a grave threat to international peace and security is more properly classed as a normative motivation for followership rather than a material one. Included in our analysis in this chapter is an identification of the normative threat assessments made of Iraq by Japan, Germany, France and the United Kingdom. These normative assessments support the analysis of legitimacy as a 'causal' factor in the decision to reject or accept US leadership examined in Chapter 4.

The chapter which follows will start with an overview of the sharing of financial and material burdens among coalition members during the crisis. From there we will move on to an examination of four case studies – that of Japan, Germany, France and the United Kingdom. In each case study we will detail the contributions made to the coalition and analyse the persuasiveness of each of the material factors mentioned above as an explanation for followership or the rejection of US leadership, as the case may be.

Sharing the burden

In contrast to the 1990–1991 Gulf Crisis, the major military and financial burdens of both prosecuting the 2003 war and rebuilding Iraq have been borne largely by the United States. Although the 'coalition of the willing' against Iraq was made up of an impressive 40 countries, in practice the vast majority of these states provided only political support rather than any direct financial or military contributions to the war effort.[6] Significantly, 21 of the 34 countries who provided military contributions in the 1991 Gulf War were not part of this coalition, with only one Arab state, Kuwait, being willing to publicly associate itself with the US.[7] In the case of the Iraq War, 340,000 US military personnel participated in offensive operations together with contingents from only three other states: the United Kingdom with 46,000 personnel; Australia deploying 2,000 mainly special operations forces and one F/A-18 aircraft squadron; and Poland contributing 200 special operations troops around Basra.[8]

In the post-conflict phase of operations, the United States continued to bear the major burden of providing security within Iraq. In October 2003, 169,000 troops were in Iraq and elsewhere in the region, with support from 21,000–29,000 non-US troops from 28 countries. Most contributions at this time came from the United Kingdom, Poland, Spain, the Netherlands, Italy and

Ukraine, with the rest sending small contingents of mainly symbolic value.[9] By November 2004, the number of non-US troops in Iraq had stabilised at around 29,000 from 29 countries, but with only one state making a contribution greater than 10,000 personnel and four making contributions of greater than 1,000 troops (see Table 5.1).

Whilst individual member states of the NATO alliance made contributions to the UN stabilisation force, NATO did not officially commit troops to Iraq in a combat capacity. Rather, in June of 2004, NATO agreed to conduct training of Iraqi security forces both within and outside of Iraqi territory.[10] However, this training mission was relatively modest, with a maximum size of 300 personnel, which by May 2005 had trained approximately 500 Iraqi officers.[11] Notably, NATO members, France, Belgium, Greece, Spain, Luxembourg and Germany refused to send training personnel to Iraq preferring to either make financial contributions to the NATO training mission in Iraq or to train Iraqi forces outside of Iraqi territory.[12]

Unlike the Persian Gulf Crisis of 1990–1991, where a substantial amount of the United State's war-fighting costs were reimbursed by other members of the coalition, the United States bore the full costs of the war itself, and in some cases subsidised the military costs of other members of the coalition.[13] In March 2003 the Bush Administration requested and received $62.6 billion for the US Department of Defense to cover the costs of the war in Iraq up to September 2003. In October 2003, the Administration's 'emergency' request for funds of $51.8 billion for the 2004 fiscal year for the war in Iraq was approved by the US Congress.[14] Additionally, the US agreed to assume the costs of deploying 15,000 non-US troops to Iraq, which in July of 2003 was estimated to cost $276 million for six months.[15]

In relation to the post-war reconstruction costs in Iraq, the United States has also shouldered the major burden. From 2003 to 2005, the US allocated approximately $28.5 billion dollars in grants towards reconstruction assistance, in addition to the amounts allocated for maintaining military forces in Iraq.[16] Following international donors' conferences in Madrid in October 2003 and Doha, Qatar in May 2004, an estimated $20.1 billion dollars in grants and loans was pledged by states to the coalition and the World Bank/UN trust fund for reconstruction costs. However, of this amount, approximately $14 billion was in the form of loans and credits rather than outright grants. The largest grants came from Japan, the United Kingdom, Canada, South Korea and the United Arab Emirates, whilst the World Bank, IMF, Japan and Saudi Arabia pledged the most in the form of loans and export credits (see Table 5.1).

Japan

During the Iraq Crisis of 2002–2003, the Japanese Government was a clear 'follower' of the United States. However, in terms of burden-sharing, the financial and military contributions made were modest, and of greatest value to the US as evidence, however unconvincing, that the coalition was broad-based. In terms of

Table 5.1 Non-US troop and financial contributions to post-war stabilisation and reconstruction in Iraq – November 2004

Country	Number of personnel	Monetary contributions to the coalition and UN/World Bank Trust Fund (millions US$)
Albania	70	–
Australia	850	120
Austria	–	1
Azerbaijan	150	–
Belgium	–	20.7
Bulgaria	485	–
Canada	–	234
China	–	25
Czech Republic	113	69
Denmark	520	201.2 (158.2 credits)
Dominican Republic	Withdrew its forces	–
El Salvador	380	–
Estonia	43	1.1
European Union	–	370 (38 for Iraqi elections)
Finland	–	5.9
France	–	10.7
Fiji	700	–
Georgia	160	–
Germany	–	155
Greece	–	9.6
Honduras	Withdrew its forces	–
Hungary	300	–
Iceland	–	3.9
IMF	–	2,500–4,250 (in loans)
India	–	30
Iran	–	10
Ireland	–	8
Italy	**3,120**	270
Japan	750	5,000 (3,500 in loans)
Kazakhstan	27	–
Kuwait	–	1,500
Latvia	120	–
Lithuania	105	0.56
Macedonia	28	–
Moldova	12	–
Mongolia	140	–
NATO	300 trainers	–
Netherlands	1,400	21
New Zealand	Withdrew its forces (61)	10
Nicaragua	Withdrew its forces (230)	–
Norway	10 (withdrew 140)	30
Pakistan	–	3.3
Philippines	Withdrew its forces (96)	–
Poland	**2,400**	–
Portugal	110	17.4
Qatar	–	100

continued

Table 5.1 continued

Country	Number of personnel	Monetary contributions to the coalition and UN/World Bank Trust Fund (millions US$)
Romania	700	0.2
Russia	–	8
Saudi Arabia	–	1,000 (500 in loans, 500 in credits)
Singapore	33	1.7
Slovakia	105	0.290
South Korea	**2,800**	260
Spain	Withdrew its forces	300
Sweden	–	54
Switzerland	–	11
Taiwan	–	4.3
Tonga	45	–
Turkey	–	50
Thailand	Withdrew its forces (443)	0.283
Ukraine	**1,700**	–
United Arab Emirates	–	215
United Kingdom	**12,000**	1,000
World Bank		$3,000–$5,000 in loans
Grand total	**29,626** in theatre in Iraq	**$20.86 billion** in grants, loans and credits

Source: Jeremy M. Sharp, 'Post-War Iraq: a Table and Chronology of Foreign Contributions', *CRS Report for Congress*, RL 32105, updated 5 November 2004, Table 1 titled 'Foreign Contributions to Reconstruction and Stabilisation in Postwar Iraq', pp. 15–17 with supplements from Steve Bowman, 'Iraq: US Military Operations and Costs', *CRS Report for Congress*, RL31701, updated 20 November 2004, Table 1 titled 'Countries Contributing Personnel to Iraq Operations', pp. 11–12, updated 20 November 2004.

military support, the Japanese Government did not participate in any warfighting activities because of constitutional restrictions which preclude Japanese defence forces acting other than in self-defence. After the UN Security Council passed Resolution 1483 (2003), which called for members to assist in the reconstruction of Iraq, the government successfully passed new legislation in the Diet to enable the Self Defense Force ('SDF') to take part in reconstruction activities in a non-combat capacity.[17] These forces were dispatched to an area least likely to require combat, at the insistence of the government, to avoid any question that the SDF was exceeding its constitutional mandate.[18] By February 2004, a 600-strong Ground Self Defence Force ('GSDF') unit was dispatched to al-Samawah in Southern Iraq to provide humanitarian and reconstruction assistance.[19] The Air Self Defence Force ('ASDF') provided logistical support for the reconstruction activities of the GSDF and transport for US troops between Kuwait and Iraq.[20]

Japan's financial contribution to the coalition came in the form of grant assistance and loans. On 16 October 2003, the Japanese Government announced that it would provide financial grants totalling approximately US$1.5 billion to meet the immediate reconstruction needs of Iraq, such as power generation, water supplies and sanitation, telecommunications and transport, health, employment and security services. Also announced was the provision of US$3.5 billion in concessional loans for assistance in 2005–2007 for infrastructure development, bringing the total financial contribution to approximately US$5 billion.[21] Japan's total contribution amounted to 10 per cent of the World Bank's estimate of reconstruction costs at the time, and made Japan the largest foreign contributor to the post-war reconstruction effort.[22]

Material threat assessment

Japanese 'followership' of the US in the Iraq Crisis cannot be explained by Walt's balance of threat hypothesis, materially defined. Japan should not have perceived Iraq as a threat based on its aggregate power and offensive power capabilities, which most states believed had been highly degraded over a decade of economic sanctions, intrusive inspections, intermittent air-strikes and military enforcement of the 'no-fly zones'. Iraq was also far from Japan geographically and was not believed to possess ballistic missile systems that were capable of reaching the Japanese mainland. Thus Japanese followership of the US, despite the fact that Iraq posed little threat to its national security, cannot be explained by the balance of threat hypothesis, defined materially.

Normative threat assessment

What we do find in Japanese statements on threat perceptions is that followership was more directly related to normative beliefs about legitimate behaviour between states. In a statement released on 20 March 2003 explaining Japan's position on the Iraq War, Prime Minister Koizumi implicitly supported the use of force against Iraq to prevent it from acquiring WMD, or to destroy its existing capabilities, with the 'prevention of the proliferation of weapons of mass destruction' described as of 'extreme importance' to the security of the international community.[23] Further, Prime Minister Koizumi also expressly supported the US view that the Iraqi threat was heightened by the possibility that it would pass on any WMD capabilities to international terrorists. In explaining his decision to support the US position, Koizumi stated that

> weapons of mass destruction ... if they fall in the hands of dictators and terrorists, it would not be the matter of tens or hundreds of lives but would be of thousands and tens of thousands of lives being threatened.... It is extremely dangerous now that we came to the conclusion that there is no willingness to disarm on the part of the Hussein regime.[24]

In other words, Japanese decision-makers were prepared to support the US position because they shared the perception that Iraq was a 'rogue' state, with the likely aggressive intent to acquire WMD and to potentially pass this technology

Alliance dependence

Japan is highly dependent for its security on its alliance with the United States, particularly because of the pacifist restrictions contained in its constitution. Whilst the gravity of the threat posed to Japan by North Korea and China cannot be compared to the Soviet threat during the Cold War, Japan remains reliant on the United States as its primary security guarantor. Over the 1990s, the North Korean nuclear threat has pushed Japan into increasing its own military capabilities, developing greater military cooperation with the United States in relation to theatre missile defence[25] and expanding regional multilateral security cooperation to supplement the US alliance.[26] Given its continuing dependence on the United States, it is not surprising that we can find evidence to show that Japanese followership in the Iraq Crisis was motivated by a fear of abandonment which outbalanced the fear of becoming entrapped in an open-ended commitment in Iraq.

In terms of the timing of contributions, in the period before the war Japan's strong political support for the US cannot be linked to heavy-handedness on the part of the Bush Administration. Japan was among the few states to overtly support the US and UK's argument that the use of force by the coalition was legally justified on the basis that Iraq's breach of its obligations under Resolution 1441 revived authority to use military force under Resolutions 678 and 687.[27] Further, Prime Minister Koizumi stated that the US had 'no other option' than to use force against Iraq.[28]

Once the war had started, however, the US Administration did place political pressure on the Japanese to contribute to the reconstruction effort in Iraq. In April 2003, Deputy Secretary of State Richard Armitage criticised Japan for being a spectator on the Iraq issue, stating that 'Japan should quit paying to see the game, and get down to the baseball diamond'.[29] In the following month, whilst visiting President Bush at the presidential ranch in Crawford, Texas, Koizumi pledged to send Japanese troops to Iraq.[30] In the course of the difficult debate in the Diet over legislation to enable the deployment,[31] Koizumi again came under pressure from the Administration to send troops to Iraq, with Armitage warning Arima Tatsuo, Japan's special ambassador to the Middle East, not to 'back off'.[32] With the governing LDP split on the issue, the ratification of the bill by the Japanese Diet in July of 2003, after five fraught weeks of deliberation, showed the government's determination to meet the expectations of its US ally.

More direct evidence of Japan's fear of abandonment comes from the public justifications for the deployment given by Prime Minister Koizumi in December 2003. Here the Prime Minister stated that Japanese security and prosperity were dependent on the enhancement of the US–Japanese alliance and 'cooperating with the international community'.[33] The deployment was needed as an expression of its commitment to maintain 'relations of trust' within the

Japan–US alliance.'[34] Thus, given Japan's direct dependence on the US for its security, the Iraq Crisis provided a useful opportunity to avoid abandonment by demonstrating its reliability as an ally, which would hopefully be rewarded in a potential future conflict in the Korean peninsula.

Economic incentives – oil dependence

In the period after the Gulf War of 1991, patterns in Japan's demand for energy supplies and sources of energy changed little. In 2003, it remained highly dependent upon oil for 49 per cent of its energy needs,[35] almost all of which was imported, with 90 per cent coming from OPEC states[36] including the UAE (22.9 per cent), Saudi Arabia (22.4 per cent), Iran (13.8 per cent), Qatar (9.2 per cent), Kuwait (6.9 per cent) and Oman (5.7 per cent).[37] The Japanese Government expected that its dependence on oil supplies from the Middle East would continue for some time[38] until alternative oil supplies could be cultivated in areas such as the Caspian Sea and Siberia.[39]

Despite this level of oil dependence, over the course of the 1990s Japan remained a consistent supporter of economic sanctions against Iraq, and did not attempt to develop friendly relations with the Iraqi regime. In these circumstances, the Japanese Government would have had little direct interest in keeping the Hussein regime in power. On the other hand, as an active participant in the reconstruction of Iraq, Japan would have increased its standing as a potential oil buyer and oil-infrastructure developer to a newly formed Iraqi government. Whilst these hypotheses are plausible, there is no evidence in the public domain to suggest that the government of Japan was in actual fact motivated by an interest in securing access to Iraq's oil fields. We cannot therefore state conclusively that access to oil was a motivating factor in Japanese 'followership' of the United States in the war against Iraq.

Germany

Unlike the 1990–1991 Gulf Crisis, the German Government explicitly rejected the leadership of the US in the Iraq Crisis by joining with other states to actively oppose the US push for a second resolution authorising the use of force. Germany made no military contributions to the coalition against Iraq, and also joined attempts by Belgium and France to thwart US efforts to involve NATO in the possible defence of Turkey. Germany later relented and provided missiles for Patriot missile batteries sent to Israel and Turkey.[40] In the post-war reconstruction phase of the conflict, the German Government, in collaboration with Russia and France, made considerable efforts to prevent the legitimisation of the US post-war occupation of Iraq. In particular, these states successfully tied their support for the creation of a UN mandated stabilisation force to the agreement by the US to allow a greater role to be played by the United Nations in the construction of a new political and economic order in Iraq, as well the setting of a clear and rapid timetable for the re-establishment of Iraqi sovereignty.[41]

Material threat assessment

Using the three material elements of the balance of threat hypothesis – aggregate power, offensive capabilities and geographic proximity – Germany should have assessed the threat to national security emanating from Iraq's military capabilities to be low. As we have discussed above (p. 112), it was widely believed that the containment strategy pursued through the UN had succeeded in degrading Iraq's military capabilities, including its ballistic missile capabilities, at least until 1998.[42] Whilst there was still uncertainty over whether Iraq had in fact taken steps to reconstitute its weapons programmes after this point, the German government remained unconvinced by US intelligence that Iraq was hiding existing WMD capabilities and that it had ties to international terrorism. Further, decision-makers believed that it was only through the continuation of the inspections process that a true assessment of the Iraqi threat could properly be made. In these circumstances, Iraq was deemed to pose a low level of direct threat to German national security. As such, the balance of threat hypothesis correctly predicted that Germany would have rejected US leadership on the issue of the forcible disarmament of Iraq.

Normative threat assessment

In terms of the assessment Iraq's 'aggressive intentions' and the potential threat this posed to international order, we find strong evidence to suggest that the German political class and public viewed the US characterisation of Iraq as a rogue element acting in concert with al-Qaeda with a high degree of scepticism. For the Germans, international terrorism was believed to pose the greatest threat to both national security and international order, with regime change in Iraq being seen to be highly damaging to the solidarity of the alliance against terrorism by alienating Islamic states.[43] As such, the balance of threat, normatively defined, does correctly predict the rejection of US leadership by Germany.

The divergence between German and US threat perceptions on Iraq and international terrorism can be traced back to the debates over whether Germany would become militarily involved in the war on Afghanistan. Here, the German coalition government of the Social Democratic Party and Greens party ('the Red–Green coalition') reacted to the September 11, 2001 attacks with both expressions of 'unconditional solidarity' in the fight against terrorism but also reticence to become entangled in 'foreign adventures' beyond Afghanistan.[44] At this point, there was already unease that the US would use the 'war on terror' as a pretext to achieve the long-held goal of regime change in Iraq, a move which Foreign Minister Fischer viewed with 'utmost scepticism'.[45] Within the German parliament, strong opposition emerged, even within the government's own ranks, to any commitment of German forces to Afghanistan, with many arguing that military action would not provide a solution to the long-term political, social and economic 'root causes' of terrorism.[46] On 6 November 1991, the government succeeded in passing legislation authorising the deployment of 3,900 troops to Afghanistan, by a narrow margin of only 20 votes.[47]

The governing coalition hardened its stance towards military action in Iraq during the campaign for re-election in September of 2002. With the SPD making a poor showing in the polls and facing a strong challenge from the centre–right alliance of the Christian Democratic Union ('CDU') and the Christian Social Union ('CSU'), the Chancellor Gerhard Schröder and his election team tapped into the widespread public opposition to the US advocacy of war against Iraq by criticising the Bush Administration for shifting policy goals from WMD disarmament to regime change,[48] denouncing the latter as 'military adventurism'. Schröder further argued that regime change would in fact draw attention away from the major threat of terrorism and undermine relations between the West and Muslim states.[49] More dramatically, Schröder began to campaign on the policy platform that, under his leadership, Germany would not participate in military action against Iraq, even if the United Nations Security Council gave its authorisation. Foreign Minister Fischer, as leader of the Greens, opposed military action against Iraq in similar terms, and also made clear on 7 August 2002 that unless a link between Iraq and al-Qaeda could be proven conclusively, the containment strategy implemented through the inspections process was adequate to deal with any potential Iraqi threat.[50]

The re-election of the coalition government in September 2002 by the tightest margin in the history of democratic Germany was directly attributed to the strong anti-war position taken by both Fischer and Schröder.[51] The German election result showed that for both the German public and the political class, the threat to international order posed by Iraq was considered to be unproven and of insufficient gravity to warrant the use of force. Among the majority of the German public, US arguments about the threat posed by Iraq and possible linkages with international terrorism were merely convenient justifications to allow the US to 'reshap[e] the balance of power in the Middle East to promote US interests'.[52] The real threat to international order was seen to be that of international terrorism, with the use of force considered counter-productive to its elimination. Thus, the rejection of US leadership by Germany can be directly related to a strong difference in threat perception, defined in terms of Iraq's material military capabilities as well as an assessment of Iraq's normative threat to international order.

Alliance dependence

In rejecting US leadership during the Iraq Crisis of 2002–2003, Germany risked damaging its long-standing alliance with the United States. The strong opposition to the US position on Iraq was a surprise given that the alliance continued to be a central pillar of German security policy, with the US playing the role of 'balancer and pacifier' within Europe.[53] Whilst Germany has actively supported the development of independent European defence capabilities, it has also consistently supported the view that these capabilities should complement rather than rival existing NATO structures.[54] Its military involvement in the NATO campaign in Kosovo and Afghanistan demonstrated the value Germany continued to place on maintaining its commitment to the US alliance.[55] Germany should therefore have more greatly feared abandonment by its stronger ally.

However, German decision-makers placed greater weight on their fear of entrapment over the course of the crisis, for two interrelated reasons. First, in the absence of an overwhelming common threat such as the Communist threat during the Cold War, the level of German alliance dependence on the US had weakened relatively. This opened up the opportunity for the development of a more self-confident and independent German foreign policy, and for demands to be made for greater consultation and consideration of its interests from its alliance partners. This trend is acknowledged to have accelerated after the election of the Red–Green coalition under Chancellor Schröder in 1998. It was this government which took the major step of participating militarily in the NATO Kosovo campaign for the purpose of demonstrating loyalty to allies, the willingness to bear responsibility for matters of international order, as well as the right to be treated on equal footing with its European partners.[56] In keeping with this greater level of self-confidence, German decision-makers can be seen to have reacted strongly against the perceived disregard of German interests by the United States which in turn fed German fears of entrapment.

In particular, Berlin was particularly resistant to the non-consultative and unilateralist style of the Bush Administration, which would have fed the fear of entrapment. By the summer of 2002, Schröder was proclaiming his government's view that Europe should be able to stand 'eye to eye' with the US, in the sense of being 'recognised, consulted, respected and taken seriously as partners'.[57] Further evidence of this came in August 2002, after a strongly worded speech by Dick Cheney calling for regime change in Iraq, where Schröder stated publicly his disappointment about hearing of the Administration's intentions from the press. He stated:

> that is why it is just not good enough if I learn from the American press about a speech which clearly states: 'we are going to do it, no matter what the world or our allies think.' That is no way to treat others ... the duty of friends is not just to agree with everything, but to say: 'we disagree on this point.'[58]

In September, Schröder again spoke of the need for consultation well in advance of any firm decisions by the US. He said;

> consultation cannot mean that I get a phone call two hours in advance only to be told, 'we're going in'.... Consultation among grown-up nations has to mean not just consultation about the how and the when, but also about whether.[59]

Second, the difference in threat perception between the US and Germany on the threat to order posed by Iraq and international terrorism fed a fear among the German leadership of becoming entrapped in a conflict which was viewed as counter-productive to Germany's own national interests. As has been discussed above, in deliberations over German involvement in the war on Afghanistan, many politicians on both the left and the right were very wary of the possibility of becoming entrapped in future conflicts in the 'war on terror' that were not calculated to be in the national interest. In particular, it was feared that the use of force against Iraq was viewed as counter-productive to the greater threat to order posed by international terrorism by potentially undermining the broad-based coalition against terror and exacerbating the 'root causes' of terrorism. It was this fear of entrapment that was demonstrated by Schröder's declaration that Germany would not participate in America's 'military adventures' and that troop deployments by Germany in Afghanistan would need to be preceded by full consultation between the allies.

What the evidence above demonstrates is that, whilst Germany continued to value its alliance with the US, it had a greater fear of becoming entrapped in a conflict that it did not believe to be in its national interests, a fear that was exacerbated by the unilateralist and non-consultative style of leadership taken by the United States. Without a common view of the gravity of the threat posed by Iraq, and the threat of proliferation of WMD to terrorist organisations, German decision-makers would have had less concern about the risk of being abandoned by its stronger ally and would have felt more room to assert an independent and assertive 'German' foreign policy that had been developing over the previous years.

Oil and trade interests

German trade interests with Iraq were unlikely to have been a significant motivating factor for decision-makers because of the miniscule amount of trade conducted between the two countries. In 2002 Germany exported 0.001 per cent of its goods and services to Iraq and imported 0.062 per cent from Iraq, most of which represented oil imports.[60] In terms of its oil dependence, Germany was the world's third-largest oil importer and depended on oil to meet 39 per cent of its energy needs, 90 per cent of which was imported. However, Middle Eastern states were not its major suppliers of oil, with the three largest sources of crude oil being Russia, Norway and the United Kingdom.[61] As already mentioned, the fact that Iraq was an insignificant oil supplier for Germany makes it unlikely that it opposed the war on Iraq to safeguard these oil contracts. There is no evidence to support this hypothesis in the public justifications used to oppose the US position, and as such oil dependence as a motivating factor provides indeterminate results in the case of Germany.

France

As has been discussed in the previous chapter, France led the opposition to the US position during the Iraq Crisis. Apart from its diplomatic efforts to oppose the use of force in the UN, including the threat of veto, in February 2003 it also used its position in NATO, along with Belgium and Germany, to attempt to block the provision of contingent military aid to Turkey in the event that the latter was attacked by Iraq.⁶² In the post-conflict phase of operations, France actively resisted efforts by the US to legitimise the Iraq War and US occupation through the involvement of the UN. It was a strong advocate for the ending of US occupation of Iraq through the rapid transfer of sovereignty to the Iraqi people, and for the oversight and control of this process by the United Nations.⁶³ France was successful in obtaining concessions on these points in the draft resolution that was to become Resolution 1511.

France refused to send forces to form part of the UN multinational force mandated under Resolution 1511, with French officials stating that because France did not approve the conditions under which the United States launched the war, it did not wish to be associated with the occupation of Iraq.⁶⁴ At the NATO summit in June 2004, France and several other allies initially opposed sending a NATO force to Iraq. Ultimately, all allies agreed upon a training mission. However, it refused to send trainers to Iraq but instead offered to train Iraqi security forces in France itself.⁶⁵

In terms of financial aid, France made some financial contribution to the postwar reconstruction effort. In June 2004 it accepted a US–German compromise plan negotiated in the context of the Paris Club to write off 80 per cent of Iraq's foreign debt; this percentage was higher than the 50 per cent of debt forgiveness that Paris had advocated, although it fell short of original US requests for nearly complete debt forgiveness for Iraq. Given that Iraq owed France US$3 billion, the concession was of some value.⁶⁶

Oil and trade interests

There has been much suggestion within the US that the opposition to the war on Iraq by the French Government was motivated by its desire to prevent the exposure of corruption at high levels in the operation of the UN 'oil for food' programme.⁶⁷ The fact that Iraq was allowed to choose which states it sold oil to, as well the states from which it would buy humanitarian goods, provided opportunities for the Iraqi Government to circumvent the sanctions regime.⁶⁸ Allegations of corruption were aired from the early days of the programme, with claims that the Hussein regime was 'demanding kickbacks from countries obtaining contracts to sell food and equipment under the program, and that the money was used to bribe public officials in other countries to support Iraq's cause, or to purchase illegal military equipment'.⁶⁹

Allegations that French policy-makers opposed the war to prevent the exposure of their corrupt dealings with the Hussein government were investigated after the war by the UN Independent Inquiry Committee into the UN Oil for Food Program ('IIC') under the Chairmanship of Paul Volker. On 27 October 2005, the final report of the IIC was released to the public and contained some damning allegations against French and Russian individuals and companies.⁷⁰

The facts uncovered by the IIC support the view that Iraq consciously singled out France and Russia as states deserving of preferential treatment in terms of oil contracts as a reward for supporting the lifting of economic sanctions.⁷¹ Over the life of the Oil For Food programme, French companies were the second-largest purchasers of oil under the programme, after Russia, contracting for approximately $4.4 billion worth of oil.[72] The IIC uncovered evidence that the French Government was aware of its preferential treatment in this regard, and took steps to preserve this unique benefit for French companies.[73] However, the possible link between French policy on Iraq and oil kickbacks fades after the autumn of 2000, when French companies effectively ended any significant purchases of Iraqi oil after the regime began to impose illicit surcharges on oil transactions.[74]

Other than giving preferential treatment to French companies, individuals based in France were selected by Iraqi Deputy Prime Minister Tariq Aziz to receive oil allocations as a reward for their pro-Iraqi activities, including anti-sanctions activities. The IIC named two individuals from the French Government who received corrupt payments from the Iraqi regime as rewards for advocating the easing of sanctions in the Security Council. The first was Jean-Bernard Mérimée, the Permanent Representative of France to the United Nations from 1991 to 1995 and special advisor on European Affairs to the United Nations.[75] The second was Mr Charles Pasqua, the former Minister of Interior in France in 1986 and 1993, as well as Senator and some time President of the Hauts-de-Seine,[76] described by the IIC as the executive council in charge of management of one of France's wealthiest and most important industrial areas.[77] Whilst Mr Pasqua had a close relationship with the French President Jacques Chirac, the IIC was unable to find any direct evidence of his or of Mr Mérimée's ability to influence French foreign policy or of any wrong-doing by high-level politicians. Thus, the IIC report does not provide sufficient evidence to support the contention that French opposition to regime change was motivated by a desire to prevent the uncovering of corrupt dealings with the Hussein regime.

Further, France's economic ties to Iraq had dissipated significantly after 2000, and by 2003 only 0.2 per cent of all trade was conducted with Iraq. In terms of oil supplies, whilst France was dependent upon oil for 37 per cent of its oil needs in 2002, its major suppliers of oil were Norway, Saudi Arabia, Russia and the United Kingdom.[78] While the US imported 56 per cent of Iraqi oil under the Oil For Food programme, France imported only 8 per cent.[79] It is difficult to argue that France would risk relations with a major ally to such a strong extent to secure oil supplies which did not significantly affect the overall French economy.

Material threat assessments

According to the balance of threat hypothesis, materially defined, the rejection of US leadership by France can be explained by the fact that the military capabilities of the Iraqi regime posed a low level of threat to French national security. As discussed in our previous cases, after more than ten years of containment, Iraq did not have the military capabilities to threaten its neighbours, let alone the delivery systems to threaten the French mainland. Whilst the issue of whether Iraq had reconstituted its WMD and ballistic missile programmes was an open question at the time, the French were unconvinced by US intelligence on the matter, and if this intelligence proved correct, in the French view the containment of Iraq could be achieved via the inspections process.[80]

Normative threat assessments

The rejection of US leadership by the French can be traced to a much lower assessment of the threat posed by Iraq and international terrorism to international order by the French people and political class than their counterparts in the US for three reasons. First, an important motivation for French divergence from US policy on Iraq is derived from a differing perception of the gravity of the threat posed by international terrorism to international order after the terrorist attacks of September 11, 2001. Whilst France showed immediate solidarity with the US after September 11, 2001, drafting UNSC Resolution 1368 (2001) and making a strong military contribution to Operation Enduring Freedom in Afghanistan,[81] its threat perceptions had not changed to the same extent as in the US, where the latter believed itself to be at war.[82] Opinion surveys conducted in 2002 showed that, whilst both Europeans and Americans believed that 'international terrorism' and 'Iraq developing WMD' were the two issues of 'critical importance' to their country's vital interests, US participants were more emphatic in this view, with 91 per cent and 86 per cent seeing these issues as critical, compared to 65 per cent and 58 per cent among Europeans.[83] As such, the attacks of September 11, 2001 had less of a paradigm-shifting effect among the French public.

Second, France also viewed military force as an inadequate or counterproductive instrument to combat the threat posed by international terrorism. Instead, what was required were policies which 'recreate hope'[84] through the alleviation of the causes of poverty.[85] French objections to spreading democracy through regime change was also tied to the view that a war on Iraq could fracture the global coalition in the 'war on terror', especially if conducted unilaterally.[86]

Finally, the French assessment of Iraq's 'aggressive intentions' diverged in significant ways from that of the US. The willingness of the French to support Resolution 1441 showed that it shared the US's view that a WMD-armed Iraq potentially posed a threat to international and regional security. However, by January 2003, prior to presentation of the first inspectors' report, it appeared that France appeared to accept that Iraq had WMD programmes in place but that the inspections process could indefinitely contain this threat.[87] In this sense, French decision-makers had a lower assessment of Iraq's 'aggressive intentions' such that the use of force was considered excessive.

Clearly what was necessary to gain French support for forcible regime change was proof of a link between Iraq and al-Qaeda.[88] President Chirac was unconvinced of this fact in September 2002,[89] a view that did not shift after the presentation of evidence by Colin Powell on 5 February 2003, with French Ambassador Levitte explaining later that France 'didn't see any imminent threat for the security of France or other European countries. We have never seen any evidence of a connection between al-Qaeda and Saddam Hussein …'[90] Thus, for the French, the gravity of the Iraqi threat based on its 'aggressive intentions' was not well-supported in evidence, and in these circumstances the inspections process was sufficient to contain any potential threat indefinitely.

Alliance dependence and asserting French independence

The French response to the Iraq Crisis demonstrated a surprisingly low fear of abandonment by the United States. In the years since the end of the Cold War, France's security dependence on the US had weakened considerably. However, NATO has continued to play a strong role in European security, despite the French push for the development of an EU Common Foreign and Security Policy ('CFSP') and independent military capabilities to implement this under the European Common Security and Defense Policy (ESDP). France's position on both policies has developed both from the practical need for Europe to be able to deal with crises in its own region, where the United States is unable or unwilling to act,[91] but also from the traditional French desire to retain an independent capacity to act in international affairs, through the exercise of leadership within a stronger European Union. As we will discuss further below, the French will to independence has been spurred by a less benign view of US hegemony, with the European Union being seen as a healthy constraint or counterweight to an otherwise unbridled US foreign policy.[92] By the time of the 2002–2003 Iraq Crisis, however, whilst the EU had taken steps to implement the ESDP, the Union's capabilities had not yet been significantly tested.[93] Further, both the key states of the United Kingdom and Germany sought to ensure that the European Union would not compete with NATO, but rather would take a secondary and complementary role.[94] As such, whilst the French dependence on the US-led NATO alliance had weakened, it had not completely disappeared. What this weakening did allow for was the assertion of an independent position on Iraq without severe consequences for her future security, relative to the likely outcome during the Cold War.

The rejection of US leadership by France should also be understood in the context of France's traditional concern with maintaining her prestige and ability to exert an independent influence over international affairs. Given that France derived much influence from its privileged position as a Permanent Member of the Security Council, French power was directly threatened by US moves to bypass the Council during the Iraq Crisis. France therefore had some interest in making this as difficult as possible.

In the lead-up to the war on Iraq, there is ample evidence to suggest that French decision-makers were well aware that the unilateralist style and policies of the Bush Administration posed a direct threat to French influence and standing internationally. In an interview given to the *New York Times* on 8 September 2002, President Chirac emphasised France's position as America's 'friend', but not its 'courtier', condemned the unilateralist US doctrine of pre-emption as 'an extraordinarily dangerous doctrine' and underscored the view that any decision on pre-emptive action could only legitimately be made by the UN Security

Council, a body which gave formal recognition to France's historical claim to great power status.[95] In the case of Resolution 1441, the efforts of the French to prevent the 'automatic' authorisation of the use of force was seen to successfully safeguard the primary authority of the Security Council, and therefore French influence, over the Iraq issue.

There is also strong evidence to suggest that the hardening of the French position against the use of force in Iraq in early 2003 stemmed directly from the perception that the US had decided on the policy of regime change, regardless of the views and interests of other states, including its own. Whilst it is clear that France preferred a diplomatic solution to the crisis, in December 2002 France had begun discussions with the US on the deployment of 15,000 French troops,[96] with President Chirac warning French armed forces to be prepared for 'any eventuality' in early January 2003.[97] What changed the French position was the realisation, after a high-level meeting between US National Security Advisor Condoleezza Rice, President Chirac's personal diplomatic advisor Maurice Gourdault-Montagne and French Ambassador to the US Jean-David Levitte, that the US had already decided on a course for regime change. Here French concerns over the effect of the use of force on the destabilisation of Arab governments, recruitment to al-Qaeda, and the lack of evidence linking al-Qaeda to Baghdad were reported to have been dismissed.[98] The open opposition of the French to the use of force in Iraq on 20 January[99] came as a response to the perception from this meeting that the US was not genuinely interested in continuing the diplomatic process, which entailed taking account of the views and interests of its ally France, as well as of the wider international community.[100] In these circumstances, if France were to allow the US to demand authorisation from the Council for the use of force by threatening to use force unilaterally, then the credibility of the Security Council would have been seriously undermined, and consequently the ability of France to influence events would have been shown to be hollow. On this basis there was a clear decision to fully oppose the US rather than raise polite diplomatic objections.

In sum, the weakening of French alliance dependence on the US since the end of the Cold war provided greater room to advance its own views and interests during the Iraq Crisis, particularly in relation to its different perception of the Iraqi threat, without strong fear of the consequences of abandonment. Further, the belief that the United States was not genuinely concerned about the interests and views of other states, particularly the views of some of its long-standing allies, spurred the French to defend its ability to influence events through its position as Permanent Member of the Security Council. In the words of UK Ambassador to the UN Sir Jeremy Greenstock, President Chirac successfully prevented the US being able to 'set a precedent whereby the UN Security Council would be put in a position of rubber-stamping a United States decision'.[101] By threatening the use of the veto and successfully leading the opposition to the US within the Council, France was able to demonstrate that it continued to have international influence, the traditional pre-occupation of French foreign policy. In the absence of a common threat perception on Iraq, and a weakening of its alliance dependence on the US, the need to defend French influence and independent action overcame any fears of future abandonment by its ally, the United States.

The United Kingdom

Throughout the Iraq Crisis and the ensuing conflict, the United Kingdom remained the most high-profile supporter of US leadership, and has backed its political support with substantial military and financial contributions in both the pre- and post-conflict phases of the crisis. In military terms, in the period before the war, the massing of US and UK troops provided the essential building blocks of coercive diplomacy on the Iraq issue. This included the deployment of a maritime contingent, a 28,000-strong ground force, and an air force consisting of 100 fighter aircraft supported by 7,000 personnel between 7 January and 6 February 2003 (see Table 5.3). Overall, by the start of hostilities, the UK contribution amounted to around 46,000 personnel out of a total of around 388,000 coalition forces, or approximately 11 per cent of the total.[102]

Table 5.2 The UK military contribution to the war in Iraq

Total UK forces in combat phase	
Land	28,000
Maritime	9,000
• 19 Royal Navy ships and submarines	
• 14 Royal Fleet Auxiliary ships	
• 43 helicopters	
Air	8,000
• 115 Aircraft	
• 27 helicopters	
National Contingent Headquarters (NCHQ) and others	1,000
Total	46,000
Air campaign	
No. of UK sorties	2,519
Coalition total	41,400
No. of UK weapons released	919
Coalition total	29,200
UK forces in theatre as at 17 November 2003	
Land	8,400
Maritime	650
Air	1,450
Total	10,500
Coalition total	160,000

Sources: UK Ministry of Defence, 'Operations in Iraq: First Reflections', July 2003, table titled 'Operations in Iraq – Provisional Statistics', p. 48 and UK Ministry of Defence, 'Operations in Iraq: Lessons for the Future', December 2003, table titled 'Force Levels', p. 84.

UK forces played an important part in the assault against Iraq.[103] The British campaign focused upon capturing the Al Faw peninsula, the Rumaylah oilfields and the strategically important port of Umm Qasr, objectives which were achieved by combined UK and US forces within two days of the start of the war.[104] The British were then responsible for securing the southern city of Basra and, by 22 April, the province was under sufficient control to allow humanitarian organisations to begin their work.[105] In post-war Iraq, UK forces were tasked with providing security for the southern part of Iraq. By mid-July 2003, UK forces totalled around 11,500 personnel in theatre, with 9,000 of these being on land.[106] In financial terms, the UK Ministry of Defence estimated the cost of combat operations up to 31 March 2003 to come to £847.2 million, whilst the costs of post-conflict operations for the financial year 2003–2004 were estimated to be £1.2 billion.[107]

Alliance dependence

The United Kingdom has cultivated a 'special relationship' with the US, a relationship which originated from the close alliance between the two countries in the Second World War and continued against the mutual threat of Communism during the Cold War. The alliance has brought significant benefits to the United Kingdom, giving it privileged access to American intelligence under the UK–USA agreement of 1947–1948, and American nuclear information which has underpinned the UK's own deterrent capabilities.[108] With the obvious imbalance in power between the two countries, the British strategy within the alliance has consisted of avoiding open disagreements with America, unlike the French, in favour of attempting to constrain and influence in private, a pattern which played out in the Iraq Crisis.[109]

Whilst it was believed that the collapse of the Soviet Union would weaken the 'special relationship', events over the course of the post-Cold War period have shown this prediction to be far from accurate. The US and UK have continued to coordinate closely in the areas of intelligence and defence, including UK involvement in the Anti Missile Defence programme, and they have cooperated on issues of international peace and security in the Security Council, including positions on Kosovo, Afghanistan and of course Iraq. In all cases the British have clearly played the role of junior partner in the alliance. Whilst the further integration of the EU and talk of it becoming a balancing pole against the US has posed a challenge to the United Kingdom's continuing alliance with the US, Prime Minister Blair took an approach that sought to preserve the alliance whilst at the same time establishing the UK's place as a European nation. The familiar phrase used by UK statesmen is that the United Kingdom should form a 'bridge' between the US and Europe. As stated by Charles Grant, Blair's vision is that of 'a stronger EU so that it can be a more useful partner to the US, helping the Americans to sort out the world's problems'.[110]

The old strategy of maintaining close ties in order to influence US policies and thereby multiply UK power was not lost on the Blair Government during the

Iraq Crisis. For example, Foreign Secretary Jack Straw stated in November 2003:

> Unless you are actually saying 'stop the world, we want to get off', there isn't anything that can be done about the fact that America has this power. The question is how do we relate to America in the most constructive way possible and what influence can we bring to bear to ensure that this power is used for the better?[111]

This awareness of the need to influence the direction of US policy was not lost on Prime Minister Blair. It was Blair who pushed the Bush Administration to internationalise the problem of Iraqi disarmament in 2002, rather than acting unilaterally.[112] Again, the Bush Administration agreed to seek a second resolution primarily because of its appreciation that the Blair Government needed the legitimacy accorded by authorisation from the UN Security Council to garner domestic support for the United Kingdom's participation in the war.[113] It is likely that the Administration also appreciated the political value that was attached to the United Kingdom's support of the US's position in the Council in terms of reducing the perception that it was acting out of self-interest rather than in the interests of maintaining international peace and security for all states. The support of the British throughout the crisis, particularly in terms of its orchestration of the 'Group of 8' letter and the letter by the 'Vilnius 10', also demonstrated to the US the value of having an ally that shared its views within the EU.[114]

Whilst the UK's fear of abandonment and the joint interest of both states in preserving the 'special relationship' are important in helping us to understand why the United Kingdom chose to join the US-led coalition against Iraq, it does not explain why UK policy-makers chose to risk expending so much political capital in advancing a policy position that had little support among the British public or the Government's own ranks.[115] The Blair Government's pro-war stance sparked the largest political protest in UK history, with one million people marching in London against the war, whilst approval of the Prime Minister's handling of the Iraq issue fell from 40 to 26 per cent between September 2002 to January 2003.[116] While the strong collaboration on diplomatic, intelligence, defence and nuclear fields the United Kingdom has with the US would have constrained the UK from stridently opposing the war, it would have been possible for the UK to have played a less-active and conspicuous part in the crisis, a part that would have been much less risky domestically. Alone, the fear of abandonment cannot explain the UK's full participation in the US-led coalition. We need to look to other variables to find a conclusive answer here.

Material assessments of threat

Of the states that we have studies so far, the UK Government was the only government that appeared to accept the US view that Iraq had in fact reconstituted its WMD and ballistic missile programmes after expelling international weapons inspectors in December 1998. However, given that the evidence put forward by the US was circumstantial and based primarily on inferences drawn from Iraq's past illegitimate behaviour, it is difficult to attribute such threat assessments to a material cause. As we have discussed in relation to France, Germany and Japan, after 12 years of economic and military sanctions it was unlikely that Iraq's aggregate power capabilities were of serious threat or that it possessed ballistic missile capabilities sufficient to deliver WMD to the UK. Rather, the belief that Iraq had reconstituted its weapons programmes, and that this posed a threat to international peace and security, were based on normative rather than material premises.

Normative threat assessments

The UK's participation in the US-led coalition can be convincingly explained by a shared perception with the US that Iraq had the 'aggressive intent' to acquire WMD, and had likely re-established this programme in the years since 1998. The arguments used by the UK to justify why Iraq continued to pose a threat to international peace and security are well known and have been dealt with in the previous chapter, so we need not go into it in detail here. What is clear from the speeches made by Prime Minister Blair during the crisis was that he believed that since 1998 Iraq had reconstituted its weapons programmes because Saddam Hussein 'continues to believe his WMD programme is essential both for internal repression and for external aggression' and that it was 'essential to his regional power'.[117] Like his American counterparts, Blair forcefully argued for the end of inspections on the grounds that Iraq's lack of cooperation showed that it did not intend to disarm, and without full cooperation the inspections would not work.[118]

Prime Minister Blair and President Bush ultimately shared a similar world view that September 11, 2001 had irreparably altered the security threats facing liberal democratic states in the West. In his 'doctrine of the International Community'[119] launched after September 11, 2001, Blair contended that Western states could now not afford to ignore problems in other parts of the world, and that the pursuit of national security should include the spread of moral values such as 'liberty, the rule of law, human rights and an open society'.[120] Blair also declared his support for 'political actions designed to remove the conditions under which such acts of evil can flourish and be tolerated', a strategy that was implemented through forcible democratic regime change in Iraq not long after.[121] Finally, on the eve of the Iraq War, Blair made clear that he placed the 'tyrannical regimes with WMD and extreme terrorist groups who profess a perverted and false view of Islam' at the top of his list of national and international security threats. Whilst he acknowledged that the intelligence linking Iraq and al-Qaeda was 'loose' he believed that the possibility of a linkage was a 'real and present danger'.[122] There is no evidence to suggest that Blair was pressured by the Bush Administration to make these statements. In his own words: 'I would never commit British troops to a war I thought was wrong or unnecessary.'[123]

Securing oil supplies and other commercial interests

The United Kingdom is a significant European oil and natural gas producer in its own right and the largest producer of petroleum and natural gas in the EU. As such, it is a net oil exporter and therefore does not depend on oil supplies from Middle Eastern countries. However, it is accepted that production from the UK's North Sea reserves of oil and gas peaked in the late 1990s and has declined consistently over several years. The lack of new discoveries has meant that the UK must face the prospect of becoming a net importer of both oil and gas by around 2010. This supports a weak argument that the UK Government may have supported the war on Iraq to secure access to Iraqi oil fields after the Hussein regime had been removed from power. Whilst this argument has some plausibility, it is not well-supported in terms of the public discourse used to justify the war by UK decision-makers. The only public statement on the significance of oil within UK national security policy was by Foreign Minister Jack Straw on 7 January 2003, in which the aim of bolstering the 'security of British and global energy supplies' was included among a list of seven medium-to-long-term strategic priorities of UK foreign policy. As one among a large number of strategic priorities, and one which would continue to be a problem for the UK regardless of which regime was in power in Iraq, it cannot be said that this provides particularly persuasive evidence that oil was a large factor in the UK Government's calculations.[124]

More generally, as Gordon and Shapiro have argued in relation to US motivations for war, the enormous costs involved in invading, occupying and rebuilding Iraq could not have been covered by the sale of Iraqi oil. It is likely that decision-makers in the pro-war countries were aware that regime change in Iraq would involve a significant economic burden that would weigh heavily for many years to come.[125] As such, a rational decision-maker would not have viewed the invasion of Iraq as a net economic benefit and the pursuit of oil security should not therefore have motivated them to support a war on Iraq.

Conclusion

In this chapter we have examined three main variables that may have affected states' decisions to either follow US leadership or to reject it: oil dependence, material assessment of threat and alliance dependence. Of these three material explanations, the most persuasive and consistent explanation for either course of action was the presence or absence of alliance dependence on the US, whilst oil dependence and material threat assessment provided inconclusive or inconsistent results with our hypotheses.

The least satisfactory of all our explanatory variables was oil dependence. It was predicted that states with a high degree of oil dependence and substantial oil contracts with the Hussein regime would have an interest in opposing regime change in Iraq. Of all the states in our sample, only France fit these criteria, in the period 1996–2000. However, in the three years preceding the war, the level of trade between the two states was miniscule, including the trade in oil which had largely ceased after 2000. Whilst the IIC enquiry into the oil for food programme did uncover corruption among public officials, it was unable to directly link this to French foreign policy. The evidence in the French case could not therefore support the oil dependence hypothesis.

Table 5.3 Normative threat assessment – threat to international order

State	Likelihood Iraq had re-armed	Link between Iraq and al-Qaeda	Likelihood of support for the US
Japan	Medium–High	Medium	Medium–High
Germany	Low	Low	Low
France	Low–Medium	Low	Low–Medium
United Kingdom	High	High	High

Table 5.4 Material assessment of threat

State	Aggregate power, offensive capabilities, geographic proximity	Likelihood of support for the US
Japan	Low	Low
Germany	Low	Low
France	Low	Low
United Kingdom	Low	Low

Table 5.5 Alliance dependence

State	Fear of abandonment	Fear of entrapment	Likelihood of support for the US
Japan	High	Low–Medium	High
Germany	Low	High	Low
France	Low	Medium	Low
United Kingdom	Medium	Low	Medium

Table 5.6 The oil factor

State	Dependence on oil as energy source	Likelihood of support for the US
Japan	High	Indeterminate
Germany	High	Indeterminate
France	High	Indeterminate
United Kingdom	Very Low	Low

A second hypothesis was that states with a heavy oil dependence that did not have oil contracts with the Hussein regime may have supported regime change to pursue opportunities for lucrative oil development contracts with a post-Hussein Iraqi government. In the cases of Germany and Japan, this hypothesis provided inconsistent results given that the former rejected US leadership and the latter was a strong follower. In any event, the evidence did not support the contention that oil was a factor in decision-making either way. Finally, whilst it was noted that, by the end of the decade, the United Kingdom is predicted to become a net oil importer and would therefore be concerned with securing reliable sources of oil, there was also little evidence in the public domain to suggest that decision-makers placed this concern highly on their list of priorities in going to war.

The second variable tested in the chapter – the balance of threat hypothesis materially defined – could also not provide a satisfactory explanation of the pattern of followership or the rejection of US leadership during the Iraq Crisis. This pattern is more accurately explained by normative assessments of the Iraqi threat made by both states, i.e. their assessment of Iraq as a threat based on its aggressive intentions and the implications this would have for international order. All appeared to hinge on whether states were willing to act on the basis that Iraq's past behaviour cast it as a rogue state that could not be deterred from acquiring WMD and potentially passing this weaponry to international terrorists. For all states, using the materially defined balance of threat hypothesis, Iraq should not have been viewed as an immediate threat to national security given that its aggregate power and offensive capabilities had been highly degraded over a decade of economic sanctions, intrusive inspections, intermittent airstrikes and military enforcement of the no-fly zones. Further, Iraq's possession of WMD was still unproven at this stage. Thus, the balance of threat defined materially can explain the rejection of US leadership by France and Germany, but cannot explain followership by Japan and the United Kingdom.

The normative threat assessments of Iraq made by these states can, however, explain the pattern of followership or the rejection of US leadership. Germany and France, the two states rejecting US leadership, clearly did not agree with the normative threat assessment of Iraq put forward by the US based on Iraq's 'aggressive intentions'. Whilst German and French decision-makers shared the perception that a WMD-armed Iraq would potentially pose a threat to international order, they were not prepared to accept that Iraq had in fact rearmed on the basis of inferences drawn from Iraq's past illegitimate behaviour. They were then also unconvinced by the circumstantial intelligence sources presented by the US to prove that Iraq had reconstituted its weapons programmes and had links with al-Qaeda, preferring instead to rely on the inspectors to verify the status of Iraq's WMD programmes and stockpiles. Both Germany and France were in fact highly sceptical of US intelligence, viewing it as a convenient pretext by the US to justify regime change in Iraq. Further, for the French, even if Iraq had reconstituted its WMD programmes, it was believed that the inspections process could contain these ambitions indefinitely. This divergence in threat perceptions may have stemmed from the fact that September 11, 2001 was far from paradigm-shifting for the French or German public and political classes, and that force was believed to be an ineffective and counterproductive instrument to tackle the root causes of terrorism. Thus, the rejection of US leadership can be attributed to the clear mismatch in the normative threat perceptions between both states and the US about the gravity of the threat posed by Iraq and the implications of its 'rogue' nature.

Similarly, followership by Japan and the United Kingdom can be explained by a sharing of the normative threat perceptions of Iraq with the US. Both states took seriously the argument that rogue regimes could not be deterred from seeking to acquire WMD and would have strong incentives to transfer this technology to international terrorists. For Japan, Iraq fit the description of a rogue state and its lack of full cooperation with the inspectors supported the inference that re-armament had in fact occurred. UK decision-makers were even more obviously prepared to infer that Iraq had 'aggressive intentions' based on its past pattern of aggression towards neighbouring states, and of obstructing international efforts to disarm it of WMD. From the evidence that we have reviewed in this chapter, it is clear that UK decision-makers, particularly Prime Minister Blair, were willing to bear strong domestic political costs to follow the US because of independently formed beliefs about the gravity of the threat posed by 'rogue' states with WMD, the possible link between such states and terrorism, and the idea that spreading liberal democratic values would help to ameliorate these threats.

The most persuasive material explanation for the pattern of followership or the rejection of US leadership was alliance dependency or lack thereof. Followership was correctly predicted where the fear of abandonment outweighed the fear of being entrapped in a conflict in which core interests were not at stake, with the opposite being true for the rejection of US leadership. Japanese followership was directly related to a strong dependence upon the United States as its only external security provider in the region. The Japanese Government appears to have responded to direct pressure from the Bush Administration to contribute to the post-war reconstruction of Iraq in recognition of the fact that participation in the coalition would enhance its alliance credentials. Whilst there is evidence that Japan feared entrapment, this fear was dampened as a result of the limitations imposed by its pacifist constitution, which provided an effective shield from demands for participation in the war itself, and allowed it to make post-war contributions that could easily be withdrawn, if necessary.

In the case of the United Kingdom, of all the material motivations examined in this chapter, alliance dependence provides the only reasonably strong explanation of followership. Given that the United Kingdom shared the same normative perception of the Iraqi threat with the US, there was little or no evidence that it feared entrapment. Whilst the United Kingdom's level of alliance dependence on the US has waned since the Cold War, the government continued to privilege the NATO alliance over the developing European security structures, and saw its influence in world politics as being tied to nurturing the special relationship with the United States. The Iraq Crisis provided the UK with an opportunity to demonstrate its loyalty as an ally and thus reduce the likelihood of US abandonment in a future conflict. However, we have argued that alliance dependence could not completely explain why the UK Government took such significant political risks domestically in following the US. There were certainly much less conspicuous ways of avoiding abandonment than becoming the US's most committed junior partner. Any explanation of UK followership must also take into account the shared normative threat perception, and the influence of international legitimacy.

Similarly, French and German rejection of US leadership can be traced directly to a weakening in their alliance dependency on the US. Whilst neither state was indifferent to their alliance with the United States, their level of dependence has weakened since the end of the Cold War, allowing both states greater freedom to express independent views, including dissatisfaction with the non-consultative and unilateralist style of the Bush Administration and to make and act upon divergent assessments of the Iraqi threat. In the French case, US unilateralism was perceived as inimical to respectful alliance relations, and to some extent French policy-makers were motivated to punish the US for neglecting their country's interests. US unilateralism also directly threatened France's influence and status within international society by downgrading the centrality and authority of the Security Council over matters concerning international security. Thus, both considerations of alliance dependence as well as identity-based considerations are likely to have motivated France to obstruct and resist the US 'vision' for Iraqi disarmament.

In the German case, the weakening of its dependence allowed for the emergence of a greater self-confidence on the part of German leaders to develop an independent foreign policy from the United States. On Iraq, the rejection of US leadership was directly connected to a fear of becoming entrapped in a conflict that was likely to be counter-productive to Germany's own strategic priorities, particularly the fear that a war on Iraq would undermine support for 'the war on terror' among Islamic states and ultimately fuel recruitment for international terrorist groups. The unilateralist style of leadership pursued by the Bush Administration further fuelled this fear of entrapment by demonstrating that the Administration was not willing to accommodate the interests and views of its alliance partners. Thus, in the German case, the fear of entrapment outweighed the fear of abandonment, leading to the rejection of US leadership on the disarmament of Iraq.

In conclusion, of the three material motivations we have examined in this chapter, only alliance dependency provided a plausible explanation of state decisions to either follow or reject US leadership in the Iraq Crisis. Those states that chose to follow the United States displayed a medium-to-high level of alliance dependency upon the United States. For those states that rejected US leadership during the crisis, both displayed a weakened appreciation of the value of the US alliance, which gave decision-makers greater room to reject the US vision on Iraqi disarmament. Oil dependency provided inconclusive results, neither explaining followership nor the rejection of US leadership in all cases. Similarly, any material assessment of the Iraqi threat would have predicted a rejection of US leadership by all states. It is only if we consider the normative assessments of the Iraqi threat – based on an assessment of its aggressive intentions and the implications this would have for international order – that we can correctly predict followership and the rejection of US leadership by each state.

6 Comparing and contrasting the Gulf Crisis and the Iraq Crisis

The overarching purpose of this book has been to explore the nature of US hegemony in the post-Cold War era. In particular we have sought to enter into the debate about whether international legitimacy truly matters in an international system dominated by a lone superpower. To do so, two key aims have been pursued. First, to examine the relationship between hegemony and international legitimacy as theoretical concepts, and specifically, to evaluate whether hegemony in the post-Cold War era is best conceptualised as a relation of dominance or of leadership. Intrinsic to the competition between these two conceptualisations is the relative weight given to the role of international legitimacy as a driver of state behaviour, interests and identities. For those advocating a view of hegemony as a relation of dominance, the stability of international order is achieved via the application of material resources by a hegemon to reward or coerce subordinate states to conform to the rules and norms associated with that order. Legitimacy plays a secondary role at best, as a tool used by the powerful to entrench unequal power relations within international law and institutions.

In contrast, for those who take a normative view of hegemony, it is international legitimacy – or shared beliefs about appropriate, rightful and proper behaviour between states – that constitutes and regulates hegemony as a socially recognised leadership role. Legitimacy constitutes hegemony by defining the expectations of proper behaviour associated with the role of leadership which, if adhered to, guides subordinate states to recognise a hegemon as having certain rights and responsibilities associated with the maintenance of international order. It therefore both constrains and regulates hegemonic power, whilst also enabling it by creating an obligation on the part of subordinate states to follow the leadership of the hegemon where order is disrupted. Further, it is the widely held belief in the legitimacy of a hegemonic order among subordinate states that underpins the stability and longevity of that order.

The second aim of the book has been to empirically evaluate which of these conceptualisations is best able to explain the practice of hegemony in the post-Cold War period through an examination of two case studies – the Gulf Crisis of 1990–1991 and the Iraq Crisis of 2002–2003 – in which the US sought to take leadership over international society. Analysis of these case studies was divided into two chapters, devoted to investigating either the possible normative or material motivations of states in choosing to follow the US or reject its leadership. Were we to find that followership or the rejection of leadership were adequately explained as a response to US threats, coercion or material rewards, then a conceptualisation of hegemony as a dominance relationship need not be challenged. However, if we were to find that a complete explanation of events required consideration of normative motivations for followership or the rejection of US leadership, then we would argue that hegemony is best understood as a leadership role in international society. Whilst it was expected that a combination of motives for followership or non-followership would be found, the main task has been to determine whether legitimacy was a significant motivation for state action and therefore added to our understanding of the practice of hegemony.

In this chapter we undertake a cross-comparison of the two case studies in order to determine the core material and normative motivations that compelled states to follow or reject US leadership. In brief, we find that the pattern of followership or the rejection of US leadership cannot be explained persuasively without consideration of two factors: the level of alliance dependency on the US of particular states together with the influence of normative beliefs about legitimate behaviour between states, and legitimate behaviour attached to the role of leadership within international society. In terms of our theoretical aims, we conclude that a conceptualisation of hegemony as a socially defined leadership role provides a more complete and compelling explanation of events in the two case studies.

Material explanations

Oil dependency

In overall terms, oil dependency did not provide a strong explanation for either followership or the rejection of leadership in either case study. In the analysis of the Gulf Crisis in Chapter 3, neither the material interest in maintaining oil supplies from the Middle East at a reasonable price or safeguarding the stability of the world oil price proved to be significant factors in motivating states to follow the United States. The United Kingdom, as a net oil exporter, could not have been motivated to follow on the basis of oil interests. UK decision-makers were concerned to safeguard the stability of world oil supplies and prices, but this is traced to a normative threat assessment of Iraq's future intent to use control of Kuwait's oil resources to raise world oil prices and enhance its regional power.

Table 6.1 Persuasiveness of the oil dependency factor

Case	United Kingdom	Japan	Germany	France
1990–1991	Low	Low	Low	Low
2002–2003	Low	Indeterminate	Indeterminate	Indeterminate

West Germany, Japan and France were all highly dependent upon oil for their energy needs and should have been sensitive to disruptions to oil supplies and concerned about the possible rise in oil prices should Iraq withhold supply.

However, none of these states in fact considered the short- or long-term likelihood of higher oil prices as being a significant threat to economic growth due to a range of factors, including confidence in measures to reduce levels of oil dependency, to diversify energy sources and to increase efficiency in energy use since the 1970s oil shocks. States such as Japan also had a sizeable oil reserve, whilst the French were confident that oil supplies below the spot price could be negotiated bilaterally by capitalising on the close ties France had nurtured with the Arab world.

In the 2002–2003 Iraq Crisis, we once more found that oil dependency provided a poor explanation for state action. Again, as a state with a very low dependence on oil imports, UK followership could not be explained by this variable. In contrast, both Japan and Germany had incentives to follow the United States because of a high level of oil dependency and an absence of strong trade relations with the Hussein regime. However, we found no clear evidence in the public discourse to suggest that Japanese followership was motivated by a desire to secure future oil supplies. Further, in choosing to reject US leadership we can say that Germany acted against a material interest in securing greater access to Iraqi oil after the war was over.

In the case of France, a prevalent explanation of its opposition to US leadership during the Iraq Crisis was that it had a strong motive to keep the Hussein regime in power to ensure that corrupt oil and trade deals were kept hidden from public view. However, whilst some level of corruption was uncovered by the Independent Inquiry Committee into the UN Oil for Food Program prior to 2000, by 2003 trade with Iraq, including oil purchases, accounted for only 0.2 per cent of French trade overall. Given the lack of a strong oil supply relationship between the regime and France, it would have had little reason to reject US leadership and more reason to in fact support regime change.

Alliance dependence and followership

Alliance dependency and the associated abandonment/entrapment dilemma proved to be the most significant and consistent explanation for the pattern of followership or the rejection of US leadership in both crises. In the Gulf Crisis, all four states had either a high or medium-high fear of abandonment by the US, whilst only France showed any notable fear of entrapment. Similarly, in the Iraq Crisis, followership in the case of the United Kingdom and Japan was explained by a medium and high fear of abandonment whilst the rejection of US leadership by Germany and France can be linked to a low fear of abandonment and high and medium fear of entrapment respectively.

The Gulf War was the first major international conflict that tested alliance relationships after the demise of the Soviet Union as the common enemy of all four states. For the three European states, Germany, France and the United

Table 6.2 Persuasiveness of the alliance dependence factor

Case	State	Abandonment	Entrapment	Prediction
1990–1991 Gulf Crisis	United Kingdom	High	Low	Followership
	Japan	High	Low	Followership
	Germany	High	Low	Followership
	France	Medium–High	Medium	Followership
2002–2003 Iraq Crisis	United Kingdom	Medium	Low	Followership
	Japan	High	Low–Medium	Followership
	German	Low	High	Rejection
	France	Low	Medium	Rejection

Kingdom, whilst there was a degree of uncertainty about the future of the NATO alliance, it was still too soon after the end of the Cold War for predictions to be made about the future trajectory of relations with the USSR or for any viable alternative security structures to have emerged. Whilst the French sought to nurture a strictly European security structure based on the WEU, both the United Kingdom and Germany sought to ensure NATO would remain the dominant of the two for different reasons. With a Conservative government at the controls, still wary of embracing the expansion of the European project into the security realm, the British sought to ensure that the US commitment to European security would not dissipate, a development that would also reduce the importance of the 'special relationship' and in turn diminish UK influence. The West Germans understood that NATO performed a dual function: safeguarding national security whilst reassuring European states and the USSR that a reunified Germany would be institutionally inhibited from once again pursuing an expansionist foreign policy. Japan, as a state constrained in its military ambitions by constitutional restrictions and the entrenchment of a pacifistic civilian culture, the US nuclear umbrella continued to be indispensable in the face of rising regional security threats from North Korea and China. All states therefore significantly feared abandonment by the US.

Alliance dependency played a significant part in spurring swift and voluntary military contributions to the coalition, but the size of these contributions can only be explained by a shared normative threat perception of Iraq with the US, as will be discussed below (pp. 139–141). In contrast, the West Germans and Japanese were highly reactive in their approach to the crisis, and it was up to the US to exploit fears of abandonment to extract financial contributions from both states. Both were subject to sustained attack for free-riding on the US's security commitments. A high correlation was found between persistent US threats – delivered by the President, Congress and Administration officials – to withdraw security benefits and the timing of announcements of sizeable financial contributions by each of these states.

Of the four states, only France showed any fear of becoming entrapped in an unpopular conflict in the Muslim world. Participation in the coalition risked damage to long-established ties with former colonies in Africa and the Middle East, thereby potentially diminishing French influence over international affairs. Attempts to distance itself from the confrontational approach of the US, the eleventh-hour diplomatic mission to Iraq to avert war, and the insistence on separate military objectives for French forces in the conduct of the war, were in part motivated to minimise the negative impact participation in the coalition would have on French influence over these states. It was argued that, ultimately, given that NATO was still of high value, France's fear of abandonment outweighed its fear of entrapment.

In the Iraq 2002–2003 crisis, alliance dependence proved to be a significant explanation for followership in the cases of the United Kingdom and Japan, whilst the absence of a strong dependence on the US by Germany and France allowed both to act on independent assessments of the Iraqi threat. Both these states feared entrapment to a much greater extent than they feared abandonment.

Of the two follower states in the Iraq Crisis, Japan continued to be highly dependent on its alliance with the United States for protection against rising security threats from North Korea and China, primarily because of the pacifist restrictions placed upon its constitution. There was some evidence of pressure being placed on Japan to contribute to the coalition, but largely this was unnecessary as Japanese leaders openly recognised that participation in the post-war reconstruction of Iraq was of central importance to demonstrating alliance solidarity with the US.

The United Kingdom still also highly valued the 'special relationship' it has developed with the US, and has insisted that the development of a European common defence capability should complement rather than compete with existing NATO structures. Public statements of both Prime Minister Blair and Foreign Minister Jack Straw made obvious that participation in the coalition did stem from a desire to influence US policy from within. However, what is also clear is that followership was not only influenced by alliance dependency, but also stemmed from normative beliefs, and a sharing of normative threat perceptions. Alliance dependency alone cannot explain the strength of material and political participation in the coalition, especially given the domestic unpopularity of the war.

In the cases of the two states which rejected US leadership, Germany and France, both surprisingly showed a low fear of abandonment, given that European military capabilities did in no way rival the capabilities of the NATO alliance. However, in the absence of a grave common threat of similar magnitude to the Cold War, perceptions of alliance dependence on the US had weakened, allowing both states greater freedom and confidence to pursue independent interests and values. Of particular importance was the fact that both states did not share US normative perceptions of the gravity of the Iraqi threat feeding fears of entrapment. Further, the unilateralist leadership style of the Bush Administration added considerable fuel to these fears of entrapment, confirming that French and German interests and views would not given due deference and accommodation by its alliance partner.

The balance of threat and followership

The third material factor tested in our empirical chapters was that of threat perception. We hypothesised that states which shared a similar threat perception to the US would be likely to 'follow' the US, whilst an absence of shared threat perception may have been a motivation for the rejection of US leadership. Using Stephen Walt's concept of the balance of threat, separation was made between material assessments of threat – based on aggregate power, geographic proximity and offensive capabilities – and normative assessments of threat based on an adversary's perceived intentions.

Followership or the rejection of US leadership cannot be credibly explained by material threat perceptions of Iraq. At the time of the Gulf Crisis, whilst Iraq possessed a considerable standing army and a proven chemical weapons capability, none of our four states could be said to have faced a direct security threat from Iraq. Iraq was not geographically proximate to any of these states and lacked the ability to project its military forces to the European continent, the British Isles or to Japan.

Similarly, at the same time as the Iraq Crisis, none of our four states should have assessed Iraq as presenting a high material threat to national security. After 12 years of economic and military sanctions, an intrusive disarmament regime and the enforcement of no-fly zones, Iraq's aggregate power and offensive capabilities were likely to have been considerably degraded. Whilst the absence of weapons inspectors from 1998–2002 may have enabled it to improve its offensive capabilities, there was a dearth of strong intelligence to confirm the true extent of these activities. Of the four states, only the UK Government appeared to accept the US view that Iraq had in fact reconstituted its WMD and ballistic missile programmes. However, given the circumstantial nature of this evidence, British assessments of the Iraqi threat were more correctly derived from a normative assessment of Iraq's likely behaviour based on its past record of regional aggression.

Normative threat assessments of Iraq's perceived intentions provided a stronger prediction of state action in the Iraq Crisis than in the Gulf Crisis. In the Gulf Crisis, the strong degree of military participation in the Gulf coalition by both the United Kingdom and France can be directly linked to a sharing of

Table 6.3 Material assessments of the Iraqi threat

Case	State	Assessment	Prediction
1990–1991 Gulf Crisis	United Kingdom	Low	Rejection
	Japan	Low	Rejection
	Germany	Low	Rejection
	France	Low	Rejection
2002–2003 Iraq Crisis	United Kingdom	Low	Rejection
	Japan	Low	Rejection
	German	Low	Rejection
	France	Low	Rejection

Table 6.4 Normative perceptions of the Iraqi threat

Case	State	Assessment	Prediction
1990–1991 Gulf Crisis	United Kingdom	High	Followership
	Japan	Low–Medium	Weak followership at best
	Germany	Low–Medium	Weak followership at best
	France	High	Followership
2002–2003 Iraq Crisis	United Kingdom	High	Followership
	Japan	Medium–High	Followership
	Germany	Low	Rejection
	France	Low–Medium	Rejection

normative threat perceptions with the US that Iraqi aggression posed a threat to international order. As noted in Chapter 3, UK Prime Minister Margaret Thatcher clearly viewed the Iraqi invasion as a serious test of a New World Order based on international law under the Charter.[1] Further, concerns about the consequences of the invasion for the stability in world oil prices derived from a perception of Iraq as an aggressive state with the intent to dominate the region through the control of territory and oil resources. French President Mitterrand also took a strong stance against Iraq's aggression, with many attributing this to the fact that members of his generation experienced personally the consequences of the appeasement of Nazi Germany at Munich.[2] Given the control of foreign policy by the office of the President, Mitterrand's personal views on the importance of upholding international law had more influence over decision-making than is the case in most states.

However, normative threat perceptions can only partially explain Japanese and German followership of the US. The leaders of both states shared in the condemnation of Iraq's aggression as a threat to international order[3] but yet, financial contributions to the coalition coincided directly with the application of veiled threats by the US to withdraw alliance-related benefits. In the Japanese case, this can partially be explained by the pacifist culture that had become entrenched in Japanese society, which made it highly reactionary, rather than proactive when it came to responding to broader security threats. The reactive nature of the German response can be partially attributed to the fact that, at this time, preparations for unification understandably took a far higher priority. It could also be argued that German strategists had not yet adjusted to the post-Cold War world and continued to view threats to national territory as being far more vital than any diffuse threat to international order. The reluctance of Germany to develop the ability to project military power beyond the NATO area was consistent with its historical development and a strict reading of its constitution. What could be argued here is that normative threat perceptions provided permissive conditions for followership, whilst the strength of contributions to the coalition is more compellingly explained by alliance dependence.

The Gulf Crisis and the Iraq Crisis 141

In the Iraq Crisis, there was a much higher correlation between normative threat perceptions of Iraqi intentions and the pattern of state action. Given the paucity of direct and reliable evidence that Iraq had reconstituted its WMD programmes between 1998 and 2002, followership or the rejection of US leadership became tied to whether states accepted US normative threat perceptions that Iraq had the aggressive intent to acquire WMD, and that its lack of full cooperation with the inspectors under Resolution 1441 proved its concealment of existing programmes and stockpiles. That is, in the face of ambiguity over Iraq's possession of WMD – the reality of the Iraqi threat – normative beliefs guided states in how to interpret and respond to this uncertainty. The two follower states, Japan and the United Kingdom, were in complete agreement with US threat perceptions and clearly believed that military action needed to be taken on this basis.

In contrast, our analysis of French and Germany motivations determined that both did not share the same normative threat perception of Iraq and terrorist groups as the US, and that this played a direct role in the decision to reject its leadership. French decision-makers were unimpressed with the veracity of US evidence put forward to prove that Iraq was concealing existing WMD capabilities and had formed strong ties to international terrorist groups. They were not prepared to make inferences about Iraq's likely intentions from its past aggression and post-1991 efforts to preserve a WMD capability. Further, it was argued that even if Iraq had reconstituted its weapons programmes, given the weak evidence linking it to al-Qaeda, the Iraqi threat could be countered by a containment policy through continued inspections and did not require the urgent use of force. The German SPD/Green coalition government concurred with this assessment and was widely seen to have won re-election on this platform. For the German public and political class, the threat posed by international terrorist groups was a much graver threat to international security, and the war in Iraq was therefore viewed as a 'military adventure' with the potential to fracture the coalition against terrorism by losing the support of Arab and Muslim states. This absence in shared threat perceptions combined with a weakened alliance dependency to propel these two states to oppose US leadership on Iraq.

Legitimacy and followership

In Chapters 2 and 4 of this book, the importance of legitimacy as a motivation for followership or the rejection of US leadership in the Gulf Crisis and Iraq Crisis was assessed, drawing from the justifications used by states in the UN Security Council and General Assembly to explain their decisions. In both cases beliefs about legitimate behaviour influenced the acceptance or rejection of two aspects of US leadership.

First, followership could be directly attributed to an acceptance of the US vision for the resolution of the common threat to international peace and security, a vision made up of proposals about legitimate end goals and the means to achieve them. Essential to followership was the belief that the goals and means advocated by the US were legitimate with respect to international norms on the use of force, the proper settlements of disputes, and the rights and responsibilities associated with state sovereignty. Conversely, we also found that the rejection of US leadership was also significantly guided by the normative beliefs in the illegitimacy of the US vision in terms of its goals and/or means.

Second, the pattern of followership or the rejection of US leadership was also strongly guided by normative beliefs about how leadership should be exercised and for what ends. US leadership was accepted by states where it was able to demonstrate a readiness to consult with other states, accommodate the interests of others where necessary, and subject the exercise of its predominant power capabilities to limitations imposed by agreed substantive and procedural norms. In particular, US respect for the multilateral decision-making procedure laid down in the UN Charter appeared to influence followership by reassuring subordinate states that leadership was sought for the purpose of achieving common rather than parochial goals. In contrast, the failure to respect shared substantive and procedural norms on the exercise of power directly spurred subordinate states to reject US claims to rightfully lead the international community. In this sense, legitimacy both constrained and enabled the exercise of hegemonic power by the United States.

The 1990–1991 crisis

In the case of the 1990–1991 Gulf Crisis, we found that followership was strong among members of both the Security Council and the broader UN membership, with the predominant justifications for this stance being normative in nature. Beliefs about legitimate behaviour influenced both the acceptance of the US vision for the restoration of international peace and security as well as acceptance of the US as a trustworthy state to occupy a leadership role over matters of international order.

The overwhelming acceptance of the US-endorsed goal of reversing the invasion was based on the belief among a strong majority of states that the Iraqi invasion breached a number of core principles of the international security order including the prohibition on the use of force, the peaceful settlement of disputes between states and respect for state sovereignty. By committing an act of aggression, Iraq had committed a grave transgression against the foundational norms of international society which needed to be reversed to bolster the credibility of the UN Charter system. It was for these reasons that all states endorsed the goal of reversing the Iraqi invasion and restoring the legitimate Kuwaiti Government.

Acceptance of the US vision on the appropriate means to be used to liberate Kuwait was also strongly influenced by normative beliefs, particularly commitments to the prohibition on the use of force, the peaceful settlement of disputes and state sovereignty. In the first instance, the imposition of economic sanctions was believed to send a sufficiently strong message, at an early stage of the crisis, that the Council was determined to reverse the invasion and defend the credibility of the collective security system. The imposition of sanctions also accorded with the normative belief that inter-state disputes should be resolved peacefully. Iraq was therefore given the opportunity to avoid war.

The decision to accept the US proposal to enforce an embargo on Iraq was also highly norm-governed. Iraq's sustained defiance of the will of the Council – by declaring Kuwait's annexation, abuse of civilians in occupied Kuwait and the taking of diplomatic hostages – was again viewed a threat to the authority of the Council and the system of collective security it represented. The majority of states that voted in favour of Resolution 665 reasoned that diplomacy backed by sanctions remained the legitimate means of liberating Kuwait, and the authorisation of military action for the limited purpose of enforcing the embargo was the surest way of allowing these peaceful means of pressuring Iraq to take effect.

Similarly, the acceptance of the US push for the forcible eviction of Iraq came only after it was accepted that all peaceful means had been exhausted, or were unlikely to succeed before irreparable damage was done to Kuwaiti assets, and to its people. In authorising the use of force, these states were satisfied that Iraq had been given every opportunity to withdraw voluntarily and that force was now only being used as a last resort.

Whilst the acceptance of US leadership depended in a large part on the judgement of states that its vision for the solution of the crisis (including goals and means) was legitimate, the US also encouraged followership by making moves to reassure other states that it was ultimately seeking their cooperation to achieve a collective interest, rather than its own parochial interests. Attempts by the Bush Administration to reassure states of its legitimate intentions and of its credentials to lead the international community took a number of forms.

First, throughout the crisis the US demonstrated both the capacity and readiness to bear a greater share of the risks and costs associated with defending international order. Whilst the Bush Administration sought to defray the burden of sanctions and military action from allies and states most threatened by the Iraqi regime, its early moves to defend Saudi Arabia and to enforce the embargo gave it greater standing to assert leadership over how to respond to the Iraqi invasion.

Second, whilst the US did attempt to influence followership by offering economic inducements or threatening to withdraw existing security or economic benefits, its leaders came to the view early in the crisis that successful leadership hinged on rousing genuine and voluntary support for the vision it proposed for the resolution of the crisis. This explained the unusual efforts made by President Bush and Secretary of State James Baker to personally persuade states of the legitimacy of the US approach to the crisis.

Third, the Administration understood that it needed to demonstrate that the US was willing to compromise on its proposals and to accommodate the interests of other states, in order to provide some reassurance that the US was not merely seeking to gather a coalition against Iraq to mask the pursuit of its own particularistic interests. There were a number of instances in which the US showed the preparedness to compromise during the crisis. In the early stages of the crisis, whilst the US had the legal right to send military forces to the Gulf at the request of the Emir of Kuwait as a measure of collective self-defence under Article 51 of the Charter, the Administration chose to abandon this justification and seek the involvement of the UN Security Council to show that it was willing to consider the views and interests of others, given that the dispute threatened the collective interest.

This intention to pursue consensus in decision-making was again displayed in negotiations over the draft of Resolution 665. Here the US agreed to include an amendment including a coordination and oversight role for the Military Staff Committee to recognise the concerns of the USSR, China, France, Malaysia, Colombia and Finland that the authorisation of force could be abused by the coalition forces. Further, the removal of the words 'minimum use of force' from Resolution 665 was accepted to allow the Chinese to appear to oppose the use of force to a Third World audience, yet in practice allow the embargo to proceed under the Security Council's authorisation. The last nod to the pursuit of consensus came with the agreement to amend the terms of Resolution 678 by delaying the deadline for Iraqi compliance, in order to accommodate and incorporate the principles of Gorbachev's 'new thinking'.

Finally, the substance of the broad US vision for international order proclaimed by the Administration appeared to reassure other states that it intended to lead an order based on cooperation and consensus to defend core agreed values. President Bush's objective of establishing a 'new world order' was premised on the view that the end of the ideological divide opened up a second opportunity to establish the post-Second World War order that had been overwhelmed by the imperatives of the Cold War. Essential to this vision was cooperation with other nations to 'deter aggression and to achieve stability' based on a 'shared commitment ... to a set of principles that undergird our relations – peaceful settlement of disputes, solidarity against aggression, reduced controlled arsenals, and just treatment of all peoples'.[4]

The 2002–2003 Iraq Crisis

Unlike the 1990–1991 Gulf Crisis, during the 2002–2003 Iraq Crisis normative beliefs about legitimate behaviour motivated a majority of states to reject the leadership of the United States. The US was largely unrecognised as a hegemonic leader for two reasons. First, it was unable to persuade a sufficient number of states that its vision for the resolution of the Iraqi threat was legitimate. Second, the US approach to leadership during the crisis failed to accord with the expectations of legitimate behaviour associated by states with this role. In this case, the general perception that the US was itself a threat to the stability of international order and sought the position of leadership to achieve its own interests, rather than the interests of the collective.

On the first issue, the US achieved partial support for its vision for the solution to the Iraq problem, with states supporting the legitimacy of the end goal but not the means to pursue it. A strong majority of the Council accepted the US perspective that the potential possession of WMD by Iraq posed a threat to the common interest in maintaining international order. The end goal of disarming Iraq was accepted on the basis of accepted beliefs about appropriate, proper and rightful behaviour of states. Iraq's failure to comply with the long list of past Council resolutions demanding WMD disarmament evidenced its defiance of the standards of behaviour expected of all states. Further, the failure of the Council to enforce its own decisions was agreed to pose a threat to international peace and security by undermining the credibility of the UN system of collective security.

However, it was on the issue of how Iraqi disarmament should be achieved that support for the US vision, and therefore US leadership, faltered. In negotiations over Resolution 1441, whilst the US plan envisaged the immediate resort to force on the first signs of Iraqi obduracy, a majority of states rejected this approach, guided by their beliefs about legitimate behaviour in the circumstances. The eventual inclusion of a two-step process within Resolution 1441 was supported by 11 out of 15 states on the basis of their belief in the peaceful settlement of disputes and the use of force as a last resort. A number of states were clearly motivated by a desire to avoid what was perceived to be an unnecessary rush to war by the US.

There was also strong evidence to suggest that a majority of the Council supported the two-step process in order to defend the role of the Security Council as the body with the legitimate right to decide on appropriate measures to defend international order. Many states were clearly reacting to the US draft resolution which would have allowed individual states – including itself – to use force on their own assessments of whether Iraq was in material breach of its obligations.

In the following year, after the presentation of inspectors' reports highly critical of the level of Iraqi cooperation, the rejection of attempts by the US to gain authorisation by the Council to use force was again strongly influenced by state beliefs about legitimate behaviour. Whilst Iraq's compliance with UNSC Resolution 1441 was generally viewed as inadequate, 11 out of 15 states in the Council believed that the inspections process should be allowed to continue in an enhanced form to give peaceful means of settling the dispute all chance to succeed. This would give Iraq a further opportunity to improve cooperation as well as giving the inspectors greater time and resources to complete their disarmament tasks. This position was strongly and consistently endorsed by a majority of the broader UN membership on the grounds that disputes between states should be settled by peaceful means.

The rejection of the US vision in this case can also be seen as a rejection of two aspects of the US vision that were viewed in themselves to dangerously undermine the core basis on which international order, and the prevention of catastrophic conflict, had been constructed after the Second World War. First, the rejection of US leadership was clearly tied to a rejection of the Bush Administration's new doctrine of pre-emption and its application to the case of Iraq. The US case for war asked states to endorse regime change on the basis that Iraq's lack of full cooperation with the inspectors, as required under Resolution 1441, had only one implication: that it had in fact reconstituted its WMD programmes between 1998 and 2002, and was now returning to the old pattern of concealment and obstruction of international disarmament efforts. Iraq's guilt was to be inferred from its evasive behaviour, rather than through the provision of direct proof that WMD programmes or stockpiles had in fact been reconstituted. The majority of states in the Council and outside of it were clearly unwilling to support the use of force where there was no proof that Iraq did in fact possess a WMD capacity, let alone whether it had plans to use it. Even if stronger evidence had emerged that Iraq did possess WMD, it is questionable whether states were willing to support the use of force to disarm it, without further evidence of an intent to use these weapons or to pass them on to international terrorist groups. We will, of course, never know the answer to this question. However, what is clear is that in the view of these states, even pre-emption as practised by the collective, was seen to dangerously weaken the core prohibition on the use of force and undermine the protections of sovereignty contained in the Charter. In these circumstances, for many states, there was little to separate pre-emption from aggression.

Finally, the US vision was also rejected by a majority of states on the grounds that the very character of a regime – as an illiberal rogue state – should not in itself be sufficient grounds to legitimise the use of force to effect democratic regime change. The use of force to spread democracy was seen to dangerously undermine the sovereignty norm and the prohibition of the use of force by allowing the preferences and ideals of one segment of international society to be forcibly applied to all. Sovereignty specifically protected the right of a polity to choose its own political system as a value in itself, but also as a pragmatic measure to minimise the range of 'just causes' for which war could be waged. No doubt, the large number of small and illiberal regimes among the UN membership also had good cause to oppose the legitimacy of a US vision that would allow democracy to be spread by force.

Whilst the vision put forward by the US Administration failed to be accepted as legitimate by a critical mass of states, additionally this failure needs to be understood within the context of the US approach to leadership during the crisis. Whilst in the first Gulf Crisis the US made concerted efforts to reassure other states of its intentions to achieve the interests of the collective, in this case efforts towards reassurance were notably lacking. As such, US behaviour was judged to be outside the bounds of appropriate, proper and rightful behaviour associated with the role of leadership in international society, leading to the rejection of its leadership aspirations. Two aspects of the US Administration's approach to leadership created the perception that the US was seeking to exploit the position of leadership for its own purposes.

First, the US claim to be acting in the best interests of the collective was undermined by its assertion of the right to use force against Iraq unilaterally, creating the perception that the US Administration intended to act without regard to the beliefs and interests of other states. As we have discussed above (p. 82), the legal basis on which the US asserted its right to act unilaterally carved out an exception to the prohibition on the use of force that was exceptionally broad and underspecified, making it unclear how pre-emption could be distinguished from aggression. Further, the assertion of a unilateral right to enforce prior Security Council resolutions usurped the role of the Security Council to ensure that force would be used to achieve the collective interests of all states. In both cases, the

US appeared to be intentionally throwing off any constraints on the use of its predominant capabilities imposed by shared rules and norms, and which unquestionably undermined its credibility to lead international society.

Second, the repeated declarations by the US of the intent to unilaterally remove the Hussein regime from Iraq throughout 2002 gave rise to the suspicion that the involvement of the UN Security Council was being sought purely for instrumental reasons. Negative perceptions of US intentions were drawn from the fact that the US appeared to be determined to act against Iraq on the basis of inferences drawn from its past behaviour and present lack of pro-active cooperation, rather than on conclusive proof. Further, as has been discussed above, the lack of consultation and accommodation of the concerns of major allies such as Germany and France on issues such as the detrimental effects of war on regional stability, the stability and governance of Iraq, and on the cohesion of the coalition against terrorism, cemented the perception that the US was seeking Council authorisation for disingenuous purposes. Ultimately, the decision by the US to go to war against Iraq without Security Council authorisation confirmed the suspicion that the US was merely seeking to acquire the legitimising effects of UN authorisation for regime change, i.e. the right to expect other states to share the burdens of the conduct of war and reconstruction in Iraq.

Striking the balance – legitimacy, material interests and hegemony

In the process of analysing the motivations for followership by states in both the Gulf Crisis and the Iraq Crisis, we have found that both material and normative interests had a significant part to play in the decision to follow or reject the leadership of the United States. The question for us here is whether consideration of the normative beliefs of states provides a substantially more complete understanding of events than consideration of material interests alone. The answer to this question is important to our overall interest in understanding the practice of US hegemony and its effects on followership in the post-Cold War period. Theoretically, it enables us to come to some conclusion about the persuasiveness of the competing theoretical conceptualisations of hegemony we have outlined above. If legitimacy has played a significant role in motivating followership or the rejection of leadership, then this supports a normative conceptualisation of hegemony as a leadership role within international society.

The Gulf Crisis provides a case in which the majority of states followed the leadership of the US against Iraq evidenced by a broad cross-section of political, financial and military participation in the coalition. In our analysis of the Gulf Crisis we found that the two strongest and most consistent motivations for followership were alliance dependence and the acceptance by states of the legitimacy of the US vision for the restoration of peace and security and of its approach to leadership. Alliance dependence convincingly accounted for followership in all cases, with the fear of abandonment overcoming any fears of entrapment by Japan, Germany, France and the United Kingdom.

Normative motives among our four states were shown to provide a strong explanation for followership for the United Kingdom and France, but less so for Japan and Germany. The highly reactive and passive response to the crisis by Germany and Japan suggests that, without US pressure applied to capitalise on the fear of abandonment, Japanese and German contributions to the Gulf coalitions would have been of a much smaller magnitude. Given that these two states politically supported the US vision for the crisis, including the implementation of all Resolutions of the Council, we would argue that the shared view of the illegitimacy of the Iraqi invasion and need to counter-aggression provided the necessary and permissive conditions for their substantial financial contributions to be made.

Whilst the United Kingdom was shown to be highly alliance dependent on the United States, we uncovered significant evidence to suggest that UK decision-makers were even more normatively outraged by the Iraqi invasion than members of the Bush Administration. We would argue that in this case both normative motivations and the material interest in supporting the US–UK alliance were of equal significance in explaining UK followership. Given the lower perception of alliance dependence in the case of France, an explanation of followership is more strongly provided by assessments of the legitimacy of the US vision and the legitimacy of its approach to leadership. In sum, of the four states chosen for deeper examination, two were significantly motivated by beliefs about legitimate, proper and appropriate behaviour of states in deciding to follow the US. Of the other two states, beliefs about legitimate behaviour allowed these states to participate in the coalition, but cannot explain the magnitude of the contributions that were eventually made.

In terms of the wider international community, we would argue that the breadth and depth of the political, financial and military contributions to the coalition can only be persuasively explained by the general acceptance of the legitimacy of the US 'vision' for the resolution to the crisis, and the pervasive belief that the US was seeking leadership to achieve the interests of the collective. Throughout the crisis the US did not need to expend significant energy towards convincing its fellow Council members of the gross illegitimacy of Iraq's actions, or of the need to reverse the invasion through economic sanctions, the enforcement of an embargo and, finally, in the use of military force. At each stage of the crisis, normative beliefs about the illegitimacy of aggression, the importance of state sovereignty, the peaceful settlement of disputes and the use of force as a last resort guided a majority of states to accept the plan proposed by the US. This consensus on the legitimate goals and means to be pursued in the crisis was strongly supported by the justifications for action given by the General Assembly and the statements of regional bodies such as the Arab League and European Union. The strength of normative beliefs in guiding followership is not negated by the relatively minor instances of inducements given to states such as Cote d'Ivoire, Zaire and China in the Council.

We have also argued that the approach to leadership taken by the US Administration guided states to recognise that it had a special leadership role within international society. The US was able to engender followership by demonstrating that it would not exploit the rights and prerogatives associated with this role, particularly the achievement of parochial interests at the expense of the interests of the community at large. It did so by consideration and incorporation of the beliefs and interests of less-powerful states within its 'vision', as well as by conforming to the rules and norms associated with the proper exercise of power. In particular, the US was responsive to criticisms about the importance of Security Council oversight of the use of force which served to reassure states that it intended to act on behalf of the interests of the international community.

In conclusion, among the four states examined in depth, followership in the 1990–1991 crisis was most strongly explained by both alliance dependence and state beliefs about legitimate behaviour in international society. Here legitimacy formed part of the necessary conditions for followership. Among the broader UN membership, including a large number of states which did not have strong alliance relationships with the US, we would argue that legitimacy played a strong role in engendering normative consensus around the US vision for the resolution to the crisis, as well as in motivating the recognition of its special leadership role. Without this normative consensus, the breadth and depth of followership would not have been attainable. That is, an explanation of followership in this case would be substantially incomplete without consideration of state beliefs about legitimate behaviour.

In relation to the Iraq Crisis, again, the two strongest and most consistent motivations for followership or the rejection of leadership were alliance dependency, or the lack thereof, and normative beliefs about legitimate state behaviour. Neither oil dependence nor the balance of threat, materially defined, could account for the pattern of state action. Threat perceptions did matter, but these perceptions were normatively driven based on an assessment of Iraq's likely aggressive intentions derived from its past illegitimate behaviour. Those states that accepted the US vision in this regard followed the US, whilst those that did not rejected US leadership.

In terms of our best-performing material motivation, alliance dependency correctly predicted both the rejection of US leadership or followership among our four chosen states, but cannot alone provide a complete explanation of state action. Following the collapse of the USSR, the level of alliance dependence by all four states had undoubtedly diminished. However, the perceptions of alliance dependence by our two follower states, Japan and the United Kingdom, still remained quite strong. In respect of UK followership, however, given the significant domestic political costs to the Blair Government associated with its support of the US, an explanation of the strength of UK followership must include the normative beliefs of key decision-makers. The UK need not have made such large and politically sensitive military contributions to the coalition to maintain its alliance with the United States.

In the cases of Germany and France, the weakening of alliance dependence on the US after the collapse of the Soviet Union provided permissive conditions for the rejection of US leadership during the crisis, but does not, however, provide positive reasons why France and Germany chose to reject US leadership. Normative beliefs provide the most persuasive explanation of the choices made by these two states in terms of their threat perceptions of Iraq and international terrorism, and their ultimate rejection of US leadership. For both these states, the US vision for the resolution of the crisis was illegitimate based on normative beliefs about the appropriate use of force in international relations. Additionally, we found evidence to suggest that both states declined to recognise the US as having a special leadership role because the latter failed to accord to their expectations of proper behaviour for an alliance partner as well as a leader of international society, by pursuing a unilateralist and uncompromising leadership style.

These normative beliefs were supported by a majority of the Security Council and the wider UN membership. Here we found that the rejection of US leadership by a broad cross-section of states was strongly motivated by the assessment that the US vision lacked legitimacy and that its motives in seeking to assert leadership over the Iraq issue were illegitimate for a state holding a special leadership role in international society. On the issue of the US vision for the Iraqi crisis, the reluctance to authorise the use of force was justified via state beliefs in the peaceful settlement of disputes and the use of force as a last resort. Further, both the doctrine of pre-emption and the use of force to spread liberal democracy were rejected as unwelcome developments in international practice which undermined the core principles of sovereignty and the prohibition on the use of force, and thereby increased the potential for greater instability in the global order.

Finally, the rejection of US leadership was found to be strongly linked to the perception that US behaviour was outside the bounds of legitimate behaviour associated with the role of leadership in international society. The repeated assertions of its right to act unilaterally, either under a doctrine of pre-emptive self-defence or to enforce the resolutions of the Security Council, demonstrated the desire of the Bush Administration to apply the US's considerable material capabilities towards the achievement of its own interests. As the crisis progressed, the unwillingness of the Administration to compromise on the use of force against Iraq, despite strong opposition among the general UN membership, served to further build on the perception that leadership had been sought for merely instrumental purposes. The inability of the US to find support for a second resolution represented an attempt by a number of states to obstruct the US from abusing its position of leadership within the Security Council to achieve its own self-interests and at the expense of the interests of other states. A majority of states effectively declined to recognise the US as having a special leadership role, denying it the right to expect other states to share the burdens of regime change in Iraq.

Thus, whilst alliance dependence provides a credible explanation for the decisions of our four states, any explanation of rejection of US leadership by France, Germany and a majority of the wider UN membership would be deficient without drawing from the beliefs of states about legitimate behaviour in international society. The rejection of US leadership by a wide cross-section of international society, including states that it considered to be strong allies, can only be persuasively explained by the beliefs of states in the legitimacy of core principles of international order which the US vision and leadership style attempted to challenge.

Theoretical implications

In this book we have contrasted two broad approaches to the conceptualisation of hegemony which differ in relation to the emphasis placed on material as opposed to ideational bases of power, the relationship between material power and norms in international society, and the methods by which international order is formed and maintained. Having analysed two post-Cold War case studies in which the United States sought to lead the international community on issues pertaining to international peace and security, we should be able to come to some conclusion about whether the actual practice of hegemony conforms to the various theoretical conceptualisations of hegemony that we have addressed.

The two case studies we have examined show a strong conformance with the alternate conceptualisations of hegemony as leadership and dominance. In the 1990–1991 crisis, the practice of US hegemony by the Bush Administration showed a recognition and appreciation of both material and normative forms of hegemonic power. Alliance dependence provided the only credible material explanation of followership, which was readily exploited by the US where necessary. In relation to a material conceptualisation of hegemony, the application of political pressure by the Administration to Germany and Japan can be seen as a form of coercion or inducement to encourage them to support its preferred goals. Whilst pressure was not directly applied to France or the United Kingdom, the fear of abandonment felt by these states can also be characterised as the fear of loss of a material benefit – a form of inducement or reward in the longer term. The coercive power of the United States was also shown to be essential to the maintenance of hegemonic order, with US military power proving to be essential to the success of the enforcement action.

A materialist conceptualisation of hegemony, however, cannot explain all aspects of the Gulf Crisis. We have shown that at least two of our in-depth case studies involved states that were highly motivated by their beliefs in legitimate behaviour of states. More importantly, our analysis of the reasons for action provided by members of the Security Council and wider UN membership showed that a belief in the legitimacy of the US vision for the crisis, as well as the expectations of proper behaviour associated with a leader in international society, played a significant role in motivating a broad range of states to follow the US in this case and to make deep contributions to the coalition effort. Political consensus around the US plan for the liberation of Kuwait was achieved with remarkably little effort – whether through arm-twisting or offering of benefits – on the part of the US. Thus, the great breadth and depth of the coalition against Iraq could not be explained by inducements and coercion alone, but must take account of the normative acceptance of US leadership.

Whilst the US could have defeated the Iraqi army without the assistance of other states, other aspects of the US plan of action required the voluntary assistance of the society of states. The almost complete implementation of economic and military sanctions was a prime example of compliance with the rules of order motivated by a logic of appropriateness rather than a logic of expected consequences. Strategies such as these simply could not have been achieved unless they were perceived to be legitimate by the majority of states.

A material conceptualisation of hegemony also does not explain why the United States perceived the need to involve the Security Council in the liberation of Kuwait. The Bush Administration was found to have a strong appreciation of the unique legitimising effects that would flow from the endorsement of the US vision by the Security Council. By successfully constructing a vision for the resolution to the crisis that was acceptable in terms of the normative beliefs of states, and by making concerted efforts to demonstrate that it could be trusted to lead international society, the US was able to utilise legitimacy as a form of power. Legitimacy was directly connected to the wide acceptance of the resolutions of the Council and with the considerable political, military and financial support the US received to restore international peace and security. Normative beliefs were found to directly correlate with the strong level of burden-sharing by a broad range of states. That is, the wide belief in the legitimacy of US leadership in the 1990–1991 crisis enabled it to maintain international order with significantly less cost than would otherwise have been the case if only material forms of power had been relied upon.

In contrast, the practice of US hegemony by the Bush Administration in the 2002–2003 Iraq Crisis strongly conformed with the material conceptualisation of hegemony as a dominance relationship by showing a lack of appreciation of the power of normative beliefs. In this case the Bush Administration strongly relied upon its material capabilities to achieve its self-defined interests. Leadership of the international community was sought at a late stage and was characterised by an obvious lack of compromise and accommodation of the interests and beliefs of other states. The decision to use force against Iraq without the authorisation of the Security Council showed clearly that the Administration believed that the US, at the peak of its powers, could achieve regime change without the support of the international community. As our materialist theorists would argue, the Iraqi crisis conformed to the idea that a hegemon is able to use its material power capabilities to enforce international order in a manner that suits its own interests. However, if we extend the period of our analysis to include the post-war reconstruction phase of the Iraqi project, this interpretation of events is found wanting. The society of states has found ways to negatively impact the achievement of the preferred goals of a hegemonic state. A focus on material factors alone does not provide a compelling explanation of why states have chosen not to share in the burdens of both the prosecution of the war and the reconstruction of Iraq.

In terms of explaining followership in the Iraq Crisis, the only compelling material explanation for followership – alliance dependency – could not in fact completely explain state action. In the UK case, alliance dependency could explain the fact of followership, but it was the shared perception of the gravity of the Iraqi threat with the US that explained the size of the UK contribution, despite the domestic opposition. Similarly, the weakening of alliance dependence on the US provided the permissive conditions for France and Germany to reject US leadership, but did not of itself explain the decision by these states to actively oppose the US position. The rejection of leadership here could only be persuasively explained by normative threat perceptions of Iraq and normative beliefs about appropriate use of force in international relations, and the respect for state sovereignty as the basis of international order. On a broader level, an understanding of the widespread rejection of US leadership by the broader international community cannot be explained without regard to these normative beliefs and threat perceptions. Further, the lack of recognition by states of a leadership role for the United States was also found to be closely tied to the normative belief that leadership should not be allowed to be exploited for the achievement of parochial interests.

Thus, whilst the practice of US hegemony by the Bush Administration conforms with a view of hegemony as a dominance relationship, the response of states to assertions of leadership by the US in the Iraq Crisis more closely conforms to the conceptualisation of hegemony as a leadership role in international society. International rules and norms were found to act as structural constraints on the maintenance of order by the hegemonic state. Whilst states could not prevent the US from using force for the purposes of regime change in Iraq, by denying the US recognition of a leadership role it was left to bear almost the full cost of maintaining order in this case alone. The illegitimacy of the war has directly affected the willingness of other states to contribute to Iraq's reconstruction, whilst the re-establishment of order and security within Iraq has been negatively affected by the view that the US is an occupying power which has attempted to colonise Iraq.

In sum, both the 1990–1991 Gulf Crisis and the 2002–2003 Iraq Crisis demonstrate that whilst a hegemon may choose to dominate or to lead international society, the normative structure in which all states act also serves to constrain and enable the ability of a hegemon to maintain international order. Where a hegemonic state fails to conform to the expectations of proper behaviour associated with the role of leadership, it can expect that the task of maintaining order will be unduly burdensome. Hence, in the Iraq Crisis, legitimacy acted as a constraint on hegemonic power by motivating states to oppose the achievement by a hegemon of its preferred goals. Even hegemonic states have limitations in their capabilities to bear the costs of maintaining order alone, as has become apparent to the Bush Administration. On the other hand, where a state is able to engender the belief in the legitimacy of the rules and norms of international order, and conforms to expectations associated with the role of leadership, it can expect subordinate states to contribute to the costs of maintaining order. In this sense, legitimacy also acts to enable hegemonic power. Thus, during the 1990–1991 Iraq Crisis, legitimacy motivated states to conform to the norms of a hegemonic order, without the expenditure of resources to induce or coerce them to do so.

In the final analysis, an understanding of hegemony is incomplete without consideration of the normative structure in which all states, including hegemonic states, act. We have found that, whilst the conceptualisation of hegemony as a dominance relationship provides us with valuable insights to understand some of the tools by which hegemonic states maintain international order, it cannot provide a complete account of events. Within the present international society, a hegemon is expected to play a leadership role, with expectations of legitimate behaviour attached to this role acting to both constrain and enable the exercise of hegemonic power. Whilst a hegemonic state, such as the United States, may disregard these expectations, by doing so it gives up the right to expect the society of states to assist it in the task of maintaining international order, and may face obstruction in its attempts to achieve its preferences. As we have seen in our case studies, the costs associated with maintaining order where a hegemon is recognised as holding a leadership role are significantly less than where hegemonic leadership is rejected. A hegemonic order is thus likely to have greater longevity and stability where subordinate states choose to follow its precepts on the basis of their belief in the legitimacy of this order and of the hegemon's leadership within it. Essential to gaining access to legitimacy as a form of power, however, is the dependence on a hegemonic state to accept certain constraints on the use of its predominant power. In other words, legitimacy can and does matter very much, even in a hegemonic system.

7 Conclusion

Barack Obama's ascent to the Presidency of the United States came at a time when stocks of goodwill towards America were at an all-time low among the global public. In December 2008, the Pew Global Attitudes Project released a report titled 'Global Public Opinion in the Bush Years' which unmistakably showed a steep decline in favourable perceptions of the United States among 26 of 33 countries polled. Worryingly for the US, some of the worst responses between 2000 and 2008 came from citizens of its traditional allies in Germany, the United Kingdom, Turkey, France, Poland, Spain and Japan, with declines in favourable perceptions ranging from 48 per cent to 17 per cent. Of note was the survey conducted in 2006 in which respondents from

> 13 of 15 countries found the American presence in Iraq to be an equal or greater danger to stability in the Middle East than the regime of Iranian President Mahmoud Almadinejad, while 11 judged it a threat to Middle East stability greater than or equal to the Israeli–Palestinian conflict.[1]

The use of force by the United States against Iraq in 2003 has unquestionably created a crisis in the legitimacy of US global leadership. Whilst the Iraq Survey Group did find evidence that Saddam Hussein intended to pursue a WMD capability should economic sanctions have been abandoned by the international community, its final determination that there were no WMD stockpiles to be found in Iraq, or clear evidence that such weapons programmes had in fact been reconstituted prior to the war,[2] gave vindication to critics of the doctrine of pre-emption who had argued that such a broad-based right to the use of force would be used to provide a convenient legal cover for the abuse of power. Further, the rise of a virulent insurgency in Iraq – stemming from perceptions that the US was an illegitimate occupying power, competition for political power among the Kurds, Shiites and Sunnis, and the exploitation of these animosities by al-Qaeda – put to rest any pretence that the US could promote democracy by force, in the Middle East or elsewhere, relatively cheaply given its material predominance. Whilst military and technological power resources did achieve regime change with relative ease, the creation of a liberal democratic polity in a country with little historical experience or indigenous entrenchment of such ideas and beliefs has been impeded by perceptions that the US has had illegitimate intentions vis-à-vis Iraq – not to bring democracy and freedom, but to occupy and control.

Why does this crisis in the legitimacy of US leadership matter, and to whom? The huge cost of quelling an insurgency whilst simultaneously creating liberal institutions and rebuilding essential infrastructure has taken a considerable toll on the US public's appetites for the costs associated with taking an active role in international affairs. Whilst the temptations of isolationism have become more and more seductive, the rehabilitation of US global leadership is in the self-interest of the US itself, but also in the interests of the broader international community, should it come in an amended form. First, from the perspective of the US, the temptations of isolationism provide an illusion of escape from problems of imperial overstretch. The threat posed by fundamentalist Islamic groups such as al-Qaeda and the risks of proliferation of WMD will not dissipate should the US retreat from international affairs. The attacks of September 11, 2001 clearly demonstrate that we do indeed live in a globalised and interconnected world, in which the problems of one region can quickly become the problems of another. From a broader perspective, whilst democracy promotion by force has been shown to be practically and normatively unwise, there is still much to be said for the post-Second World War belief of American strategists that it is in America's interest to promote values of openness, freedom and democracy to forge a world safe for America, i.e. to make the world more like itself.[3]

From the perspective of the broader international community – the prospective followers – US leadership should still be needed and wanted, albeit in a restrained form harnessed also for the pursuit of the collective interest. The distaste for unilateralism in US foreign policy stemmed partially from the recognition that many of the world's most difficult security challenges – from climate change and Kyoto, to ending impunity for gross human rights violations under the ICC, to the problem of WMD proliferation among others – are examples of truly global problems requiring international cooperation for their resolution. As the state with the greatest material capacity to take leadership over these issues and to effectively provide a greater share of the global public good of international order, US unilateralism was both disappointing but also a serious impediment to cooperation to solve these shared problems. Given the nature of these shared security problems, it is likely that the international community would be open to US interest in taking a constructive leadership role.

How then can US leadership be rehabilitated? In Gow and Bellou's terms, how can the alter's image – the perception of US leadership among purported followers – be transformed? In the early days of the Obama Administration, this challenge is being approached through the lens of a 'smart power' strategy. In her confirmation hearing statement, Secretary of State Hillary Clinton explained that smart power meant the use of

> the full range of tools at our disposal – diplomatic, economic, military, political, legal, and cultural – picking the right tool, or combination of tools, for each situation. With smart power, diplomacy will be the vanguard of foreign

policy.... One need only look to North Korea, Iran, the Middle East and the Balkans to appreciate the absolute necessity of tough-minded, intelligent diplomacy – and the failures that result when that kind of diplomatic effort is absent. And one need only consider the assortment of problems we must tackle in 2009 – from fighting terrorism to climate change to global financial crises – to understand the importance of cooperative engagement.... We will lead with diplomacy because it's the smart approach. But we also know that military force will sometimes be necessary, and we will rely on it to protect our people and our interests when and where needed, as a last resort.[4]

In other words, for the Obama Administration smart power means a return to diplomacy and cooperative engagement first and foremost, with the use of force in reserve as a last resort.

The concept of smart power was first comprehensively introduced by Richard Armitage and Joseph Nye[5] as a combination of both hard and soft power. Whilst hard power is the deployment of material resources to affect the behaviour of others (in the traditional realist view of power) through the application of carrots and sticks, soft power is defined as 'the ability to affect others to obtain the outcomes one wants through attraction rather than coercion or payment'.[6] According to Nye, the power to attract others to want what America wants depends upon perceptions of its culture, its domestic values and external policies.[7] In terms of perceptions, legitimacy is an inherent element of the potential attractiveness of US policies and leadership.

This book has demonstrated the neglect of legitimacy as a form of power under the leadership of the second Bush Administration. There are a number of core insights that can be drawn from the analysis we have undertaken of the relationship between legitimacy and hegemonic power that are pertinent to the question of what could make US leadership attractive once more. All of these insights begin with the recognition that an analysis of US power cannot be undertaken without consideration of the social context in which it is deployed. Hegemonic power is now exercised in an international society with a highly developed sense of shared interest in a stable international order, and more importantly of a commitment to shared values about the prevention and regulation of warfare and the appropriate use of power on behalf of the collective. Whilst material power will always have a central role in providing a hegemonic state with the capacity to achieve its interests – through coercion and inducement – in a thickly enmeshed international society the capacity to influence is also highly dependent upon legitimacy.

This book has demonstrated that the social structure of international society – which includes shared beliefs about legitimate behaviour between its subjects and of legitimate membership – both constrains and enables the exercise of hegemonic power in three ways. First, in both cases it has been established that US leadership is more likely to be accepted by subordinate states where the goals it sought to achieve for the collective was consistent with shared normative beliefs about legitimate behaviour. The US proposal of the liberation of Kuwait as the end goal for the collective in the Gulf Crisis was largely accepted by a strong majority of states because it furthered shared normative commitments to core principles of international order: to sovereignty, non-interference, the peaceful settlement of disputes and the responsibility to combat aggression. In the Iraq Crisis, normative beliefs about legitimate behaviour allowed the US to push for Iraqi disarmament, but became a structural barrier to attempts to frame Iraqi sovereignty as conditional and therefore subject to democratic regime change by force. Second, normative beliefs about the legitimate means to pursue these goals also constrained and enabled US leadership in both crises. Legitimacy provided the impetus which swung a broad-based coalition behind the US preference for the use of force to liberate Kuwait once it was apparent that all peaceful means had been exhausted. On the contrary, beliefs about the legitimate use of force between states precluded the participation of a broad majority of states from joining the Iraq coalition because of a failure to demonstrate that war was being advocated as a last resort.

Third, in the present international society, legitimacy clearly circumscribes the behaviour expected of states seeking to hold a leadership position within it. Just as domestic societies have sought to restrain the abuse of power through the establishment of agreed rules, in international society both informal and formal rules have emerged to restrict the use of force by the powerful and to ensure leadership is exercised for the pursuit of the collective interest. The first Bush Administration showed a strong appreciation of legitimacy as a form of power, and took steps to ensure that US leadership was normatively accepted and recognised. Here the Administration appreciated that the end of the Cold War required an adjustment of the US approach to leadership to emphasise elements of partnership and collective engagement. As Secretary of State James Baker stated after the 1991 Gulf War: 'To put it simply: We led, we had partners and together we succeeded. US leadership of collective engagement avoids the dangerous extremes of fallacious omnipotence or misplaced multilateralism.'[8] A conscious attempt to lead through partnership, consultation, compromise and engagement, together with a vision of international order which confirmed a commitment to the core principles of the UN Charter, served to reassure subordinate states that the US could be trusted to lead for the purpose of achieving the interests of the collective.

In contrast, warnings against overestimating the value of material predominance – the connotations of arrogance implicit in Baker's reference to 'fallacious omnipotence' – were clearly lost on the second Bush Administration. An overreliance on material power, a failure to recognise the social nature of international society, and the heightened sense of impending danger generated by the September 11, 2001 attacks combined to create an approach to leadership far removed from practices of collaboration, consultation and compromise. A core lesson to be learnt here is that a core driver of followership is the perception that a potential leader seeks this role to achieve the collective interest, and will act responsibly in the exercise of the enhanced rights and prerogatives that come with it. Perceptions of leadership intent can in fact feed into perceptions of threat. Just as states were divided over Iraq's future intentions and threatening disposition, the uncompromising approach to leadership taken by the administration of George W. Bush, and the declaration of a legal doctrine which would unshackle the US from the constraints of international law on the use of force, created a perception of the US as a threat to order rather than protector of order with the intent to use the position of leadership for its own parochial interests rather than the interests of the collective.

The Iraq Crisis also made it clear that the legitimacy of hegemonic leadership has become more clearly tied to multilateral processes as a proof of right intentions. The formal procedural controls over the use of force and the freedom of action of the most powerful states within the UN Charter have become more and more firmly entrenched into the structure of international society. The collective legitimisation provided by the authorisation of the use of force by the UNSC has become a valuable prize. As the Iraq War has shown, the absence of collective legitimisation has had significant impacts upon the ability of the US to restore order in Iraq. The hegemon has been left to bear the significant costs of rebuilding Iraq alone, and has stretched its capacity to maintain order in other theatres of equal importance, such as Afghanistan.

Finally, in the broader context of the war on terror, the legitimacy of US leadership has been found wanting because of an inconsistency between its foreign policy prescriptions and the core values with which it has long been identified. The American story of exceptionalism projects the image of an ideal polity based on individual freedom and democratically accountable government. The attempt to actively avoid international human rights and humanitarian obligations towards al-Qaeda and Taliban forces captured in Afghanistan, the practice of extraordinary rendition, and the treatment of prisoners in Abu Ghraib have opened the US up to the charge that American exceptionalism applies only to Americans. There is also a real tension between a commitment to freedom and democracy at home, whilst promoting foreign policies that would impose liberal democracy on others by force. This erosion of the commitment to an international society in which diversity is protected by the institution of sovereignty has undermined US credentials to lead international society.

Whilst we are still in the early days of the Obama Administration, it is plain that re-establishing the legitimacy of US leadership over international society is a key aim of foreign policy. Already, the Administration has taken some bold decisions in an attempt to break from the past. In the first months after taking office, Obama has ordered the closure of Guantanamo Bay by early 2010, released details of the interrogation methods used on prisoners there (the so-called 'torture memos'), abandoned the use of controversial interrogation techniques such as waterboarding, withdrawn US troops from Iraqi cities in July 2009 and committed to ending the US military presence in Iraq by 2012.

Even more dramatic have been the direct overtures made by the President to the Iranian people in March 2009[9] and his efforts to re-define America's relationship with the Muslim world in a ground-breaking speech given in Cairo in

June 2009. Here Obama spoke frankly about US mistakes and future intentions in relation to the war on Afghanistan, international terrorism, Iraq and the Arab–Israeli conflict, and committed to 'fight against negative stereotypes of Islam wherever they appear'. Of note was his description of the war on Iraq as a 'war of choice' which had 'reminded America of the need to use diplomacy and build international consensus to resolve our problems whenever possible', and the declaration that the US had 'no claim' on Iraq's 'territory or resources' and recognised it as 'a partner, and never as a patron'. Further, Obama made clear that democracy promotion by force would no longer have a place in US foreign policy, stating unequivocally that 'no system of government can or should be imposed upon one nation by any other'.[10] Whilst it is still too early to tell whether these policy shifts and diplomatic overtures will rehabilitate the credibility of US leadership, it is at least apparent that the importance of legitimacy to hegemonic power is not lost on the Obama Administration.

Finally, putting questions of policy aside for the moment, this book has by its very nature delved into the old materialist versus idealist debate running through international relations scholarship. Whilst the end of the Cold War brought with it hopes of a new era of state cooperation through the operation of international institutions and commitment to international law, the rise of a global hegemon with the drive to change the dominant rules of international order provided, in the words of Dunne, 'a critical test for those who believe that states are increasingly caught up in a normative web spun from cosmopolitan thread'.[11] In the aftermath of the Iraq War, scholars were beginning to speculate on the demise of international society based on a plurality of equal sovereign states and to take the realist view that law and morality, and implicitly legitimacy, was indeed contingent on power.[12] This book has demonstrated unambiguously that a plural international society is certainly not dead, and that there is no simple linear relationship between the possession of material resources and the achievement of preferred interests by a hegemonic state. Power is now wielded in an international society constituted and regulated by shared conceptions of legitimacy which both constrain and enable hegemonic power. As Raymond Aron insightfully observed: 'Either a great power will not tolerate equals, and then must proceed to the last degree of empire, or else it consents to stand first among sovereign units, and must win acceptance for such pre-eminence.'[13] At this stage it appears that President Obama has chosen the second path and, if so, the prospects for the reinvigoration of US leadership of international society are looking promising.

Notes

1 Introduction and theoretical framework

1 Charles Kindleberger, *The World in Depression 1929–1939*, Berkeley: University of California Press 1973; Charles Kindleberger, 'Systems of International Economic Organization', in David Calleo (ed.) *Money and the Coming World Order*, New York: New York University Press 1976; Stephen Krasner, 'State Power and Structure of International Trade', *World Politics*, 28(3), April 1976, 317–343; Stephen Krasner, *International Regimes*, Ithaca: Cornell University Press 1983; Robert Keohane, *After Hegemony*, New Jersey: Princeton University Press 1984; Robert Gilpin, *US Power and Multinational Corporation*, New York: Basic Books 1975.

2 David Calleo, *Beyond American Hegemony: the Future of the Western Alliance*, New York: Basic Books 1987; Paul Kennedy, *The Rise and Fall of the Great Powers: Economic Change and Military Conflict from 1500 to 2000*, USA: Vintage Books 1989; Robert Gilpin, *The Political Economy of International Relations*, New Jersey: Princeton University Press 1987; Robert O. Keohane, *After Hegemony: Cooperation and Discord in the World Political Economy*, New Jersey: Princeton University Press 1984; Charles P. Kindleberger, *Marshall Plan Days*, Boston: Allen & Unwin 1987; Robert Gilpin, *US Power and Multinational Corporations*, New York: Basic Books 1975; Imanuel Wallerstein with Samir Amin, Giovanni Arrighi and Andre Gunder Frank, *Dynamics of Global Crisis*, London: Macmillan 1982; G. John Ikenberry, 'Rethinking the Origins of American Hegemony', *Political Science Quarterly*, 104(3), Fall 1989, 375–400; Walter R. Mead, *Mortal Spendor: The American Empire In Transition*, Boston: Houghton Mifflin Company 1987; Susan Strange, 'The Persistent Myth of Lost Hegemony', *International Organisation*, 41(4), autumn 1987, 551–574; Bruce Russett, 'The Mysterious Case of Vanishing Hegemony, or, Is Mark Twain Really Dead?', *International Organization*, 38(2), spring 1985, 207–231; Samuel P. Huntington, 'The US – Decline or Renewal?', *Foreign Affairs*, 67, winter 1988–1989, 76–96; Henry Nau, *The Myth of America's Decline: Leading the World Economy into the 1990s*, New York: Oxford University Press 1990; Joseph S. Nye, Jr, *Bound to Lead: the Changing Nature of American Power*, New York: Basic Books 1990.

3 In September 1996, the US conducted a missile attack on Iraqi air defences south of Baghdad in response to an Iraqi attack on the northern city of Irbil which was within the 'no-fly' zone.

4 Charles Krauthammer, 'The Unipolar Moment', *Foreign Affairs*, 70(1), 1990/1991, 23–33.

5 William Pfaff, 'The Question of Hegemony', *Foreign Affairs*, 80(1), January–February 2001, 221–232, p. 221.

6 Tim Dunne, 'Society and Hierarchy in International Relations', *International Relations*, 17(3), 303–320; Paul Rogers, 'Right for America, Right for the World', *The World Today*, 58(2), February 2002, 13–15.

7 Ian Clark, *Legitimacy in International Society*, Oxford: Oxford University Press 2005; Ian Hurd, *After Anarchy: Legitimacy and Power in the United Nations Security Council*, New Jersey: Princeton University Press 2008.
8 Mark Suchman, 'Managing Legitimacy: Strategic and Institutional Approaches', *Academy of Management Review*, 20(3), 1995, 571–610, p. 574, quoted in Ian Hurd, 'Legitimacy and Authority in International Politics', *International Organization*, 53(2), spring 1999, 379–408, p. 387.
9 Hedley Bull, *The Anarchical Society: a Study of Order in World Politics*, London: Macmillan Press Ltd 1995, p. 13.
10 Ian Clark, *Legitimacy in International Society*, Oxford: Oxford University Press 2005, p. 24.
11 David Beetham, *The Legitimation of Power*, New Jersey: Humanities Press International Inc. 1991, p. 3.
12 Ibid., p. 17.
13 David P. Rapkin, 'The Contested Concept of Hegemonic Leadership', in David P. Rapkin (ed.) *World Leadership and Hegemony*, Boulder: Lynne Reiner Publishers 1990, p. 1.
14 William E. Connolly, *The Terms of Political Discourse*, Oxford: Martin Robertson 1974, p. 10.
15 For a survey of hegemony as a normative concept within world systems theory, long-cycle theory, Gramscian approaches to international relations, structural realist and liberal approaches see David P. Rapkin, op. cit.
16 Ibid.
17 Kenneth Waltz, *Theory of International Politics*, Reading: Addison-Wesley Pub. Co. 1979, 97–101.
18 Ibid.
19 Ibid., pp. 34–35.
20 John Mearsheimer, *The Tragedy of Great Power Politics*, New York: W.W. Norton & Company 2001, pp. 33 and 40.
21 Ibid., p. 35.
22 Whilst Waltz does not explicitly use the term 'hegemony', we can deduce that within the terms of his structural realism, hegemony is synonymous with unipolarity.
23 In *Theory of International Politics*, Waltz argues that a world hegemony would not be allowed to form 'because balancing, not bandwagoning, is the behavior induced by the system. The first concern of states is not to maximize power but to maintain their positions in the system' (Kenneth Waltz, op. cit., p. 126).
24 Ibid., p. 127.
25 Kenneth Waltz, 'The Anarchic Structure of World Politics', reproduced in R. Art and R. Jervis, *International Politics: Enduring Concepts and Contemporary Issues*, New York: Pearson/Longman 1979/2005, 7th edn, p. 32.
26 John Mearsheimer, *The Tragedy of Great Power Politics*, New York: W.W. Norton and Co. 2001, p. 49.
27 David Baldwin, 'Power and International Relations', in Walter Carlsnaes, Thomas Risse and Beth A. Simmons (eds) *Handbook of International Relations*, London: Sage Publications 2002, pp. 178 and 179.
28 John Mearsheimer, op. cit., p. 60; Kenneth Waltz, op. cit., 1979, pp. 191–192. Waltz offers another definition of power as follows: 'an agent is powerful to the extent that he affects others more than they affect him.' However, it is difficult to see how this definition overcomes his own objection of confusing process and outcome. One is still measuring power by its intended outcomes; see p. 192.
29 David Baldwin, op. cit., p. 178.
30 Kenneth Waltz, op. cit., 1979, pp. 191–192; David Baldwin, op. cit., pp. 183–184.
31 John Mearsheimer, op. cit., p. 60.

32 Ibid.
33 Kenneth Waltz, 1979, op. cit., *Theory of International Politics*, p. 192.
34 David Lake argues that there are two approaches within hegemonic stability theory: leadership theory and hegemony theory. The first encompasses the emphasis on hegemony and provision of public goods. The second is focused on explaining patterns of economic openness in the international economy and posits that the relative openness of the international economy is directly related to the actions of a hegemonic state in changing the policy preferences of other states towards free trade. The first approach will be focused upon here. David A. Lake, 'Leadership, Hegemony, and the International Economy: Naked Emperor or Tattered Monarch with Potential?', *International Studies Quarterly*, 37(4), December 1993, 459–489.
35 Charles P. Kindleberger, op. cit., 1973, p. 305.
36 Duncan Snidal, 'The Limits of Hegemonic Stability Theory,' *International Organization*, 39(4), autumn 1985, 579–614, p. 581; Charles P. Kindleberger, op. cit., 1973, p. 305; David A. Lake, op. cit., p. 462; Kindleberger argues that the 1929–1939 depression was caused by the unwillingness of the United States, the dominant economic power of the time, to step in and provide the public goods necessary to keep the world economy stable by '(a)maintaining a relatively open market for distress goods; (b) providing counter-cyclical long-term lending; and (c) discounting in crisis' (Charles P. Kindleberger, op. cit., p. 292).
37 Mancur Olson, *The Logic of Collective Action*, Cambridge: Harvard University Press 1965, referred to in Duncan Snidal, op. cit., p. 581.
38 Robert Gilpin, *War and Change in World Politics*, Cambridge: Cambridge University Press, 1982, p. 34.
39 Duncan Snidal, op. cit., p. 588.
40 Duncan Snidal, op. cit., p. 601; David A. Lake, op. cit., pp. 463–466.
41 Robert O. Keohane, 'The Theory of Hegemonic Stability and Changes in International Economic Regimes, 1967–1977', in Ole Holsti, Randolph Siverson and Alexander George (eds), *Change in the International System*, Boulder: Westview Press 1980, 131–162, p. 132.
42 Robert O. Keohane, *After Hegemony: Cooperation and Discord in the World Political Economy*, New Jersey: Princeton University Press 1984, p. 32.
43 Ibid.; Robert Gilpin, op. cit., 1982, p. 13.
44 Robert Gilpin, op. cit., 1982, p. 29.
45 Ibid., p. 30.
46 Ibid., p. 34.
47 Ibid.
48 Ibid., p. 31.
49 Stefano Guzzini, *Realism in International Relations and International Political Economy: the Continuing Story of a Death Foretold*, London: Routledge 1998, 155–156.
50 Robert O. Keohane, op. cit., 1984, p. 64.
51 Hans J. Morgenthau, *Politics Among Nations: the Struggle for Power and Peace*, New York: Alfred A. Knopf, 5th edn, revised, pp. 30–31.
52 Ibid., p. 32.
53 Ibid., p. 237.
54 Ibid., chapter 16, 'International Morality', pp. 236–263.
55 Ibid., pp. 10–11.
56 Ibid., p. 282.
57 Antonio Gramsci, *Selections from the Prison Notebooks*, edited and translated by Derek Boothman, Minneapolis: University of Minnesota Press 1995.
58 James Martin, *Gramsci's Political Analysis: a Critical Introduction*, Basingstoke and London: Macmillan Press Ltd 1998, p. 65.
59 Prison Notebook 19, paragraph 24, quoted in James Martin, ibid., p. 70.

60 Joseph V. Femia, *Gramsci's Political Thought: Hegemony, Consciousness and the Revolutionary Process*, Oxford: Clarendon Press 1981, p. 24.
61 Bacharach and Baratz, 'Two Faces of Power', *American Political Science Review*, 56, 1962, 947–952; Jeffrey C. Isaac, *Power and Marxist Theory: a Realist View*, Ithaca: Cornell University Press 1987; Stephen Lukes, *Power: a Radical View*, Houndsmills, Basingstoke, Hampshire and New York: Palgrave Macmillan 2005.
62 Robert W. Cox, 'Gramsci, Hegemony and International Relations: an Essay in Method', *Millennium: Journal of International Studies*, 12(2), 1983, 162–175, p. 171.
63 Ibid., p. 171; Robert W. Cox, *Production, Power and World Order: Social Forces in the Making of History*, New York: Columbia University Press 1987, p. 7.
64 Robert W. Cox, op. cit., 1983, p. 172.
65 James Martin, op. cit., p. 77.
66 Prison Notebook 7, paragraph 21, quoted in James Martin, op. cit., pp. 79 and 82.
67 Robert W. Cox, op. cit., 1983, p. 168.
68 Martha Finnemore and Kathryn Sikkink, 'Taking Stock: the Constructivist Research Program in International Relations and Comparative Politics', *Annual Review of Political Science*, 4, 2001, 391–416, p. 393.
69 Emanuel Adler, 'Constructivism and International Relations', in Walter Carlsnaes, Thomas Risse and Beth A. Simmons (eds) *Handbook of International Relations*, London; Thousand Oaks: Sage Publications 2002, pp. 97–98.
70 David Marsh and Paul Furlong, 'A Skin not a Sweater: Ontology and Epistemology in Political Science', in David Marsh and Gerry Stoker (eds) *Theory and Methods in Political Science*, Houndsmills, Basingstoke, Hampshire, New York: Palgrave Macmillan 2002, 2nd edn, p. 26.
71 Alexander Wendt, *Social Theory of International Politics*, Cambridge: Cambridge University Press 1999, p. 1; Finnemore and Sikkink, op. cit., pp. 392–393; Emanuel Adler, op. cit.
72 Alexander Wendt, ibid., pp. 110–111; John Searle, *The Construction of Social Reality*, New York: Free Press 1995, pp. 55–56.
73 Emmanuel Adler, 'Seizing the Middle Ground: Constructivism in World Politics', *European Journal of International Relations*, 3(3), 1997, 319–363; Alexander Wendt, 'Constructing International Politics', *International Security*, 20(1), 1995, 71–81, p. 73. Note however that radical constructivists do not agree with this position and take the view that material forces alone do not have independent effects on international politics.
74 Ibid., Alexander Wendt, 1995, p. 73.
75 Alexander Wendt, 'Anarchy Is What States Make Of It: the Social Construction of World Politics', *International Organization*, 46, 1992, 391–425; Nicholas Onuf, *World of Our Making: Rules and Rule in Social Theory and International Relations*, Columbia: University of South Carolina Press 1989.
76 Alexander Wendt, op. cit., 1999, p. 1; Finnemore and Sikkink, op. cit., pp. 392–393.
77 Peter Katzenstein, 'Introduction', in Peter Katzenstein (ed.) *The Culture of National Security: Norms and Identity in World Politics*, New York: Columbia University Press 1996, p. 5.
78 Ronald L. Jepperson, Alexander Wendt and Peter J. Katzenstein, 'Norms, Identity and Culture in National Security', in Peter Katzenstein (ed.), ibid., p. 54.
79 James G. March and Johan P. Olsen, 'The Institutional Dynamics of International Political Orders', *International Organization*, 52(4), autumn 1998, 943–969, p. 949.
80 The questions asked by the individual actor are: '(1) What are my alternatives? (2) What are my values? (3) What are the consequences of my alternatives for my values? (4) Choose the alternative that has the best consequences' (James G. March and Johan P. Olsen, *Rediscovering Institutions: the Organizational Basis of Politics*, New York: Free Press 1989, p. 23).

81 Martha Finnemore and Katherine Sikkink, 'International Norm Dynamics and Political Change', *International Organization*, 52(4), autumn 1998, 887–917, p. 912.
82 James March and Johan Olsen, op. cit., 1998, p. 951.
83 Finnemore and Sikkink, op. cit., 1998, p. 912.
84 Ibid., p. 914.
85 Alexander Wendt, op. cit., 1992, p. 400; Alexander Wendt, op. cit., 1999, chapter 6.
86 Alexander Wendt, op. cit., 1999, pp. 279–297.
87 Ian Hurd, 'Legitimacy and Authority in International Politics', *International Organization*, 53(2), spring 1999, 379–408, pp. 379, 385.
88 Ian Hurd, ibid., p. 387; Desmond P. Ellis, 'The Hobbesian Problem of Order: a critical Appraisal of the Normative Solution', *American Sociological Review*, 36(4), 1971, 692–703, p. 693.
89 Morgenthau, op. cit., Part 4, 'Limitations of National Power: the Balance of Power'; Kenneth Waltz, op. cit., 1979, pp. 123–128.
90 Bruce Cronin, 'The Paradox of Hegemony: America's Ambiguous Relationship with the United Nations', *European Journal of International Relations*, 7(1), 2001, 103–130, p. 106; Christopher Layne, 'The Unipolar Illusion: Why New Great Powers Will Rise', in Sean Lynn-Jones and Steven Miller (eds) *The Cold War and After: Prospects for Peace*, expanded edition, Cambridge: MIT Press 1993, pp. 252–253; Robert Gilpin, op. cit., 1981.
91 What I have termed legitimate power is described by Reus-Smit as authoritative power. That is, power resting on the 'normative belief on the part of an actor that a command or rule ought to be obeyed'. Christian Reus-Smit, *American Power and World* Order, Cambridge: Polity Press 2004, p. 58.
92 Ian Hurd, op. cit., p. 387.
93 Ian Hurd, ibid., p. 388.
94 See section on Gramscian approaches in this chapter and also the work of Hedley Bull on the role of the Great Powers within international society. Hedley Bull, *The Anarchical Society: a Study of Order in World Politics*, London: Macmillan Press 1995, 2nd edn, chapter 9; Martin Wight, *Power Politics*, London: Leicester University Press 1978, 1995 edn, pp. 43–44.
95 Bruce Cronin, op. cit., p. 108; Christian Reus-Smit, op. cit., p. 65; Jean-Marc Coicaud, *Legitimacy and Politics: a Contribution to the Study of Political Right and Political Responsibility*, Cambridge: Cambridge University Press 2004, p. 11.
96 Bruce Cronin, op. cit., p. 111; Hedley Bull, op. cit., pp. 196 and 221–222. In respect of the latter, Reus-Smit argues that the entrenched norms of procedural justice in the post-1945 world are that of multilateralism and contractual international law. Christian Reus Smit, 'The Constitutional Structure of International Society and the Nature of Fundamental Institutions', *International Organization*, 51(4), autumn 1997, 555–589, p. 566.
97 Ronald L. Jepperson, Alexander Wendt and Peter J. Katzenstein, op. cit., p. 54; Francesca Cancian, *What Are Norms? A Study of Beliefs and Action in a Maya Community*, Cambridge: Cambridge University Press 1975, pp. 137–138.
98 Innis Claude, *Swords into Plowshares: the Problems and Progress of International Organization*, New York: Random House 1956, 2nd edn, p. 81; Hedley Bull, op. cit., pp. 228–229.
99 John Ruggie, *Constructing the World Polity: Essays on International Institutionalization*, London: Routledge 1998, p. 97.
100 Ibid.
101 Ibid.
102 Ronald L. Jepperson, Alexander Wendt and Peter J. Katzenstein, op. cit., pp. 52–53.
103 James Gow and Fotini Bellou, 'Image and Intervention, Leadership and Legitimacy: the Dynamics of Euro-Atlantic Engagement with Challenges to International Peace and Security', *Civil Wars*, 6(2), 2003, 33–52, p. 34.

104 Gregory A. Raymond, 'Problems and Prospects in the Study of International Norms', *Mershon International Studies Review*, 41, 1997, 205–245, p. 220.
105 Nicholas J. Wheeler, *Saving Strangers: Humanitarian Intervention in International Society*, Oxford: Oxford University Press 2000; Martha Finnemore, 'Constructing Norms of Humanitarian Intervention', in Peter J. Katzenstein (ed.) *The Culture of National Security: Norms and Identity in World Politics*, New York: Columbia University Press 1996, p. 159.
106 Martha Finnemore, ibid., p. 159.
107 Quentin Skinner, 'Analysis of Political Thought and Action', in J. Tully (ed.) *Meaning and Context: Quentin Skinner and his Critics*, Cambridge: Polity Press 1988, p. 117, quoted in Nicholas J. Wheeler, op. cit., p. 9.
108 Nicholas J. Wheeler, op. cit., p. 9.

2 Legitimacy and hegemony in the Gulf Crisis of 1990–1991

1 These states were: Argentina, Australia, Bahrain, Bangladesh, Belgium, Canada, Czechoslovakia, Denmark, Egypt, France, Germany, Greece, Hong Kong, Hungary, Italy, Japan, South Korea, Kuwait, Luxembourg, Morocco, Netherlands, New Zealand, Niger, Norway, Oman, Pakistan, Poland, Portugal, Qatar, Romania, Saudi Arabia, Senegal, Sierra Leone, Singapore, Spain, Sweden, Syria, Turkey, the UAE and the UK. The Afghan Mujahideen also took part in the defence of Saudi Arabia (Government of the United Kingdom, *Statement on the Defence Estimates: Britain's Defence in the 90s*, vol. 1, Cm 1559–1, London: HMSO 1991).
2 Quoted in Martin Walker, 'The U.S. and the Persian Gulf Crisis', *World Policy Journal*, 7, Fall 1990, p. 791.
3 Lawrence Freedman and Efraim Karsh, *The Gulf Conflict*, London and Boston: Faber and Faber 1993, p. 67; Ken Matthews, *The Gulf Conflict and International Relations*, London: Routledge 1993, p. 33.
4 Ibid.; 'Canada, Colombia, Cote d'Ivoire, Ethiopia, Finland, France, Malaysia, United Kingdom of Great Britain and Northern Ireland and United States of America: draft resolution', UN Document S/21425, 2 August 1990; 'Provisional Verbatim Record of the 2932nd Meeting of the Security Council', UN Doc. S/PV.2932.
5 'Provisional verbatim record of the 2932nd Meeting of the Security Council', 2 August 1990, UN Document S/PV.2932, pp. 14–15.
6 Ibid., p. 17.
7 Ibid., p. 21.
8 Ibid., p. 22.
9 States referring to the peaceful settlement of disputes were: France, China, Finland, USSR, Romania and Yemen; states referring to the prohibition on the use of force were: Columbia, Malaysia, Finland, Romania and Yemen; and states referring to the prohibition against the aggressive use of force were the USA, Canada, Malaysia, UK, and Finland (ibid.).
10 Ibid., p. 16.
11 'Gulf Cooperation Council: Ministerial Council Statement on 3 August 1990, The Gulf Crisis', reproduced in A.G. Noorani (ed.) *The Gulf Wars: Documents and Analysis*, New York: Advent Books 1991, pp. 26–27.
12 'Statement by the Twelve Member States of the European Community Issued Within the Framework of European Political Cooperation', 2 August 1990, reprinted in E. Lauterpacht CBE, QC, C.J. Greenwood, Marc Weller and Daniel Bethlehem (eds) *The Kuwait Crisis: Basic Documents*, United Kingdom: Cambridge Grotius Publications Limited 1991, p. 308.
13 'The Arab League's Resolution of 3 August 1990', reproduced in A.G. Noorani, op. cit., p. 52.

14 Statement of Canada, '45th Session of the General Assembly', 26 September, UN Document A/45/PV.9, p. 22.
15 Statement of Luxembourg, ibid., p. 106.
16 Statement of Poland, '45th Session of the General Assembly', 24 September 1990, UN Document A/45/PV.4, p. 73.
17 'Canada, Colombia, Cote d'Ivoire, Ethiopia, Finland, France, Malaysia, the United Kingdom of Great Britain and Northern Ireland, the United States of America and Zaire: Draft Resolution', 6 August 1990, UN Doc. S/21441.
18 UN Security Council Resolution 661 (1990), 6 August 1990, UN Document S/21441.
19 George Bush and Brent Scowcroft, *A World Transformed*, New York: Vintage Books 1998, p. 303.
20 Ibid., p. 316.
21 'Executive Order 12722, Blocking Iraqi Government Property and Prohibiting Transactions with Iraq', and 'Executive Order 12723, Blocking Kuwaiti Government Property', 2 August 1990, in E. Lauterpacht, C.J. Greenwood, Marc Weller and Daniel Bethlehem (eds) *The Kuwait Crisis Basic Documents*, Cambridge: Grotius Publications Limited 1991, pp. 224–225.
22 George Bush, 'Message to the Congress on the Declaration of a National Emergency with Respect to Iraq', 3 August 1990. George Bush Presidential Library and Museum, http://bushlibrary.tamu.edu.
23 US Secretary of State James Baker particularly underlines that the US believed it could have taken a unilateral position on the invasion under Article 51 of the Charter, but chose to take a coalition approach to dealing with the crisis. The latter was crucial in bolstering the 'credibility' of the US position, not only in the Arab world but also within the United States; and, without international backing in the Security Council, Baker was convinced that the US would not have been able to 'attract the breadth of support' that it did. President Bush is reported to have said in this context: '[i]nternational sanctions will give us security cover. They will give some spine to Saudi Arabia and others to take difficult actions, like closing the pipeline' (James A. Baker III with Thomas M. Defrank, *The Politics of Diplomacy: Revolution, War and Peace 1989–1992*, New York: G.P. Putnam and Sons 1995, p. 279).
24 Bush and Scowcroft, op. cit., p. 326.
25 'EC hits Iraq with ban on oil and arms', *Observer* 5 August 1990, and 'EC takes swift action in sweeping embargo aimed at halting Iraq', *Wall Street Journal* 6 August 1990; Renaud Dehousse, 'European Political Cooperation in 1989–1990', *European Journal of International Law*, 205, 1992, p. 209; 'European Union Press Statement Concerning the Invasion of Kuwait by Iraq', *European Foreign Policy Bulletin*, Doc. 90/297, 4 August 1990.
26 Ilan Greilsammer, 'European Reactions to the Gulf Challenge', in Gad Garzilai (ed.) *The Gulf Crisis and its Global Aftermath*, New York: Routledge 1993, p. 211.
27 'Statutory Instrument 1990 No. 1591: The Control of Gold, Securities, Payments and Credits (Kuwait) Directions', 2 August 1990, in E. Lauterpacht, C.J. Greenwood, Marc Weller and Daniel Bethlehem (eds), op. cit., p. 202; 'Statutory Instruments 1990 No. 1616: The Control of Gold, Securities, Payments and Credits (Republic of Iraq) Directions, 4 August 1990', in E. Lauterpacht CBE, QC, C.J. Greenwood, Marc Weller and Daniel Bethlehem (eds), op. cit., p. 202.
28 'Remarks and a Question-and-Answer Session with Reporters in Aspen, Colorado, Following a Meeting with Prime Minister Margaret Thatcher of the United Kingdom', 2 August 1990, George Bush Presidential Library and Museum, http://bushlibrary.tamu.edu.
29 'Joint Statement of the USA and the USSR', 6 August 1990, UN Document A/45/399.

30 Bush and Scowcroft, op. cit., p. 331.
31 'Provisional Verbatim Record of the 2933rd Meeting of the Security Council', UN Document S/PV.2933, 6 August 1990, p. 16.
32 President George Bush, 'Speech to Congress', 6 March 1991.
33 UN Document S/PV.2933, op. cit., p. 17.
34 Ibid., pp. 29–30.
35 Ibid., p. 18.
36 Ibid., pp. 24–25.
37 Ibid., p. 33.
38 Economic sanctions were adopted against Southern Rhodesia following its unilateral declaration of independence in 1965. Freedman and Karsh, op. cit., p. 83.
39 Statement of France, UN Document S/PV.2933, op. cit., p. 21.
40 Statement of Canada, ibid., pp. 24–25.
41 Statement of the United Kingdom, ibid., p. 27.
42 Statement of Malaysia, ibid., p. 22.
43 Statement of Spain, 'Address to the 45th Session of the General Assembly', UN Document A/45/PV.9, p. 119.
44 Statement of Japan, 'Address to the 45th Session of the General Assembly', UN Document A/45/PV.7; Statement of the Federal Republic of Germany, 'Address to the 45th Session of the General Assembly', UN Document A/45/PV.8, p. 22.
45 Security Council Resolution 661, paragraphs 5, 6 and 7.
46 Canada, Cote d'Ivoire, Finland, France, the United Kingdom, the United States and Zaire, 'Draft Resolution on measures to implement Security Council Resolution 661 (1990), especially its provisions related to shipping', UN Document S/21640, 25 August 1990.
47 Ibid.
48 Freedman and Karsh, op. cit., pp. 143–144. Within the region, Jordan was the weakest link in maintaining the embargo as it was highly dependent on oil supplies from Iraq. In the end, the United Kingdom came to Jordan's aid, providing $2 billion compensation for losses in revenue that it claimed.
49 'Statement by Press Secretary Fitzwater on the Persian Gulf Crisis', 12 August 1990, *The President Bush Library and Museum*, http://bushlibrary.tamu.edu; 'The President's News Conference', 14 August 1990, The President Bush Library and Museum, http://bushlibrary.tamu.edu; Bush and Scowcroft, op. cit., p. 336.
50 A special warning notice issued on 17 August 1990 by the United States to all commercial shipping operators in the Gulf asserted the right to enforce the sanctions regime created by Resolution 661 under an 'inherent right of collective self-defense recognised under Article 51 of the UN Charter', and asserted that the '[f]ailure of a ship to proceed as directed will result in the use of the minimum level of force necessary to ensure compliance'. E. Lauterpacht, C.J. Greenwood, Marc Weller and Daniel Bethlehem (eds), op. cit.
51 Bush and Scowcroft, op. cit., p. 345.
52 James Baker states that Richard Cheney, Colin Powell and Brent Scowcroft opposed his view that further UN authorisation should be sought. James A. Baker, op. cit., p. 287; Bush and Scowcroft, op. cit., p. 351; Margaret Thatcher, *The Downing Street Years*, London: HarperCollins Publishers 1993, p. 821.
53 Baker stated in his memoirs: '[w]ithout more explicit UN authorisation, I was sure the Soviets would bolt from the coalition, a calamity that would surely threaten our entire strategy' (James A. Baker, op. cit., p. 286).
54 Ibid.
55 Freedman and Karsh, op. cit., p. 147.
56 Article 43 of the UN Charter.
57 Article 47 of the UN Charter.
58 See 'Canada, Cote d'Ivoire, Finland, France, United Kingdom, United States and

Zaire: Draft Resolution', UN Document S/21640, 25 August 1990 and Security Council Resolution 665 (1990) 25 August 1990, UN Document S/RES/0665 which are identical.
59 Robert O. Freedman, 'Moscow and the Iraqi Invasion of Kuwait', in Robert O. Freedman (ed.) *The Middle East After Iraq's Invasion of Kuwait*, Gainsville: University of Florida Press 1993, p. 75.
60 'Statement by the USSR Ministry for Foreign Affairs', UN Document S/21479, 9 August 1990.
61 James Gow, 'The Soviet Involvement', in James Gow (ed.) *Iraq, the Gulf Conflict and the World Community*, New York: Macmillan Pub. Co. 1992, p. 125.
62 Robert O. Freedman, op. cit., p. 86.
63 James Baker, *The Politics of Diplomacy*, op. cit., p. 287.
64 Security Council Resolution 665 (1990), as well as the earlier 'Statement by the USSR Ministry for Foreign Affairs', UN Document S/21479, 9 August 1990.
65 Eduard Shevardnadze, 'Speech to the General Assembly', UN Document A/45/PV.6, 18 September 1990.
66 J. Mohan Malik, 'Peking's Response to the Gulf Crisis', *Issue and Studies*, 27(9), September 1991, 107–128, p. 110.
67 Statement of China, 'Provisional Verbatim Record of the 2933rd Meeting of the Security Council', UN Document S/PV.2933, 6 August 1990, p. 28.
68 'Statement of China's Premier Li P'eng', *Xinhua*, 17 August 1990, reproduced in *Daily Report: China*, 20 August 1990.
69 J. Mohan Malik, op. cit., p. 111.
70 Shih Chun-yu, 'China's Performance in Handling Gulf Crisis', *Ta Kung Pao* (Hong Kong), 31 August 1990, quoted in J. Mohan Malik, ibid., p. 112.
71 Statement of China, 'Provisional Verbatim Record of the 2,938th Meeting of the Security Council', UN Document S/PV.2938, 25 August 1990, pp. 54–55.
72 Paragraph 4, UN Security Council Resolution 665 (1990), UN Document S/21640, 25 August 1990; Freedman and Karsh, op. cit., p. 150; David Cox (ed.) *The Use of Force by the Security Council for Enforcement and Deterrent Purposes: A Conference Report*, Toronto: Canadian Centre for Arms Control and Disarmament 1991.
73 Statements of Finland, Soviet Union, USA, Canada, Zaire and the United Kingdom, 'Provisional Verbatim Record of the 2,938th Meeting of the Security Council', UN Document S/PV.2938, 25 August 1990.
74 Ibid.
75 Statement of Cuba, ibid., pp. 12 and 17; Statement of Yemen, ibid., p. 7.
76 Statement of Zaire, ibid., p. 38.
77 Statement of the United Kingdom, ibid., p. 48.
78 Statement of Canada, ibid., p. 33; Statement of the US, ibid., p. 31.
79 Statement of France, ibid., p. 32.
80 Statement of Cuba, ibid., p. 14.
81 Statement of Cuba, ibid., pp. 18–20; Statement of Yemen, ibid., pp. 8–10.
82 Statement of Yemen, ibid., pp. 13–15.
83 Statement of the USSR, ibid., p. 43.
84 See Oscar Schacter, Thomas M. Franck and Faiza Patel, 'UN Police Action in Lieu of War: "The Old Order Changeth"', *American Journal of International Law*, 81(1), 1994, 63–74, for further discussion of the legal position on the authorisation of the use of force by the Security Council.
85 Bush and Scowcroft, op. cit., pp. 377–388.
86 President Bush stated that he was emotionally affected by hearing about Iraqi atrocities in Kuwait, and the treatment of diplomatic hostages, and recalled that

> at some point it came through to me that this was not a matter of shades of gray, or of trying to see the other side's point of view. It was good versus evil, right

versus wrong. I'm sure the change strengthened my determination not to let the invasion stand and encouraged me to contemplate the use of force to reverse it.

(Bush and Scowcroft, op. cit., p. 374)

87 James A. Baker, op. cit., p. 301.
88 Ibid., p. 303.
89 Bush and Scowcroft, op. cit., pp. 385–386.
90 James A. Baker, op. cit., p. 304.
91 'Provisional Verbatim Record of the 2963rd Meeting of the Security Council', UN Document S/PV.2963, 29 November 1990.
92 James A. Baker, op. cit., p. 305.
93 Ibid., p. 316.
94 Ibid., pp. 319–320.
95 Ibid., p. 232.
96 Ibid., pp. 314–315.
97 Yitzhak Shichor, 'China and the Gulf Crisis', *Problems of Communism*, 40(6), November–December 1991, 80–90; Lillian Craig Harris, 'The Gulf Crisis and China's Middle East Dilemma', *The Pacific Review*, 4(2), 1991, 116–125.
98 See James A. Baker, op. cit., p. 309, for an account of the early November meeting between the two.
99 Ibid., p. 316.
100 Ibid., p. 310. Baker met with Shevardnadze on 8 November 1990 in Moscow.
101 Ibid., p. 313.
102 Statement of Yemen, 'Provisional Verbatim Record of the 2963rd Meeting of the Security Council', UN Document S/PV.2963, 29 November 1990, p. 33; Statement of Cuba, UN Document S/PV.2963, p. 53.
103 Statements of France and Canada, ibid., pp. 66 and 69 respectively.
104 Statement of Colombia, ibid., p. 41; Statement of Malaysia, ibid., p. 75; Statement of Cote d'Ivoire, ibid., p. 87; Statement the UK, ibid., p. 81; Statement Canada, ibid., p. 69; Statement of Finland, ibid., pp. 84–85.
105 Statement of USSR, ibid., p. 92.
106 Statement of USA, ibid., p. 102.
107 Statement of France, ibid., pp. 66–67.
108 Statement of Zaire, ibid., p. 46; Statement of Ethiopia, ibid., pp. 49–50; Statement of Canada, ibid., p. 71.
109 Statement of Cuba, ibid., pp. 59–60; Statement of Yemen, ibid., pp. 34–35.
110 Statement of China, ibid., p. 62.
111 Ibid., p. 63.
112 Statement of Kuwait, ibid., pp. 12–13; Statement of Ethiopia, ibid., p. 51.
113 Statement of Ethiopia, ibid., p. 51; Statement of Malaysia, ibid., p. 76.
114 Statement of Malaysia, ibid., p. 76.
115 Statement Ethiopia, ibid., p. 51.
116 Statement of France, ibid., p. 67; Similar statements were made by the USSR, ibid., p. 91; Malaysia, ibid., p. 78; Canada, ibid., p. 74; Colombia, ibid., p. 42; UK, ibid., p. 82; Finland, ibid., pp. 84–85; Cote d'Ivoire, ibid., p. 88; Romania, ibid., pp. 99–100; USA, ibid., p. 103.
117 Statement of Colombia, ibid., p. 41.
118 Statement of the USSR, ibid., p. 91.
119 Andrew Fenton Cooper, Richard A. Higgott, and Kim Richard Nossal, 'Bound to Follow? Leadership and Followership in the Gulf Conflict', *Political Science Quarterly*, 106(3), 1991, 391–410, p. 395; G. John Ikenberry, 'The Future of International Leadership', *Political Science Quarterly*, 111(3), Fall 1996, 385–408, p. 386.
120 Table 2.1 was collated from the records of the 45th Session of the United Nations in 1990/1991. All statements were made between the end of September to the end of October 1990. The following UN Documents contain the text of the addresses

to the General Assembly made by states in this sample: Argentina A/45/PV.5; Australia A/45/PV.17; Bahrain A/45/PV.15; Brazil A/45/PV.4; Canada A/45/PV.9; China A/45/PV.12; Denmark A/45/PV.7; Egypt A/45/PV.21; European Community A/45/PV.6; France A/45/PV.4; Federal Republic of Germany A/45/PV.8; Greece A/45/PV.11; Hungary 3 October 1990 A/45/PV.18; India 28 September 1990 A/45/PV.13; Indonesia 24 September 1990 A/45/PV.5; Japan 25 September A/45/PV.7; Luxembourg 26 September 1990 A/45/PV.9; Morocco 4 October 1990 A/45/PV.21; Netherlands 26 September 1990 A/45/PV.9; New Zealand 1 October 1990 A/45/PV.14; Niger 28 September 1990 A/45/PV.15; Norway 27 September 1990 A/45/PV.11; Oman 27 September 1990 A/45/PV.11; Pakistan 28 September 1990 A/45/PV.12; Poland 24 September 1990 A/45/PV.4; Qatar 5 October 1990 A/45/PV.22; Saudi Arabia 2 October 1990 A/45/PV.16; Senegal 4 October A/45/PV. 21; Sierra Leone 10 October 1990 A/45/PV.28; Singapore 3 October 1990 A/45/PV.19; Spain 26 September A/45/PV.9; Sweden 28 September 1990 A/45/PV.13; Syrian Arab Republic 2 October 1990 A/45/PV.16; Turkey 26 September 1990 A/45/PV.9; United Arab Emirates 3 October 1990 A/45/PV.19; United Kingdom 26 September 1990 A/45/PV.9; USSR 25 September 1990 A/45/PV.6.
121 Table 2.2 was collated from the records of the 45th Session of the United Nations in 1990/1991. All statements were made between the end of September to the end of October 1990. Ibid.
122 Mr Al-Nuaimi spoke of the UAE's support for the resolutions of the Security Council, but did not specifically mention support for sanctions.

3 Material factors and followership in the Gulf Crisis

1 See Andrew Bennett, Joseph Lepgold and Danny Unger (eds) *Friends In Need: Burden Sharing in the Persian Gulf War*, New York: St Martin's Press 1997, chapter 1.
2 Michael Sterner, 'Navigating the Gulf', *Foreign Policy*, 81, winter 1990–1991, 39–52. For accounts of the causes of the Gulf War of 1991, see John K. Cooley, 'Pre-War Gulf Diplomacy', *Survival*, 33(2), March/April 1991, 125–139, p. 127; Steve A. Yetiv, *The Persian Gulf Crisis*, Westport, London: Greenwood Press 1997; Ken Matthews, *The Gulf Conflict and the World Community*, London, New York: Brasseys 1993; Alex Danchev and Dan Keohane, *International Perspectives on the Gulf Conflict 1990–1991*, London: Macmillan Press 1994; Alberto Bin, Richard Hill and Archer Jones, *Desert Storm: a Forgotten War*, Westport, London: Praeger Publishers 1998; James Gow (ed.) *Iraq, The Gulf Conflict and the World Community*, London, New York: Brasseys 1993.
3 Bennett, Lepgold, and Unger (eds), op. cit., p. 9.
4 Charles A. Kupchan, 'NATO and the Persian Gulf: Examining Intra-Alliance Behaviour', *International Organization*, 42(2), spring 1988, 317–346, pp. 324–325; Glenn Snyder, 'The Security Dilemma in Alliance Politics', *World Politics*, 36(4), July 1984, 461–495, pp. 466–467.
5 Glenn Snyder, ibid., pp. 466–467.
6 Ibid., p. 467.
7 Bennett, Lepgold and Unger, op. cit., p. 13; Michael Mandelbaum, *The Nuclear Revolution: International Politics Before and After Hiroshima*, New York: Cambridge University Press 1981, pp. 151–152.
8 Charles A. Kupchan, op. cit., p. 325.
9 Bennett, Lepgold and Unger, op. cit., pp. 12–13.
10 Stephen M. Walt, *The Origins of Alliances*, Ithaca: Cornell University Press 1987, p. 22; Stephen M. Walt, 'Alliances in Theory and Practice: What Lies Ahead', *Journal of International Affairs*, 43(1), summer 1981, 1–17.

172 *Notes*

11. Peter J. Katzenstein, 'Introduction', in Peter J. Katzenstein (ed.) *The Culture of National Security*, New York: Columbia University Press 1986, p. 27; Alexander Wendt, *Social Theory of International Politics*, Cambridge: Cambridge University Press 1999, p. 106.
12. For example, using balance of threat theory to explain the formation of a Western alliance against the Soviet Union, Walt includes as evidence of aggressive intentions: 'repressive nature of the Soviet regime', 'Soviet postwar diplomacy' which 'reinforced an image of aggressiveness', and interventions in Hungary, Czechoslovakia, Poland and Afghanistan (Stephen Walt, op. cit., 1981, p. 7).
13. United States General Accounting Office, 'Report to the Chairman, Committee on Armed Services, House of Representatives: Operation Desert Shield/Storm Update on Costs and Funding Requirements', *GAO/NSAID* 92–194, May 1992, p. 1; see also Hearing Before the Committee on Ways and Means, House of Representatives 102nd Congress, 'Foreign Contributions to the Costs of the Persian Gulf War', *USGPO* 102–165, 31 July 1991, p. 24, in which the US Department of Defense estimated the cost of Operation Desert Storm and Operation Desert Shield to be $42.2 billion as of May 1991.
14. United States General Accounting Office, op. cit., pp. 8 and 10; Hearing Before the Committee on Ways and Means, op. cit., Table 13, p. 39.
15. See Appendix 3.1.
16. Ronald D. Asmus, 'Germany After the Gulf War', *A Rand Note*, N-3391-AF, Santa Monica, CA 1991, p. 12 based on figures from the US Office of Management and Budget. See also Julian Thompson, 'The Military Coalition', in James Gow (ed.) *Iraq, the Gulf Conflict and the World* Community, London: Brassey's for Centre for Defence Studies 1993, for alternative force contribution figures; Anthony Cordesman and Abraham Wagner provide slightly different statistics again in their book, *The Lessons of Modern War Volume IV: The Gulf War*, Boulder: Westview Press 1996, p. 116.
17. Based on amounts received by the US as of May 1992 rather than amounts pledged. United States General Accounting Office, ibid., p. 10.
18. Ronald D. Asmus, 'Germany After the Gulf War', *A Rand Note*, N-3391-AF, 1991, p. 12.
19. Inacker, *Unter Ausschluß der Öffentlichkeit*, pp. 104–105, quoted in Gunther Hellman, 'Germany and Alliance Burden Sharing in the Gulf War', in Bennett, Lepgold and Unger, op. cit, p. 168; Paul E. Gallis, 'German Foreign Policy After the Gulf War: Implications for US Interests', *CRS Report for Congress,* 91-451 F, 30 May 1991, 'Summary' section (page not numbered).
20. Ibid., Inacker, pp. 104–105.
21. Ronald D. Asmus, op. cit., p. 12.
22. Max Otte with Jurgen Greve, *A Rising Middle Power? German Foreign Policy in Transformation, 1989–1999*, New York: St Martin's Press 2000, p. 93.
23. Ibid., p. 93.
24. Op. cit., Ronald D. Asmus, p. 12.
25. Op. cit., Paul E. Gallis, p. 5.
26. Op. cit., Gunther Hellman, p. 187, note 37.
27. Scott Erb, *German Foreign Policy: Navigating a New Era*, London: Lynne Reinner Publishers 2003, p. 154.
28. Gunther Hellman, op. cit., p. 173; Paul E. Gallis, op. cit., p. 6.
29. Gunther Hellmann, p. 37. Statistics from Statistisches Bundesamt (ed.) *Datenreport 1992. Zahlen und Fakten über die Bundesrepublik* Deutschland, Bonn: Bundeszentrale für Poltische Bildung 1992, pp. 391–400.
30. 'Letter Dated 14 August 1990 from the Chargé d'affaires a.i.i. of the Permanent Mission of the German Democratic Republic to the United Nations Addressed to the Secretary General', UN Document A/45/417, 14 August 1990; 'Letter Dated 3

August 1990 from the Chargé d'affaires a.i. of the Permanent Mission of the German Democratic Republic to the United Nations Addressed to the Secretary General', UN Document A/45/377, 3 August 1990.
31 Nicholas Doughty, 'NATO ministers start emergency talks on Gulf Crisis', *Reuters News* 10 August 1990.
32 The governing coalition consisted of the Christian Democratic Union (CDU) led by Chancellor Kohl and Free Democratic Party (FDP) led by Foreign Minister Hans-Dietrich Genscher.
33 Jeffrey S. Lantis, *Strategic Dilemmas and the Evolution of German Foreign Policy Since Unification*, Westport and London: Praeger Publishers 2002, p. 26; Paul E. Gallis, op. cit., p. 18.
34 Hobart Rowen, 'The Gulf Crisis: No Excuse ...', *Washington Post* 6 September 1990; Walter S. Mossberg, Urban C. Lehner and Frederick Kempe, 'Footing the Bill: Some in US ask Why Germany, Japan Bear So Little of Gulf Cost', *Wall Street Journal* 11 January 1991.
35 John M. Goshko and Dan Balz, 'Allies Aid Needed in Gulf, Hill Warns; American Reportedly Shot Iraqi Soldier', *Washington Post* 6 September 1990.
36 Ronald D. Asmus, op. cit., p. 13.
37 Patrick E. Tyler and David Hoffmann, 'US Asking Allies to Share the Costs', *Washington Post* 30 August 1990, pp. A1, A36.
38 James A. Baker III with Thomas M. Defrank, *The Politics of Diplomacy: Revolution, War and Peace 1989–1992*, New York: G.P. Putnam and Sons 1995, p. 299.
39 Gunther Hellmann, op. cit., p. 175.
40 James A. Baker III with Thomas M. Defrank, op. cit., p. 299; Steve James, 'Baker sees more German aid, backs ban for Iraq Embargo-busters', *Reuters News* 15 September 1990.
41 Gunther Hellmann, op. cit., p. 176.
42 John Palmer, 'US Signals cuts on number of troops to be stationed in Western Europe', *Guardian* 11 September 1990.
43 Jeffrey S. Lantis, op. cit., p. 27; Gunther Hellman, op. cit., p. 174.
44 James A. Baker III with Thomas M. Defrank, op. cit., p. 299; Steve James, op. cit.
45 Jeffrey S. Lantis, op. cit., p. 37.
46 Ronald D. Asmus, op. cit., p. 13.
47 Stephen Daggett and Gary J. Pagliano, 'Persian Gulf War: US Costs and Allied Financial Contributions', *CRS Issue Brief*, IB91019, 26 March 1991, p. 12.
48 Op. cit., Scott Erb, p. 152.
49 Ibid.
50 Excerpt of this interview found in Jeffrey S. Lantis, op. cit., p. 31 and p. 36; see also similar statements in his later memoirs, Hans-Dietrich Genscher, *Rebuilding a House Divided*, New York: Broadway Books 1998, p. 85.
51 Hans-Dietrich Genscher, ibid., p. 85; see also Jeffrey S. Lantis, op. cit., p. 36.
52 Jeffrey J. Anderson and John B. Goodman, 'Mars or Minerva? A United Germany', in Robert O. Keohane, Joseph S. Nye, and Stanley Hoffmann (eds) *After the Cold War: International Institutions and State Strategies in Europe, 1989–1991*, Cambridge and London: Harvard University Press 1993, p. 42.
53 Hans-Dietrich Genscher, op. cit., p. 86.
54 The final ratification of the 2-Plus-4 treaty by the USSR did not in fact occur until 15 March 1991. See Jonathan P.G. Bach, *Between Sovereignty and Integration: German Foreign Policy and National Identity After 1989*, New York: St Martin's Press 1999, p. 124; Hans-Dietrich Genscher, op. cit., p. 85; Helga Haftendorn, *Coming of Age: German Foreign Policy Since 1945*, Lanham: Rowman and Littlefield Publishers 2006, pp. 284–286.
55 Nina Philippi, 'Civilian Power and War: the German Debate About Out-of-Area Operations 1990–99', in Sebastian Harnisch and Hanns W. Maull (eds) *Germany as*

174 *Notes*

        a Civilian Power: the Foreign Policy of the Berlin Republic, Manchester and New York: Manchester University Press 2001, p. 51; Paul E. Gallis, op. cit., pp. 1–2.
56 Anthony Cordesman and Abraham Wagner, *The Lessons of Modern War Volume IV: the Gulf War*, Boulder: Westview Press 1996, p. 113.
57 See ibid., p. 116, for a comparison of the Iraqi and UN coalition forces at the start of the Gulf War.
58 Ibid., pp. 850–851.
59 Scott Erb, op. cit., pp. 151–152.
60 Steven R. Weisman, 'Confrontation in Gulf: Japan promises grants of food but lack of arms aid nettles US', *New York Times* 30 August 1990.
61 Danny Unger, 'Japan and Gulf War: Making the World Safe for Japan–US Relations', in Bennett, Lepgold and Unger, op. cit., p. 143; Mossberg, Lehner and Kempe, op. cit.; Courtney Purrington, 'Tokyo's Policy Responses During the Gulf Crisis', *Asian Survey*, 31(4), April 1991, 307–323, pp. 309–11.
62 Figures quoted vary from 60–70 per cent. Unger, ibid. p. 144; 'The Iraqi invasion: Tokyo sees no threat to its reserves of oil', *New York Times* 3 August 1990.
63 Ibid.
64 Jonathan Fuerbringer, 'Invasion shakes up markets', *New York Times* 3 August 1990.
65 Larry A. Niksch and Robert G. Sutter, 'Japan's Response to the Persian Gulf Crisis: Implications for US–Japan Relations', *CRS Report for Congress*, 91–444 F, 23 May 1991, p. 6.
66 'The Iraqi invasion; Tokyo sees no threat to its reserves of oil', *New York Times* 3 August 1990; 'Japan Falls in Cautiously Behind Bush', *Middle East Economic Digest* 24 August 1990.
67 Ibid.
68 Eugene Brown, 'Fire On the Other Side of the River: Japan and the Persian Gulf War', in Robert O. Freedman (ed.) *The Middle East After Iraq's Invasion of Kuwait*, Gainesville: Florida University Press 1993, p. 140.
69 Colin Narbrough, 'Gulf events put energy supply in focus', *The Times* 13 August 1990.
70 Eugene Brown, op. cit., p. 140.
71 Steven R. Weisman, 'The world; Japan counts the costs of Gulf action – or inaction', *New York Times* 27 January 1991; Victor Fic, 'The Japanese PKO Bill', *Asian Defence Journal*, 11, 1992, 28–33, p. 30; Kazuyoshi Abe, 'The Japanese Business Community's Response to the Gulf War', *Japanese Review of International Affairs*, 5(2), Fall/winter 1991, 177–200.
72 Masaru Tamamoto, 'Trial of an Ideal: Japan's Debate Over the Gulf Crisis', *World Policy Journal*, 8(1), winter 1990, 89–106, p. 93.
73 Reinhard Drifte, *Japan's Foreign Policy in the 1990s: From Economic Superpower to What Power?*, New York: St Martin's Press 1996, p. 50.
74 Ibid., p. 66.
75 Ibid., p. 50.
76 Danny Unger, op. cit., pp. 147–150.
77 Johanna Neuman, 'Bush's carrot is financial aid; Germany, Japan asked to aid Arabs', *USA Today* 15 August 1990.
78 Mossberg, Lehner and Kempe, op. cit.; Michael Blaker, 'Japan's Diplomatic Style', in Gerald Curtis (ed.) *Japan's Foreign Policy After the Cold War*, Armonk: M.E. Sharpe 1993, p. 22.
79 'Bonn heeds US call to share financial burden of the Gulf Crisis', *Financial Times* 1 September 1990.
80 Terence Hunt, 'Bush asks allies to help pay in Gulf, says "New World Order" could result', *Associated Press* 30 August 1990; 'President puts pressure on allies to help foot Gulf crisis bill', *The Times* 31 August 1990; 'Government warns Allies over bill for military build-up in Gulf', *The Times* 7 September 1990.

81 'Japan to US: Don't link troop presence to Gulf contribution', *Straits Times* 14 September 1990; Fred Kaplan, 'As Gulf costs rise, so does US ire at Germany, Japan', *Boston Globe* 14 September 1990; Louise Lief, Carla Anne Robbins and Jim Impoco, 'Tin-cup diplomacy as the cost of confronting Iraq mounts, the US finds donors', *US News and World Report* 17 September 1990.
82 Larry A. Niksch and Robert G. Sutter, 'Japan's Response to the Persian Gulf Crisis: Implications for US–Japan Relations', *CRS Report for Congress*, 91–444 F, 23 May 1991, p. 5.
83 Danny Unger, op. cit., p. 149.
84 *New York Times* 27 January 1991, p. 21, quoted in Danny Unger, 'Japan and the Gulf War', op. cit., p. 48.
85 Niksch and Sutter, op. cit., p. 5; Courtney Purrington, April 1991, p. 310.
86 Article 9, Japanese Constitution.
87 Masaru Tamamoto, op. cit., p. 91. The 1954 Self Defense Forces law also states that military forces cannot be sent to other countries. Niksch and Sutter, op. cit., p. 12.
88 Masaru Tamamoto, ibid., p. 100.
89 Victor Fic, 'The Japanese PKO Bill', *Asian Defence Journal*, 11, 1992, 28–33, p. 30.
90 Masaru Tamamoto, op. cit., p. 93; Eugene Brown, op. cit., pp. 137–138; Christopher W. Hughes, *Japan's Re-emergence as a 'Normal' Military Power*, Adelphi Paper 368–369, London: International Institute for Strategic Studies, 2004, Chapter 2.
91 Courtney Purrington, 'Tokyo's Policy Responses During the Gulf War and the Impact of the "Iraqi Shock" on Japan', *Pacific Affairs*, 65(2), summer, 1992, 161–181, pp. 171–172; Eugene Brown, op. cit., pp. 140–141.
92 Francois Heisbourg, 'France and the Gulf Crisis', in Nicole Gnesotto and John Roper (eds) *Western Europe and the Gulf*, Paris: Western European Union Institute for Security Studies 1992, p. 23; Isabelle Grunberg, 'Still a Reluctant Ally? France's Participation in the Gulf War Coalition', in Bennett, Lepgold and Unger, op. cit., p. 116.
93 'Opposing Forces in the Gulf', *Associated Press*, 29 August 1990.
94 Francois Heisbourg, op. cit., p. 23.
95 'Still in Step, Mostly – Promised Release of Iraqi-Held Hostages May Be Ploy to Split Western Alliance', *The Economist* 27 October 1990; Isabelle Grunberg, op. cit., p. 117.
96 Alan Riding, 'War in the Gulf: France; France's troops now at US call', *New York Times* 17 January 1991.
97 Ibid.
98 Alan Riding, 'War in the Gulf: Europe; France says US bombers can now use airspace', *New York Times* 2 February 1991; Isabelle Grunberg, op. cit., p. 118.
99 Francois Heisbourg, ibid., p. 25; Isabelle Grunberg, op. cit., p. 118.
100 'MEED Special Report on France – Overcoming Dependence on Oil', *Middle East Economic Digest* 12 October 1990.
101 In 1989, France's major suppliers were as follows: Saudi Arabia 18.7 per cent, Norway 11.3 per cent, Iran 11 per cent, Iraq 8.1 per cent, USSR 7.2 per cent, Nigeria 4.5 per cent, Gabon 4.4 per cent, UK 4 per cent, Algeria 3.7 per cent, Mexico 3.7 per cent, Libya 3.5 per cent, Cameroon 3.1 per cent, UAE 2.8 per cent, Dubai 1.1 per cent, Syria 1.1 per cent, Venezuela 0.7 per cent. 'France buys only 45 percent of its oil from the Middle East', *Le Figaro* 3 August 1990.
102 'France and the Middle East', *Middle East Economic Digest* 26 September 1987.
103 'MEED Special Report on France – Overcoming Dependence on Oil', op. cit.
104 'France buys only 45 percent of its oil from the Middle East', *Le Figaro* 3 August 1990.
105 'France and the Middle East', *Middle East Economic Digest* 26 September 1987.
106 Isabelle Grunberg, op. cit., pp. 120–121; Barzan el Tikriti, originally quoted from Josette Alia and Christine Clerc, *La guerre de Mitterrand: la derniere grande illusion*, Paris: Orban 1991, pp. 140–141.

107 'Still in Step, Mostly – Promised Release of Iraqi-Held Hostages May Be Ploy to Split Western Alliance', *The Economist* 27 October 1990.
108 Alan Riding, 'Confrontation in the Gulf: France; Paris stressing independent role', *New York Times* 18 August 1990; 'Gulf crisis blocks France/Iraq debt accord', *Reuters News* 23 August 1990; 'Invasion of Kuwait the death blow for French friendship', *The Times* 4 August 1990.
109 Ronald Tiersky, *Francois Mitterrand: the Last French President*, New York: St Martin's Press 2000, p. 201.
110 Francois Heisbourg, op. cit., p. 18.
111 Stanley Hoffman, 'French Dilemmas and Strategies in the New Europe', in Robert O. Keohane, Stanley Hoffman and Joseph Nye (eds) *After the Cold War: International Institutions and State Strategies in Europe 1989–1991*, Cambridge: Harvard University Press 1993, pp. 128–129; Barbara S. Balaj, 'France and the Gulf War', *Mediterranean Quarterly*, 4, summer 1993, 96–116, pp. 108–109.
112 Francois Heisbourg, op. cit., p. 19.
113 Including Ryadh, Cairo, Amman, Damascus, Yemen, Algiers, Tunis and Rabat. Alan Riding, 'Confrontation in the Gulf: France; Paris stressing independent role', *New York Times* 18 August 1990.
114 Ibid.
115 Francois Heisbourg, op. cit., p. 26.
116 Flora Lewis, 'Mitterrand's cynical Gaullist posturing', *New York Times* 16 January 1991; Alan Riding, 'War in the Gulf: France; French policy upsets friend and foe, at home and abroad', *New York Times* 24 January 1991.
117 Alan Riding, 'Confrontation in the Gulf: France; Paris stressing independent role', *New York Times* 18 August 1990.
118 Isabelle Grunberg, op. cit., p. 118; Alan Riding, 'War in the Gulf: France; France's troops now at US call', *New York Times* 17 January 1991.
119 Barbara S. Balaj, op. cit., p. 107.
120 Francois Heisbourg, op. cit., p. 20.
121 Stanley Hoffman, op. cit., p. 136.
122 Theodore Robert Posner, *Current French Security Policy: the Gaullist Legacy*, New York, Westport, Connecticut, London: Greenwood Press 1991; Christian Reus-Smit, *The Moral Purpose of the State: Culture, Social Identity, and Institutional Rationality in International Relations*, New Jersey: Princeton University Press 1999, chapter 7.
123 Roland Dumas, quoted in Posner, ibid., p. 81. See Roland Dumas, 'One Germany – if Europe agrees', *New York Times* 13 March 1990.
124 'The Gulf Crisis: a Roundtable Discussion', *France Magazine*, spring 1991, p. 10; Barbara S. Balaj, op. cit., p. 108.
125 Theodore Robert Posner, op. cit., pp. 3, 6; Isabelle Grunberg, op. cit., p. 123; Fredrik Wetterqvist, *French Security and Defence Policy: Current Developments and Future Prospects*, Sundbyberg, Sweden: National Defence Research Establishment, Department of Defence Analysis 1990, p. 42.
126 Willem Van Eekelen, 'WEU and the Gulf Crisis', *Survival*, 32(6), November/December 1990, 519–532; Trevor C. Salmon, 'Europeans, the EC and the Gulf', in James Gow, op. cit., p. 97; Arnaud Jacomet, 'The Role of WEU in the Gulf Crisis', in Nicole Gnesotto and John Roper (eds), op. cit.
127 Stanley Hoffman, op. cit., p. 137.
128 Anoushiravan Ehteshami, 'The Arab States and the Middle East Balance of Power', in James Gow, op. cit., p. 60.
129 General Sir Peter de la Billiere, 'The Gulf Conflict: Planning and Execution', *RUSI Journal*, 136, 1991, p. 7.
130 'Speech by UK Prime Minister Margaret Thatcher, opening the two-day debate on the Gulf Crisis in the House of Commons on 6 September 1990', reproduced in Ref-

erence Services, Central Office of Information, *Britain and the Gulf Crisis*, London: HMSO Publications 1993; Craig R. Whitney, 'Confrontation in the Gulf; Thatcher warns Europe over Gulf', *New York Times* 31 August 1990.
131 'Announcement on 14 September by UK Secretary of State for Defence, Tom King, of the Government's decision to send an armoured brigade to Saudi Arabia', reproduced in Reference Services, ibid., p. 22.
132 Sources of figures found in Anthony Cordesman and Abraham Wagner, op. cit., pp. 156–166.
133 'Parliamentary statement on 22 November by UK Secretary of State for Defence, Tom King on further deployments of British forces to the Gulf', reproduced in Reference Services, ibid.
134 'Announcement on 14 September by UK Secretary of State for Defence, Tom King, of the Government's decision to send an armoured brigade to Saudi Arabia', reproduced in Reference Services, ibid., p. 22.
135 Reference Services, ibid., p. 27.
136 Reference Services, ibid., pp. 27 and 28.
137 UK Ministry of Defence, *National Audit Office Report by the Comptroller and Auditor General*, London: HMSO 2 December 1992, p. 2.
138 Ibid., table 3.
139 'Higher oil prices unlikely to prompt recession', *The Economist* 11 August 1990; 'The winners and the losers if the price of a barrel of oil keeps rising', *Guardian* 6 August 1990.
140 'The Autumn Statement – Oil Production Expected To Fall', *Financial Times* 9 November 1990.
141 'Review of developments by the Foreign and Commonwealth Secretary, Douglas Hurd, in his speech opening the second House of Commons debate on 11 December 1990', selections reproduced in Reference Services, op. cit., p. 68.
142 'Speech by Prime Minister, Margaret Thatcher 6 September 1990', Reference Services, op. cit., p. 58.
143 Speech by Margaret Thatcher 6 September 1990, ibid.; 'Prime Minister John Major's statement to the House on 17 January 1991 on the outbreak of hostilities in the Gulf', reproduced in Reference Services, op. cit.
144 Speech by UK Prime Minister Margaret Thatcher, 6 September 1990, ibid.; George Bush and Brent Scowcroft, *A World Transformed*, New York: Vintage Books 1999, p. 319, where Margaret Thatcher is quoted as saying in a meeting with Bush in the early days of August 1990: 'They [Iraq] won't stop here, they see a chance to take a major share of oil. It's got to be stopped. We must do everything possible.' At the meeting it was Thatcher who urged Bush to go to the UN to ask for a resolution on economic sanctions.
145 'Gulf Crisis Prompts Strengthening of the Thatcher–Bush Relationship', *The Economist* 1 September 1990.
146 Joseph Lepgold, 'Britain in Desert Storm', in Bennett, Lepgold and Unger (eds), op. cit., p. 74.
147 John Dumbrell, *A Special Relationship: Anglo-American Relations in the Cold War and After*, Houndmills, Basingstoke, Hampshire and New York: Palgrave Macmillan 2005, p. 106; Margaret Thatcher, *The Downing Street Years*, London: HarperCollins 1993, pp. 768 and 783.
148 John Dumbrell, ibid.
149 Louise Richardson, 'British State Strategies After the Cold War', in Robert O. Keohane, Joseph S. Nye and Stanley Hoffman (eds), op. cit., p. 151.
150 John Dumbrell, op. cit., p. 108; Louise Fawcett and Robert O'Neill, 'Britain, the Gulf Crisis and European Security', in Nicole Gnesotto and John Roper (eds), op. cit., p. 145.
151 John Dumbrell, ibid., p. 108.

152 Louise Richardson, op. cit., pp. 159–162.
153 Louise Fawcett and Robert O'Neill, op. cit., p. 147.
154 *The Times* 31 August 1990, p. 1, quoted in Louise Fawcett and Robert O'Neill, ibid.
155 UK Foreign Secretary Douglas Hurd, 'Saddam Hussein: Standing up to the bully of Iraq', *Daily Telegraph* 24 August 1990.
156 *The Daily Telegraph*, 1 March 1991, quoted in Louise Fawcett and Robert O'Neill, op. cit., p. 15.
157 Michael R. Gordon, 'Greater threats from lesser powers', *New York Times* 8 April 1990.
158 'Customs' Action Will Not Stop Iraqi Supergun Programme', *The Engineer* 26 April 1990; 'Iraq slams British claims over supergun, hints at trade war', *Reuters News* 1 April 1990; '"Supergun" poses only limited threat', *Independent* 20 April 1990; 'Iraq says it made an atom "trigger"', *New York Times* 9 May 1990.
159 Ibid. See also 'Iraq said to build launchers for its 400-mile missiles', *New York Times* 30 March 1990.

4 Legitimacy and the Iraq Crisis

1 Of particular importance was the defection of Saddam Hussein's son-in-law, General Hussein Kamal, in 1995. He revealed the extent of the regime's efforts to conceal and deny the existence of its WMD programmes to both the IAEA and UNSCOM. See 'Letter Dated 25 January 1999 from the Executive Chairman of the Special Commission Established by the Secretary-General Pursuant to Paragraph 9 (b) (i) of Security Council Resolution 687 (1991) Addressed to the President of the Security Council', UN Document S/1999/94, 29 January 1999; 'IAEA/UNSCOM Interview with General Hussein Kamal', 22 August 1995, www.casi.org.uk/info/unscom950822.pdf.
2 Richard Butler, *The Greatest Threat: Iraq, Weapons of Mass Destruction and the Crisis of Global Security*, New York: Public Affairs 2000, pp. 51, 52, 67 and 83; Daniel Byman, Kenneth Pollack and Matthew Waxman, 'Coercing Saddam Hussein: Lessons from the Past', *Survival*, 40(3), 1998, 127–151, pp. 139–140; James Bone, 'Iraq defies UN over weapons inspections', *The Times* 17 September 1998.
3 James M Goshko, 'US stands alone in seeking force against Iraq', *Washington Post* 21 September 1998; Lawrence Freedman, 'War in Iraq: Selling the Threat', *Survival*, 46(2), 7–49, pp. 11–12.
4 Bradley Graham and Dana Priest, 'US targets sites crucial to weapons-making', *Washington Post* 17 December 1998; 'Saddam's Iraq Key Events: 16–19 Desert Fox December', 2002, *BBC News Online*, http://news.bbc.co.uk/2/shared/spl/hi/middle_east/02/iraq_events/html/desert_fox.stm.
5 The Whitehouse, *The National Security Strategy of the United States of America*, September 2002 (henceforth referred to as the *NSS*); Nicholas J. Wheeler, 'The Bush Doctrine', *Asian Perspective*, 27(4), 2003, 183–216, p. 185.
6 Bob Woodward, Robert G. Kaiser and David B. Ottaway, 'U.S. fears Bin Laden made nuclear strides; concern over "dirty bomb" affects security', *Washington Post* 4 December 2001; Kamran Khan and Molly Moore, '2 nuclear experts briefed Bin Laden, Pakistanis say', *Washington Post Foreign Service* 12 December 2001; Michael Getler, 'The dirty bomb and the alert', *Washington Post*, 9 December 2001.
7 *NSS*, op. cit.
8 Ibid., p. 14.
9 US President George W. Bush, 'Speech to the UN General Assembly on 12 September 2002', reproduced in Micah L. Sifry and Christopher Cerf (eds) *The Iraq War Reader: History, Documents, Opinions*, New York, London: Touchstone Book, Simon & Schuster 2003, p. 316.

10 *NSS*, op. cit., p. 15.
11 Ibid.
12 Nicholas J. Wheeler, op. cit., p. 186; John Ikenberry, 'The Lures of Pre-emption', *Foreign Affairs*, 81(5), September/October 2002, 44–60, p. 51.
13 *NSS*, op. cit., p. 6.
14 Ian Brownlie, *International Law and the Use of Force by States*, Oxford: Oxford University Press 1963, p. 264; Phillip Jessup, *A Modern Law of Nations*, New York: The Macmillan Company, 1952, pp. 165–167; B.V.A. Röling, 'On the Prohibition of the Use of Force', in A.R. Blackshield (ed.) *Legal Change: Essays in Honour of Julius Stone*, New York: Butterworths 1983, p. 276.
15 Rosalyn Higgins, *Problems and Process: International Law and How We Use It*, Clarendon: Clarendon Press 1994, p. 242; Antonio Cassese, *International Law in a Divided World*, Oxford: Oxford University Press 1986, p. 231.
16 Myres S. McDougal, 'The Soviet–Cuban Quarantine and Self-Defence', *American Journal of International Law*, 57(3), 1963, 597–604, pp. 600–601.
17 Antonio Cassese, *International Law*, Oxford: Oxford University Press 2005 p. 358.
18 R.Y. Jennings, 'The Caroline and McLeod cases', *American Journal of International Law*, 32(1), 1938, 82–89, p. 82; Donald R. Rothwell, 'Anticipatory Self-Defence in the Age of International Terrorism', *Queensland Law Journal*, 24, 2005, 337–353, p. 339; Abraham D. Sofaer, 'On the Necessity of Pre-emption', *European Journal of International Law*, 14(2), 2003, 209–226, p. 219; McDougal, op. cit., p. 598.
19 Cassese, 2005, op. cit., p. 359.
20 Ibid., p. 231.
21 Christine Gray, *International Law and the Use of Force*, Clarendon: Oxford University Press 2000, pp. 112–113.
22 Israel, 'Letter Dated 8 June 1981 from the Permanent Representative of Israel to the United Nations Addressed to the President of the Security Council', UN Document S/14510; UN Security Council, 'Security Council Official Records 2,288th Meeting', UN Document S/PV.2288, 19 June 1981, para. 44–75.
23 UN Security Council, 'Security Council Official Records 2,280th Meeting', UN Document S/PV 2280, 12 June 1981, para. 64–69.
24 UN General Assembly Resolution 36/27, 13 November 1981.
25 Between 15 and 19 June 1981, 38 states gave their views on the use of force by Israel (including members of the Security Council). The six states were the United Kingdom, United States, Ireland, Sierra Leone, Uganda and Niger. UN Document S/PV. 2280, op. cit.; UN Document S/PV. 2288, op. cit.; United Nations Security Council, 'Security Council Official Records 2282nd Meeting', 15 June 1981, UN Document S/PV. 2283; United Nations Security Council, 'Security Council Official Records 2283rd Meeting', 15 June 1981, UN Document S/PV.2283.
26 US Joint Chiefs of Staff, *Department of Defense Dictionary of Military and Associated Terms*, Joint Publication 1–02, Washington, DC: Government Printing Office 2009, p. 432.
27 Cassese, op. cit., 1986, p. 232.
28 *NSS*, op. cit., p. 15.
29 Ibid.
30 Cassese, op. cit., 1986, p. 137.
31 James Gow, *Defending the West*, Cambridge: Polity Press 2005, pp. 41–42.
32 Nicholas J. Wheeler, *Saving Strangers: Humanitarian Intervention in International Society*, Oxford: Oxford University Press 2000.
33 International Commission on Intervention and State Sovereignty, *The Responsibility to Protect*, Ottawa: International Development Research Centre 2001; Kofi A. Annan, 'Reflections on Intervention', 35th Annual Ditchley Foundation Lecture, 26 June 1998, reprinted in Kofi Annan, *The Question of Intervention: Statements by the Secretary General*, New York: United Nations 1999, p. 6.

34 Richard Haas, 'Existing Rights, Evolving Responsibilities', remarks to the School of Foreign Service and the Mortara Center for International Studies, Georgetown University, Washington, 15 January 2003, quoted in Nicholas Wheeler, op. cit., 2003, p. 197.
35 Walter B. Slocombe, 'Force, Pre-emption and Legitimacy', *Survival*, 45(1), spring 2003, 117–130, p. 124.
36 Nicholas Wheeler, op. cit., 2003, p. 198; Edward Luttwak, 'The New Calculus of Pre-emption', *Survival*, 44(4), winter 2002–2003, 53–79, p. 59.
37 UN Document S/PV.39955, 16 December 1998; Marc Weller, 'The US, Iraq and the Use of Force in a Unipolar World', *Survival*, 41 (4), winter 1999–2000, 81–100, pp. 84, 86 and 87.
38 Various authors, 'Editorial Comments: Nato's Kosovo Intervention', *American Journal of International Law*, 93, 1999, 828–861; Antonio Cassese, 'Ex Injuries Ius Oritur: Are We Moving Towards International Legitimation of Forcible Humanitarian Countermeasures in the World Community?', *European Journal of International Law*, 10(1), 1999, 23–30.
39 '4,644th Meeting of the Security Council', UN Document S/PV.4644, 8 November 2002, p. 3.
40 Dick Cheney, speech before the Veterans of Foreign Wars in Nashville, Tennessee, 26 August 2002.
41 These drafts were not officially tabled in the Security Council, but can be found on the website of Campaign Against Sanctions on Iraq (CASI) at www.casi.org.uk/info/scriraq.html#2002.
42 UN Security Council Resolution 1441 (2002), UN Document S/2002/1198, 7 November 2002, Operational paragraph 3.
43 Ibid., paragraph 9.
44 James G. March and Johan P. Olsen, *Rediscovering Institutions: the Organisational Basis of Politics*, New York: Free Press 1989, p. 23.
45 Ibid.
46 Kofi Annan, 'Address to the UN General Assembly', *UN Press Release*, SG/SM/8378-GA/10045, 12 September 2002.
47 '4,644th Meeting of the Security Council', UN Document S/PV.4644, 8 November 2002, p. 5.
48 Ibid., p. 8; 'Chinese, Russian Ministers Discuss Iraq – UK, US Officials Meet Chinese Officials', *BBC Monitoring Newsfile* 30 September 2002.
49 UN Document S/PV.4644, op. cit., p. 4.
50 In his statement to the Security Council, Mr Negroponte of the US remarked:

> If the Security Council fails to act decisively in the event of further Iraqi violations, this resolution does not constrain any Member State from acting to defend itself against the threat posed by Iraq or to enforce relevant United Nations resolutions and protect world peace and security.
>
> (Ibid., p. 3)

51 Ibid., p. 5.
52 Ibid., p. 9.
53 Ibid., p. 12.
54 Tyler Marshall, Maggie Farley and Doyle McManus, 'A war of words led to unanimous Iraq vote; the long-sought UN resolution shows the extent of US power – and its limits', *Los Angeles Times* 1 November 2002.
55 'Interview of President Jacques Chirac', *New York Times* 8 September 2002.
56 James Bone, 'Britain risks rift with US over regime change – War on Terror', *The Times* 24 September 2002.
57 Security Council Resolution 1441 (2002), UN Document S/Res/1441(2002) paragraph 2.

58 Ibid.
59 Ibid., paragraph 4.
60 The demand for unrestricted access to all relevant sites and information explicitly revoked the earlier agreement to exempt 'Presidential Sites' from inspection agreed to under Resolution 1154 (1998). Ibid., paragraph 7.
61 IAEA, 'IAEA Update Report for the Security Council Pursuant to Resolution 1441 (2002)', 20 January 2003, UN Document S/2003/95, paragraphs 4 and 65.
62 Ibid., paragraphs 27 and 62.
63 Ibid., paragraph 70.
64 Ibid., paragraph 71.
65 'An Update on Inspection – Executive Chairman of UNMOVIC, Dr Hans Blix', 27 January 2003, available at www.un.org/depts/unmovic/Bx27.htm.
66 Ibid.
67 Ibid.
68 Ibid.
69 'Iraq Failed Two Key Tests of UN Compliance, Negroponte Says', US State Department (Washington File) 27 January 2003; 'Transcript – Little Hope Iraq Intends to Comply, Negroponte Says', US State Department (Washington File) 27 January 2003; US Department of State, Office of the Spokesman, 'Remarks, Secretary of State Colin L. Powell', Washington, DC, 27 January 2003; UK Foreign and Commonwealth Office, 'Foreign Secretary Straw, Statement and 10-question List', 28 January 2003, www.fco.gov.uk.
70 Julia Preston, 'US set to push for a UN debate on war with Iraq', *New York Times* 30 January 2003; 'Transcript of Russian Permanent Representative to the UN Sergei Lavrov's Live Interview on the Vremya (Channel One) Television Program Regarding the Outcome of the UN Security Council Meeting Held on 27 January 2003', Russian Foreign Ministry Transcript, Document 200–27–2003, 27 January 2003; 'After Briefing by Inspectors, Security Council Plans to Consult on Iraq Wednesday', *UN News Service* 27 January 2003; Chinese Ministry of Foreign Affairs, 'Statement of the Chinese Foreign Ministry Spokesperson', 28 January 2003, www.fmprcgov.cn.
71 'What they said – world reaction – Iraq', *The Times* 29 January 2003.
72 US Department of State, Office of the Spokesman, 'Remarks: Secretary of State Colin L. Powell to the United Nations Security Council', 5 February 2003, www.un.int/usa/03print_clp0205.htm.
73 Ibid.
74 Walter Pincus, 'Alleged Al Qaeda ties questioned', *Washington Post* 7 February 2003.
75 United States, United Kingdom and Spain, 'Draft resolution: Released by the US Mission to the United Nations', 24 February 2003, US Department of State website, www.state.gov/p/10/rls/othr/17937.htm; 'Spain, United Kingdom of Great Britain and Northern Ireland and the United States of America: Draft Resolution', UN Document S/2003/215, 7 March 2003, OP3.
76 'Annex II to the Letter Dated 28 February 2003 from the Permanent Representatives of China and the Russian Federation to the United Nations Addressed to the Secretary General', UN Document S/2003/238, 28 February 2003.
77 'Annex to the Letter Dated 24 February 2003 from the Permanent Representatives of France, Germany and the Russian Federation to the United Nations Addressed to the President of the Security Council: Memorandum', UN Document S/2003/214, 24 February 2003.
78 'Joint Declaration from Russia, Germany and France', Russian Foreign Ministry Document 333–11–02–2003, 11 February 2003; 'Annex to the Letter Dated 5 March 2003 from the Permanent Representatives of France, Germany and the Russian Federation to the United Nations Addressed to the President of the Security Council',

UN Document S/2003/253; Robert J. McCartney, 'France denounces US and its allies', *Washington Post* 18 March 2003; Karen de Young and Colum Lynch, 'Bush lobbies for deal on Iraq', *Washington Post* 12 March 2003.
79 See 'Annex to the Letter Dated 18 March 2003 from the Permanent Representatives of Portugal, Spain, the United Kingdom of Great Britain and Northern Ireland and the United States of America to the United Nations Addressed to the President of the Security Council', UN Document S/2003/347, 18 March 2003.
80 Statement of the US, '4,714th Meeting of the Security Council', UN Document S/PV.4714, 7 March 2003, pp. 14–15; Statement of Spain, '4,714th Meeting of the Security Council', UN Document S/PV.4714, 7 March 2003, p. 23.
81 Statement of Spain, ibid., p. 24; Statement of the US, ibid., p. 14; Statement of the United Kingdom, ibid., p. 26.
82 Statement of the US, ibid., p. 15; Statement of Spain, ibid., p. 24.
83 Warren Hodge, 'Blair, facing dissent in party, dismisses French–German Plan', *New York Times* 26 February 2003.
84 Mohamed ElBaradei, 'Statement to the United Nations Security Council: the Status of Nuclear Inspections in Iraq', 14 February 2003, IAEA website, http://iaea.org/NewsCenter/Statements/2003/ebsp2003n005.shtml.
85 Statement of Spain, UN Document S/PV.4714, op. cit., p. 24.
86 Statement of the United States, ibid., p. 116.
87 Statement of Spain, ibid., p. 24.
88 Ambassador Dumisani Kumalo of South Africa on Behalf of the Non-Aligned Movement, 'Statement to the Security Council on the Situation Between Iraq and Kuwait', 4,709th Meeting of the Security Council, 18 February 2003, UN Document S/PV.4709; Non-Aligned Movement, 'XII Conference of Heads of State or Government – Statement on Iraq', 25 February 2003, www.berama.com/events/newnam2003/readspeech.shtml?declare/dc2202_iraq.
89 Statement of Malaysia on Behalf of the NAM, '4,726th Meeting of the Security Council', 26 March 2003, UN Document S/PV. 4726, p. 7; Statement of Mr Mahmassani, League of Arab States, 4,726th Meeting of the Security Council, 26 March 2003, UN Document S/PV. 4726, p. 8; 'Annex to the Letter Dated 24 March 2003 from the Permanent Observer of the League of Arab States to the United Nations Addressed to the President of the Security Council', 26 March 2003, UN Document S/2003/365, paragraph 2.
90 Steven Erlanger, 'No-one has a clear idea about what the effects would be', *New York Times* 5 September 2002; '4,714th Meeting of the Security Council', 7 March 2003, UN Document S/PV.4714, p. 120.
91 UN Document S/PV.4714, op. cit., pp. 17 and 10.
92 Steven Erlanger, op. cit.
93 Ibid.
94 Ibid. Schroeder further stated that he believed that the threat from Saddam Hussein was 'overestimated' by Condoleezza Rice, and that a return of the inspectors would ensure that 'we could discover what the real situation was and not have to rely on surmises or intelligence reports'.
95 President Bush, 'Remarks to the American Enterprise Institute', Washington, DC, 26 February 2003, quoted in Ron Huisken, 'The Road to War on Iraq', *Canberra Papers on Strategy & Defence*, 148, 2005, p. 36.
96 Ibid., p. 37.
97 See 'Interview with Jacques Chirac', *New York Times* 4 September 2002.
98 '2,726th Meeting of the Security Council', 26 March 2003, UN Document, S/PV.4726 (Resumption 1), p. 27.
99 Malaysia on behalf of the Non-Aligned Movement, 'Statement to the 4,717th Meeting of the Security Council', 11 March 2003, UN Document S/PV.4717, p. 9.
100 Ibid., p. 7.

101 Angola implicitly supported the French/Russian/German position by acknowledging that improvements in Iraqi cooperation were associated with specific benchmarks and dates, 'signaling the makings of a model for strengthening the scope and the intrusiveness of inspections' (Mr Chikoti, Angola, 4,714th Meeting of the Security Council, UN Document S/PV.4714, p. 28).

102 Whilst not explicitly stating its support for the French/Russian/German Memorandum, Cameroon expressed support for its main element, that is, the continuation of inspections within a limited timeframe. Mr Beling-Eboutou, Cameroon, 4,714th Meeting of the Security Council, UN Document S/PV.4714, p. 29.

103 Guinea stated its support for continued inspections, but believed that they could not go on indefinitely.

104 The Pakistani delegate did not state explicitly that his country supported the French/Russian/German position but did express support for its core elements, that is, the continuation of inspections, the setting of key outstanding disarmament tasks, to be completed within a 'relatively short time frame'. Mr Akram, Pakistan, 4,714th Meeting of the Security Council, UN Document S/PV.4714, p. 32.

105 The EU statement at the Security Council stated that inspections could not go on indefinitely, implicitly showing support for the setting of a deadline.

106 The Canadian delegate put forward a compromise solution to the Council at the 4,417th meeting on 11 March, which involved the setting of key disarmament tasks requiring active, effective and substantive Iraqi cooperation within three weeks. Force would be authorised in the event of a failure to comply. Canada, 4,717th Meeting of the Security Council, 11 March 2003, S/PV.4714, p. 20.

107 Indonesia associated itself with the statement made by Malaysia in its capacity as Chair of the Non-Aligned Movement. Indonesia, 4,717th Meeting of the Security Council, 11 March 2003, S/PV.4714, p. 29.

108 Norway, 4,717th Meeting of the Security Council, 11 March 2003, S/PV.4714, p. 23. The Norwegian delegate expressed support for further inspections on the basis that a short time limit and clear achievable criteria for Iraq to comply with Resolution 1441 (2002) be set.

109 Turkey aligned itself with the statement of the European Union as well as making further comments on its position. Turkey, 4,717th Meeting of the Security Council, 11 March 2003, S/PV.4714, p. 22.

110 I have placed El Salvador among the countries that supported the use of force even though the statement of its representative did not state this explicitly. In the statement made to the Security Council, El Salvador emphasised that Iraq had not fully complied with resolutions of the Council, that this represented a defiance of its authority and stated that 'Given that persistent defiance, the Security Council, pursuant to Chapter VII of the Charter, must assume its lofty responsibilities and give effect to its decisions'. It also stated that inspections could not go on indefinitely. El Salvador, 4,717th Meeting of the Security Council, 11 March 2003, S/PV.4717, p. 10.

111 The representative of Iceland did not explicitly state his support for the use of force against Iraq. However, he did take a strong position in stating that Iraq had not actively cooperated, was in violation of Resolution 1441, and that the UN could not tolerate its 'relentless obstruction' any further, and called for the UN to show determination. See Mr Ingolfsson, Iceland, 4,717th Meeting of the Security Council, 11 March 2003, UN Document S/PV.4717, p. 27

5 Material factors and the Iraq Crisis of 2002–2003

1 Andrew Bennett, Joseph Lepgold and Danny Unger (eds) *Friends In Need: Burden Sharing in the Persian Gulf War*, New York: St Martin's Press 1997, p. 12; Glenn Snyder, 'The Security Dilemma in Alliance Politics', *World Politics*,

36(4), July 1984, 461–495; Michael Mandelbaum, *The Nuclear Revolution: International Politics Before and After Hiroshima*, New York: Cambridge University Press 1981, pp. 151–152; Charles A. Kupchan, 'NATO and the Persian Gulf: Examining Intra-Alliance Behaviour', *International Organization*, 42(2), spring 1988, pp. 324–325.
2 See Bennett, Lepgold and Unger, ibid., pp. 12–13.
3 Stephen M. Walt, *The Origins of Alliances*, Ithaca: Cornell University Press 1987, p. 22; Stephen M. Walt, 'Alliances in Theory and Practice: What Lies Ahead?', *Journal of International Affairs*, summer 1989, 43(1), 1–17, p. 5.
4 See Charles A. Kupchan, 'NATO and the Persian Gulf: Examining Intra-Alliance Behaviour', *International Organization*, spring 1988), 42(2), 317–346, p. 324. Kupchan derives an external threat hypothesis from balance of power theory which has been adapted here to take into account Walt's modification of balance of power theory.
5 See Chapter 2; Alexander Wendt, *Social Theory of International Politics*, op. cit.; Peter J. Katzenstein, *The Culture of National Security: Norms and Identity in World Politics*, op. cit.
6 The full list of countries in support of the war: Afghanistan, Albania, Australia, Azerbaijan, Bulgaria, Colombia, Costa Rica, the Czech Republic, Denmark, Dominican Republic, El Salvador, Eritrea, Estonia, Ethiopia, Georgia, Honduras, Hungary, Iceland, Italy, Japan, Kuwait, Latvia, Lithuania, Macedonia, Marshall Islands, Micronesia, Mongolia, the Netherlands, Nicaragua, Palau, the Philippines, Poland, Portugal, Romania, Rwanda, Singapore, Slovakia, Solomon Islands, South Korea, Turkey, Uganda, United Kingdom, Uzbekistan.
7 Steve Schifferes, 'US Says "Coalition of the Willing" Grows', *BBC News* 21 March 2003, http://newsvote.bbc.co.uk/mpapps/pagetools/print/news.bbc.co.uk/2/hi/americas/2870487.
8 Steve Bowman, 'Iraq: US Military Operations', *CRS Report For Congress*, RL31701, updated 20 November 2004.
9 Steve Bowman, 'Iraq: US Military Operations', *CRS Report For Congress*, RL31701, updated 2 October 2003, p. 7; 'GIs doubt foreign troop readiness', *Chicago Tribune* 7 September 2003.
10 Steve Bowman, 'Iraq: Military Operations and Costs', *CRS Report for Congress*, RL31701, updated 20 November 2004, p. 11.
11 Jeremy Sharp and Christopher M. Blanchard, 'Post-War Iraq: Foreign Contributions to Training, Peacekeeping, and Reconstruction', *CRS Report for Congress*, RL32105, updated 6 June 2005, p. 3.
12 Jeremy Sharp and Christopher M. Blanchard, ibid., p. 4.
13 Of note was the subsidisation of the Polish deployment. Jeremy M. Sharp, 'Post-War Iraq: a Table and Chronology of Foreign Contributions', *CRS Report for Congress*, RL 32105, updated 5 November 2004, p. 2.
14 Steve Bowman, op. cit., November 2004, p. 13.
15 Steve Bowman, ibid., p. 11.
16 Curt Tarnoff, 'Iraq: Recent Developments in Reconstruction Assistance', *CRS Report for Congress*, updated 12 August 2005, p. 2.
17 The relevant legislation is titled the Law Concerning Special Measures on Humanitarian and Reconstruction Assistance ('LCSMHRA') 2003. See C.W. Hughes, *Japan's Re-emergence as a 'Normal' Military Power*, Adelphi Paper 368–369, London: International Institute for Strategic Studies 2004, p. 128.
18 'Press Conference by Prime Minister Junichiro Koizumi (Decision on the Extension of the Basic Plan Regarding Humanitarian and Reconstruction Assistance of the Self Defense Forces in Iraq)', 9 December 2004, website of the Prime Minister of Japan and his Cabinet, http://wwwkantei.go.jp/foreign/koizumispeech/2004/12/09press_e.html.

19 'Prime Minister Koizumi Encourages Japan Ground Self-Defense Force (JGSDF) to be Dispatched to Iraq', 1 February 2004, website of the Prime Minister of Japan and his Cabinet, www.kantei.go.jp/foreign/koizumiphoto/2004/02/01asahikawa_e. html.
20 C.W. Hughes, 'Japan's Security Policy, the US-Japan Alliance, and the 'War On Terror': Incrementalism Confirmed or Radical Leap?', *Australian Journal of International Affairs*, 58(4), 427–445, p. 428; see 'The Outline of the Basic Plan Regarding Response Measures Based on the Law Concerning the Special Measures on Humanitarian and Reconstruction Assistance in Iraq', 3 December 2003, website of the Prime Minister of Japan and his Cabinet, www.kantei.go.jp/foreign/policy/2003/031209housin_e.html.
21 'Japan's Assistance to Iraq (Fact Sheet)', 30 January 2006, the Government of Japan, available at the website of the Ministry of Foreign Affairs of Japan, www.infojapan.org/region/middle_e/iraq/issue2003/assistance/assist0601.pdf; 'Japan's Assistance for the Reconstruction of Iraq (Assistance to Meet the Medium-Term Reconstruction Needs of Iraq)', 24 October 2003, website of the Prime Minister of Japan and his Cabinet, www.kantei.go.jp/foreign/tyokan/2003/1024press_e. html.
22 Robert Uriu, 'Japan in 2003: Muddling Ahead?', *Asian Survey*, 44(1), 168–181, p. 179.
23 See 'Statement by Prime Minister Junichiro Koizumi: Cabinet decision', 20 March 2003, website of the Prime Minister of Japan and his Cabinet, www.kantai.go.jp/foreign/koizumispeech/2003/03/20danwa_e.html.
24 'Prime Minister Junichiro Koizumi's Interview on the Issue of Iraq', 18 March 2003, website of the Prime Minister of Japan and his Cabinet, www.kanteigo.jp/foreign/koizumispeech/2003/03/18interview_e.html.
25 See Tsuchiyama Jitsuo, 'Ironies in Japanese Defense and Disarmament Policy', in Inoguchi Takashi and Purnendra Jain (eds) *Japanese Foreign Policy Today: a Reader*, New York: Palgrave 2000, 137–151, p. 149.
26 Akaha Tsuneo, 'US–Japan Relations in the Post-Cold War Era: Ambiguous Adjustment to a Changing Strategic Environment', in Inoguchi Takashi and Purnendra Jain (eds), ibid., p. 183; Robert Uriu, op. cit., p. 177.
27 'Prime Minister Junichiro Koizumi's Interview on the Issue of Iraq', 18 March 2003, website of the Prime Minister of Japan and his Cabinet, www.kanteigo.jp/foreign/koizumispeech/2003/03/18interview_e.html.
28 'Prime Minister Junichiro Koizumi's Interview on the Issue of Iraq', 18 March 2003, website of the Prime Minister of Japan and his Cabinet, www.kanteigo.jp/foreign/koizumispeech/2003/03/18interview_e.html.
29 *Yomiuri Shimbun*, 11 June 2003, quoted in Gavan McCormack, 'Remilitarizing Japan', *New Left Review*, 29, September/October 2004, 29–45, p. 34.
30 Gavan McCormack, ibid., p. 34.
31 See Christopher W. Hughes, op. cit., pp. 128 and 130; Gavan McCormack, ibid., p. 36.
32 *Kyodo*, 15 September 2003; *Asahi Shimbun*, 9 October 2003, quoted in Gavan McCormack, ibid., p. 35.
33 'Press Conference by Prime Minister Junichiro Koizumi: the Basic Plan Regarding the Measures Based on the Law Concerning the Special Measure on Humanitarian and Reconstruction Assistance in Iraq', 9 December 2003, website of the Prime Minister of Japan and his Cabinet, www.kantei.go.jp/foreign/koizumispeech/2003/12/09press_e. html.
34 Ibid.
35 Japanese Agency for Natural Resources and Energy, Ministry of Economy, Trade and Industry, 'Energy in Japan 2003', 2003, www.enecho.meti.go.jp.
36 Ibid., p. 25.

37 Ibid., p. 21.
38 US Energy Information Administration, 'Japan', *Country Analysis Briefs*, November 2005, p. 3, www.eia.doe.gov.
39 The Ministry of Foreign Affairs of Japan, 'Strategy and Approaches of Japan's Energy Diplomacy,' April 2004, website of the MOFA, www.mofa.go.jp/policy/energy/diplomacy.html; 'Special Report Japan – Energy', *Mead Weekly Special Report* 14 December 2001.
40 Michael R. Gordon, 'German intelligence gave US Iraqi defense plan, report says', *New York Times* 27 February 2006.
41 Resolution 1511 (2003).
42 See Scott Erb, *German Foreign Policy: Navigating a New Era*, London: Lynne Rienner Publishers 2003, p. 204.
43 See 'Policy Statement by Federal Chancellor Gerhard Schroder in the German Bundestag on the Current International Situation', 13 February 2003, www.germany.info/phprint.php.
44 Sebastian Harnisch, 'Germany Non-Proliferation Policy and the Iraq Conflict', *German Politics*, 13(1), March 2004, 1–34, p. 6.
45 Quoted in ibid., p. 7.
46 Piotr Buras and Kerry Longhurst, 'The Berlin Republic, Iraq and the Use of Force', *European Security*, 13(3), 2004, 215–245, pp. 233–234.
47 Buras and Longhurst, ibid.; Harnisch, op. cit., pp. 6–7.
48 Steven Erlanger, 'Schroder cautions Bush on "big mistake" over Iraq', *International Herald Tribune* 5 September 2002.
49 Piotr Buras and Kerry Longhurst, op. cit., p. 236; Steven Erlanger, ibid.
50 'Remarks by Joschka Fischer, German Foreign Minister', *Süddeutsche Zeitung* 7 August 2002, www.iraqwatch.org, www.iraqwatch.org/government/Germany/germany-mfa-fischer-080702.htm.
51 Harnisch, op. cit., p. 12; Buras and Longhurst, op. cit., p. 236.
52 Scott Erb, op. cit., p. 204.
53 Helga Haftendorn, *Coming of Age: German Foreign Policy Since 1945*, Lanham: Rowman & Littlefield Publishers 2006, p. 386.
54 Norman Bowman, 'Multilateralism, Multipolarity, and Regionalism: the French Foreign Policy Discourse', *Mediterranean Quarterly*, 16, winter 2005, 94–116, pp. 105–106.
55 Hanns W. Maull, 'Germany's Foreign Policy, Post-Kosovo: Still a "Civilian Power"?', in Sebastian Harnisch and Hanns W. Maull (eds) *Germany as a Civilian Power? The Foreign Policy of the Berlin Republic*, Manchester and New York: Manchester University Press 2001, p. 117.
56 Buras and Longhurst, op. cit., p. 227, with reference to comments by Chancellor Schroder in Gunter Hofmann, 'Es lebe der kleine Unterschied', *Der Zeit* March 2003.
57 Tuomas Forsberg, 'German Foreign Policy and the War on Iraq: Anti-Americanism, Pacifism or Emancipation?', *Security Dialogue*, 36(2), 2005, 213–231, p. 224, in reference to Nikolaus Blome, '"Operation Augenhöhe" des Bundeskanzlers' ['The Chancellor's "Operation Eye-level"'], *Die Welt* 25 September 2003.
58 Forsberg, ibid., p. 224, quoting from an interview with Gerhard Schroder in, Steven Erlanger, 'German leader's warning: war plan is a huge mistake', *New York Times* 5 September 2002.
59 Steven Erlanger, 'German leader's warning: war plan is a huge mistake', *New York Times* 5 September 2002.
60 Philip H. Gordon and Jeremy Shapiro, *Allies at War: America, Europe and the Crisis over Iraq*, Washington, DC: Brookings Institution Press 2004, p. 78.

61 See US Energy Information Administration, 'Germany – Country Analysis Brief', November 2005, www.eia.doe.gov/emeu/cabs/Germany/Background.html.
62 Charles Cogan, 'The Iraq Crisis and France: Heaven-Sent Opportunity or Problem From Hell?', *French Politics, Culture and Society*, 22(3), Fall 2004, 121–134, p. 127.
63 Paul Gallis, *France: Factors Shaping Foreign Policy, and Issues in US–French Relations*, CRS Report for Congress, RL 32464, 10 January 2005, p. 23, quoting from 'Paris–Washington, deux diagnostics opposés sur la situation en Irak', *Le Monde* 25 September 2003 and De Villepin, 'Discours d'ouverture', Conference of ambassadors at the Ministry of Foreign Affairs, Paris, 28 August 2003.
64 Paul Gallis, op. cit.
65 'Allies Support Iraq with Troop Training', NATO Brussels, 29 June 2004.
66 'Give me liberty or give me debt', *Financial Times* 10 June 2004; 'French president spells out limits on Iraq support', *Financial Times* 11 June 2004.
67 Under the rules of the programme, Iraq was allowed to sell its oil at a price considered fair by the United Nations and the proceeds of each sale were deposited into a UN-controlled escrow account to be used to purchase largely humanitarian goods.
68 See Independent Inquiry Committee into the UN Oil for Food Programme, *Manipulation of the Oil For Food Programme by the Iraqi Regime: Oil Transactions and Illicit Payments, Humanitarian Goods Transactions and Illicit Payments, the Escrow Bank and the Inspection Companies, Other UN Related Issues*, 27 October 2005, www.iic-offp.org.
69 Paul Gallis, op. cit., pp. 19–20.
70 Independent Inquiry Committee into the UN Oil for Food Programme, op. cit.
71 Ibid., p. 2.
72 Paul Gallis, op. cit., p. 20.
73 Independent Inquiry Committee into the UN Oil for Food Programme, op. cit., p. 47.
74 Ibid.
75 Ibid., pp. 47 and 49. It was during Mr Mérimée's tenure as Permanent Representative to the UN for France that Resolution 986 was passed by the Security Council which instituted the Oil for Food Programme. Ibid., p. 50.
76 Senator intermittently between 1977 to 1999, and since 2004; and President intermittently from 1973 to 2004.
77 Independent Inquiry Committee into the UN Oil for Food Programme, op. cit., p. 53; see also Phil Hershcorn, 'Europeans Accused in Iraq report', 12 May 2005, www.cnn.com, www.cnn.com/2005/LAW/05/12/senate.oilforfood/.
78 Energy Information Administration, 'France – Country Analysis Brief', March 2005, www.eia.doe.gov.
79 French Ambassador Jean-David Levitte, 'France/United States Relations: the United States and France Transformed', Press Conference, Rice University, Houston, 22 May 2003, reproduced at the website of the French Embassy in the United States, www.ambafrance-us.org/news/statmnts/2003/levitte_us052203.asp.
80 See Chapter 4; Michael Brenner, 'The CSFP Factor: a Comparison of United States and French Strategies', *Cooperation and Conflict*, 38(3), 2003, 187–209, p. 202.
81 See Embassy of France in the United States, 'National Defense', website of the French Embassy in the US, www.ambafrance-us.org/atoz/defense.asp, last accessed April 2005.
82 See the Bush Administration's 2002 *National Security Strategy*.
83 The Chicago Council on Foreign Relations, 'Europeans See the World as Americans do, But Critical of US Foreign Policy', 4 September 2002, www.worldviews.org/key_findings/transatlantic_report.htm.
84 Interview given by Dominique de Villepin, Minister of Foreign Affairs, to *Le Monde* Newspaper, 30 July 2002, website of the Embassy of France in the United States, www.ambafrance-us.org/news/statmnts/2002/villepin073002.asp.

188 *Notes*

85 Contradictory views on the connection between poverty and terrorism were expressed by Jacques Chirac in March and September 2002. See 'Q&A/Jacques Chirac: What Message for the Globalization Talks? "Liberty, equality, fraternity"', *International Herald Tribune* 20 March 2002 and 'Interview of President Jacques Chirac', *New York Times* 8 September 2002.
86 'Interview of President Jacques Chirac', ibid.
87 On 20 January, French Foreign Minister Dominique de Villepin stated:

> If war is the only way to resolve this problem, we are going down a dead end. Already we know for a fact that Iraq's weapons of mass destruction programs are being largely blocked, even frozen. We must do everything to strengthen this process (and not) move forward out of impatience over a solution in Iraq to move towards military intervention. We believe that today nothing justifies envisaging military action.
> (Quoted in Glenn Kessler and Colum Lynch, 'France vows to block resolution on Iraq war', *Washington Post* 21 January 2003)

88 Paul Gallis, op. cit., p. 22, from interviews; Thierry Tardy, 'France and the United States: the Inevitable Clash?', *International Journal*, 59(1), winter 2003–2004, pp. 6–7.
89 'Interview of President Jacques Chirac', *New York Times* 8 September 2002.
90 French Ambassador to the United States, Jean-David Levitte, 'The United States and France in a World Transformed', speech given at Rice University, Houston, Texas, United States, 22 May 2003, www.ambafrance-us.org/news/statmnts/2003/levitte_us052203.asp.
91 Paul Gallis, op. cit., p. 14.
92 Michael Brenner, op. cit., p. 198; Helga Haftendorn and Michael Kolkmann, 'German Policy in a Strategic Triangle: Berlin, Paris, Washington ... and What About London?', *Cambridge Review of International Affairs*, 17(3), October 2004, 467–480, p. 476; Jolyon Howorth, 'France, Britain and the Euro-Atlantic Crisis', *Survival*, 45(4), winter 2003–2004, 173–192, p. 175.
93 Jolyon Howorth, ibid., pp. 178–179.
94 Jolyon Howorth, ibid., p. 179 and 182.
95 'Interview of President Jacques Chirac', *New York Times* 8 September 2002; Alex Macleod, 'Just Defending National Interests? Understanding French Policy Towards Iraq Since the End of the Gulf War', *Journal of International Relations and Development*, 7, 2004, 356–387, p. 373, with reference to Jacques Chirac, 'Discours de Monsieur Jacques Chirac, Président de la Républic, Troyes Aube', 14 October, www.elysee.fr/cgi-bin/auracom/aurweb/search/file?aur_file=discours/2002/0210TROYhtml.
96 'The divided West: war in Iraq – how the die was cast before transatlantic diplomacy failed', *Financial Times* 27 May 2003.
97 'French troops readied for war', *Guardian* 7 January 2003.
98 'War in Iraq – how the die was cast before transatlantic diplomacy failed – the divided west – part one', *Financial Times* 27 May 2003.
99 Ibid.
100 In the first week of January, Gerard Araud, Director of Strategic Affairs and Security in the Foreign Ministry told Foreign Minister Dominique Villepin of this belief, stating: 'We seem to be acting as though we believe the train has not left the station. In fact, it has already departed. All we are doing is lying down on the tracks in front of it.' Quoted in 'The divided West: war in Iraq – how the die was cast before transatlantic diplomacy failed', *Financial Times* 27 May 2003.
101 Sir Jeremy Greenstock, quoted in Charles Cogan, op. cit., p. 124.
102 See section entitled 'Burden-sharing' in this chapter (pp. 108–112). Based on figures of 340,000 US troops, 46,000 UK troops, 2,000 Australian and 200 Polish special forces.

103 See UK Ministry of Defence, *Operations in Iraq: First Reflections*, London: Directorate of Corporate Communications DCCS (Pubs) 7 July 2003, pp. 14 and 17 for detailed information on the objectives and activities of the UK Air Force and Navy.
104 UK Ministry of Defence, *Operations in Iraq: First Reflections*, ibid., p. 11.
105 Ibid., p. 12.
106 See UK Ministry of Defence, *Operations in Iraq: Lessons for the Future*, London: Directorate of Corporate Communications DCCS (Pubs) December 2003, p. 66. By February 2007, the UK had 7,100 troops in Iraq with plans to reduce this number to 5,500 by the summer of 2007. See 'Blair announces troops cut', *BBC Online* 21 February 2007, http://news.bbc.co.uk/2/hi/uk_news/6380933.stm.
107 UK Ministry of Defence, *Operations in Iraq: Lessons for the Future*, op. cit., p. 71.
108 John Dumbrell, 'The US–UK "Special Relationship" in a World Twice Transformed', *Cambridge Review of International Affairs*, 17(3), October 2004, 437–450, pp. 437–438.
109 Samuel Azubuike, '"The Poodle Theory" and the Anglo-American "Special Relationship"', *International Studies*, 42(2), 2005/2006, 123–139, pp. 128–129; John Baylis, 'The "Special Relationship": a Diverting British Myth?', in Cyril Buffet and Beatrice Heuser (eds) *Haunted by History: Myths in International Relations*, Oxford: Berghahn Books 1998, pp. 119–125; David Reynolds, 'A "Special Relationship"? America, Britain and the International Order Since the Second World War', *International Affairs*, 62(1), 1985, 1–20, p. 2; Jane M.O. Sharp, 'Tony Blair, Iraq and the Special Relationship: Poodle or Partner?', *International Journal*, 59(1), winter 2003–2004, 59–86; William Wallace, 'The Collapse of British Foreign Policy', *International Affairs*, 82(1), 2005, 52–68.
110 Charles Grant, *Transatlantic Rift: How to Bring the Two Sides Together*, London: Centre for European Reform, 2003, quoted in John Dumbrell, op. cit., p. 442; Alister Miskimmon, 'Continuity in the Face of Upheaval – British Strategic Culture and the Impact of the Blair Government', *European Security*, 13(3), 273–299, p. 283.
111 'The View from America', *Observer*, 16 November 2003.
112 Bob Woodward, *Plan of Attack*, New York: Simon & Schuster 2004.
113 'The divided west: Blair's mission impossible – the doomed effort to win a second UN resolution', *Financial Times* 29 May 2003.
114 The French claim to represent Europe was challenged by the publishing of the open letter by the United Kingdom, Spain and six other European states in the *Wall Street Journal*, and a second open letter from ten Central and Eastern European states effectively declaring support for the US position. See 'The rift turns nasty – the plot that split old and new Europe asunder', *Financial Times* 28 May 2003.
115 Warren Hoge, 'Parliament backs Blair on Iraq, but vote bares rift in Labour Party', *New York Times* 27 February 2003; Warren Hoge, 'Blair's stand on Iraq costs him popularity at home', *New York Times* 26 January 2003; Warren Hoge, 'Blair's stand on Iraq hurts him politically but seems unlikely to topple him', *New York Times* 21 February 2003; Philip Webster, Roland Watson and James Bone, 'Cooke ready to quit over war in Iraq', *The Times* 14 March 2003; Melissa Kite, 'Departing Minister warns of isolation', *The Times* 19 March 2003.
116 Philip Gordon and Jeremy Shapiro, op. cit., p. 144; Tony Blair, 'Speech to the House of Commons Opening Debate on the Iraq Crisis', *The Guardian Online*, http://politics.guardian.co.uk/print/0,3858,4627766-111381,00.html.
117 Tony Blair, 'Statement to the House of Commons', 25 February 2003, www.pm.gov.uk/output/page3088.asp.
118 Ibid. In reference to the calls by France, Germany and Russia for more time for inspections, Blair stated: 'Iraq is a country with a land mass roughly the size of France. The idea that the inspectors could conceivably sniff out the weapons and documentation relating to them without the help of the Iraqi authorities is absurd.'

190 *Notes*

119 British Prime Minister Tony Blair, Speech to the Economic Club of Chicago, 'Doctrine of the International Community', 22 April 1999.
120 Ibid.
121 Tony Blair, 'Speech at the Lord Mayor's Banquet', 13 November 2001, *Guardian Unlimited Online*, http://politics.guardian.co.uk/speeches/story/0,11126,592735,00.html; UK Prime Minister Tony Blair, Speech to the Labour Party Annual Conference, 'Let Us Re-Order This World Around Us', 2 October 2001.
122 Tony Blair, 'Speech Opening Debate on the Iraq Crisis at the House of Commons', 18 March 2003, www.pm.gov.uk/output/Page3294.asp.
123 Speech to the UK ambassadors in London, *Guardian* 7 January 2003, quoted in Samuel Azubuike, op. cit., p. 132.
124 'Threat of war – Straw admits oil is a key priority', *Guardian* 7 January 2003.
125 Philip Gordon and Jeremy Shapiro, op. cit., *Allies at War*, p. 81.

6 Comparing and contrasting the Gulf Crisis of 1990–1991 and the Iraq Crisis of 2002–2003: final conclusion

1 See Chapter 3.
2 See Chapter 3 and Francois Heisbourg, 'France and the Gulf Crisis', in Nicole Gnesotto and John Roper (eds) *Western Europe and the Gulf: a Study of West European Reactions to the Gulf War*, Alecon: Institute for Security Studies of the WEU 1992, p. 20.
3 In January 1991 President Kaifu described Iraq's behaviour as 'a brutal display of belligerence' and stated that Japan had to 'uphold the just principle that the aggressor must never be condoned in the international community' (*Far Eastern Economic Review*, 7 February 1991, pp. 10–11, quoted in Danny Unger, 'Japan and the Gulf War: Making the World Safe for Japan–US Relations', in Bennett, Lepgold and Unger (eds), op. cit., p. 140.
4 President George Bush, 'Speech at Air University, Maxwell Air Force Base', 13 April 1991 (US Information Service).

7 Conclusion

1 The Pew Global Attitudes Project, 'Global Public Opinion in the Bush Years (2001–2008)', Washington, DC: The Pew Research Centre 18 December 2008, p. 3.
2 Iraq Survey Group, *Comprehensive Report of the Special Advisor to the DCI on Iraq's WMD*, 30 September 2004, key findings in volume II 'Nuclear' chapter, volume III 'Iraq's Chemical Warfare Program' and 'Biological Warfare', www.globalsecurity.org/wmd/library/report/2004/isg-final-report/.
3 Simon Bromley, *American Power and the Prospects for International Order*, Cambridge: Polity Press 2008, pp. 1–2.
4 'Transcript – Confirmation Hearing: Hillary Clinton', *New York Times* 13 January 2009.
5 Richard L. Armitage and Joseph S. Nye Jr (co-chairs), *CSIS Commission on Smart Power: a Smarter, More Secure America*, Washington, DC: Center for Strategic and International Studies 2007.
6 Joseph S. Nye Jr, 'Public Diplomacy and Soft Power', *AAPSS*, 616, March 2008, 94–109, p. 94.
7 Ibid., p. 96.
8 James A. Baker, 'A Summons to Leadership', speech before the Chicago Council of Foreign Relations, Chicago, Illinois, 21 April 1992, quoted in Gow and Bellou, op. cit., p. 38.
9 President Barack Obama, 'Videotaped Remarks by the President in Celebration of Nowruz', 20 March 2009.

10 President Barack Obama, 'Obama's Speech in Cairo', *New York Times* 4 June 2009.
11 Tim Dunne, 'Society and Hierarchy in International Relations', *International Relations*, 17(3), 303–320, p. 304.
12 Ibid., pp. 305–306.
13 Raymond Aron, *Peace and War: a Theory of International Relations*, London: Weidenfeld and Nicolson, 1966, p. 70, quoted in Andrew Hurrell, 'Legitimacy and the Use of Force: Can the Circle be Squared?', *Review of International Studies*, 31, 2005, 15–32, p. 31.

Index

abandonment, fear of 22, 50, 57, 61, 66, 69–75, 92, 107, 113–14, 116, 122–4, 126, 129, 131–2, 136–8, 147–8
Abu Ghraib Prison 159
Afghanistan 78, 81–2, 92, 115, 117–18, 125, 159–60, 172, 184
aggression: illegitimacy of 28, 69, 148; illegitimate act of 55, 92
aggressive intentions 51, 108, 115, 121–2, 130–1, 133, 172
aggressive use of force 31, 39, 42, 81–2, 166
al-Qaeda 78, 83, 90, 92–3, 96, 115–16, 121, 123, 127, 130, 141, 155–6, 159
Algeria 65
alliance dependence 22–3, 50, 55, 57, 60, 64, 69, 71–4, 106–7, 113, 116, 128, 131–2, 135–8, 147–52
Almadinejad, Mahmoud 155
Annan, Kofi 77, 86
Anti Missile Defence 125
anticipatory self-defence 79–80, 82, 179; *see also* use of force
Arab–Israeli conflict 160
Armitage, Richard 113, 157, 190
Aron, Raymond 160, 191
Aziz, Tariq 120

Bahrain 48, 52, 67, 74, 166, 171
Baker, James A. 24, 30, 34–5, 40–1, 56, 143, 158
balance of power 6, 59, 116
balance of threat hypothesis 50–1, 58, 62–3, 66, 70, 72, 106–7, 112–13, 115, 120, 130, 139, 149
Baldwin, David 162
Belgium 48, 74, 109–10, 114, 118, 166
Bellou, Fotini 20, 156, 165, 190
Bennett, Andrew 50

Blair, Tony 91, 125–7, 131, 138, 149
Blair Government 125–6, 149
Blix, Hans 89–90
Bosnia 81
Brazil 28, 48
Bull, Hedley 4
burden sharing: Gulf Crisis 49–50, 56, 61, 140, 148–9, 151; Iraq Crisis 108–12, 114–15, 118–19, 124–5, 137, 153, 155–6
Bush Administration: George H.W. 40, 45, 56, 61, 62, 65, 69–70, 73, 113, 143–4, 148, 150–3; George W. 1–2, 77, 82, 83–4, 109, 116–17, 126–7, 131–2, 146, 150, 157

Cairo Speech 159, 176, 191; *see also* Obama, Barack
Canada 27, 31, 34, 37, 40, 42, 48, 54, 80, 100, 105, 109–10
Caroline Case, *The* 79, 81
Chapter VII 26, 30, 33–4, 38, 81, 183
Cheney, Richard 55, 84, 117, 168, 180
China 30, 32, 34, 36, 39–42, 48, 61, 73, 77, 87, 90–1, 95, 110, 113, 137–8, 144, 169–71, 180–1
Chirac, Jacques 87–8, 120–3
Christian Democratic Union (Germany) 116
Churchill, Winston 31
Clinton, Hillary 156
'Coalition of the Willing', Iraq War 1991 108–9
Cold War 1–3, 18, 23, 31, 35, 42, 56, 66, 69–70, 122–3, 131–2, 134, 137–8
collective security 24, 28, 32, 35, 37, 42, 45, 55, 81–2, 86, 94, 142–3, 145
collective self-defence 34, 143
Colombia 27, 40, 42, 144

Index 193

constructivism 2, 11, 13–18, 19
Cote d'Ivoire 40, 42, 44, 148
Cox, Robert W. 12
Cronin, Bruce 17
Cuba 29, 33, 37–8, 40–2, 169–70

De Gaulle, Charles 65–6
democracy promotion 156, 160
democratic regime change 93–5, 127, 146, 158
Dumas, Roland 66

European Community (EC) 27, 30, 55, 64–5
economic sanctions 8, 16, 25, 29–34, 36–7, 39–45, 48, 54–5, 58, 61, 77, 107, 112, 119–20, 142–3
Egypt 48, 51–4, 56, 58–9, 80,
El Salvador 102, 110
economic embargo 24, 28, 33–5, 37–9, 45, 54, 63–4, 69, 143–4, 148
enforcement: blockade of Iraq 1990 36, 34, 39, 69
entrapment: fear of 22, 50, 71–3, 107, 117–18, 129, 131–2, 136, 138, 147
Ethiopia 28, 40, 43
European Union 32, 66, 48, 99, 110, 122, 125–6, 128, 148
European Union Common Security and Defense Policy 122
European Security 69–70, 74, 122, 137

Fahd, King (Saudi Arabia) 67
Finland 27, 38, 40, 42, 110, 144, 166–70
Finnemore, Martha 20
Fischer, Joschka 115–16
followership, of the US 2, 6, 19–23, 25, 29, 44–5, 49–75, 106–9, 111–33, 135–6, 138–42, 147–9, 151–3, 158
France 48–9, 52–4, 63–6, 71–4, 84–5, 87–93, 95–8, 108–10, 118–23, 127–32, 135–40, 147–51; 'will to independence' 64, 122

Genscher, Hans-Dietrich 57, 73, 173
Germany 22–3, 48–9, 51–8, 61, 66, 72, 90–3, 108–10, 114–18, 130, 136, 147–8, 150–1, 173–5, 181, 186; '2-Plus-4' treaty 56; Greens Party 115, 117, 141; Red-Green Coalition 115, 117; Social Democratic Party (SPD) 115; unification of 54, 56–8, 73, 140, 173
Gilpin, Robert 8–9
Gorbachev, Mikhail 35, 41, 58, 144

Gordon, Philip 128
Gourdault-Montagne, Maurice 123
Gow, James 20, 156
Gramsci, Antonio 11–13
Great Powers 18
Greece 48, 74, 109–10, 166, 171
Greenstock, Jeremy 123
Guantanamo Bay 159
Gulf coalition (Gulf War 1991) 45, 49–52, 54, 58, 65, 67, 139, 148
Gulf War, 1991 20, 39, 70, 77–8, 108, 158
Gulf Cooperation Council (GCC) 27, 53
Gulf Crisis, 1990–1991 3, 24–45, 48–51, 58, 60–1, 63, 69, 71, 74–5, 106–9, 134–54, 166–71, 173–7, 190

Haas, Richard 82
Haiti 81
hegemon 2, 5–9, 11, 13, 15–18, 20, 23, 76, 94, 96, 134, 152–4, 159
Hegemonic Stability Theory (HST) 2, 8–10
hegemonic states 2, 7–11, 16–17, 20, 152–4, 157, 160, 163
hegemonic systems 8, 16, 154: operation of 4–5, 20, 23
hegemony 1–3, 5–21, 23–45, 48–9, 71, 74–96, 106, 122, 134–5, 147, 151–4; as a dominance relationship 6, 25, 49, 71, 74–5, 106, 135, 152–4; constructivist approaches to 2, 3, 5, 13–16, 17, 151–4; essentially contested concept 5; Gramscian approaches to 11–13; legitimacy and 2, 4–5, 15–18, 19, 21, 24–48, 75–105, 141–7, 151–4; materialist approaches to 2, 6, 23, 151–4
hegemonic leadership 2, 5, 9, 15, 17–18, 21, 23, 24, 75–6, 94, 96, 144, 151–4, 159
hegemonic power 1, 2–3, 5, 8, 15–18, 23, 134, 142, 151, 153–4, 157, 160
HST *see* Hegemonic Stability Theory
Human rights 43, 46, 81, 93–4, 127, 156, 159
Hurd, Douglas 68, 70,
Hurd, Ian 16
Hussein regime (Iraq) 39, 41–3, 72, 75, 77–8, 80, 107, 112, 114, 119–20, 128, 130, 136, 147
Hussein, Saddam 1, 58–60, 64, 68–9, 72, 84, 121, 127, 155, 178, 182

International Atomic Energy Agency (IAEA) 76–7, 85, 88–9, 93

Iceland 102, 110
Independent Inquiry Committee into the UN Oil for Food Program (IIC) 119–20, 129, 136
imminence 80–1; *see also* anticipatory self-defence
India 28, 48, 110
Indonesia 28, 48, 100
insurgency 155–6
International Donors' Conference (Iraq) 109
international law 10–11, 27, 31–3, 46, 64, 79, 91, 134, 140, 159–60; principle of necessity 36, 38, 79–80, 90; principle of proportionality 36, 38, 79
international legitimacy 2–3, 4–5, 23, 44, 84, 134, 106, 132, 134
international order 1–3, 5, 7–8, 15–19, 27, 29, 32, 44–5, 57–8, 78, 94–5, 115–17, 121, 129–30, 140, 142–5, 151–4, 158
international relations, study of 3–5, 6, 20
international society 2–6, 13, 15–19, 21–3, 44, 49, 51, 69, 95–6, 106, 134–5, 146–7, 149–54, 157–60; leadership role within *see* hegemony
international system 2–5, 7–9, 15–16, 31, 134
international terrorism 115–18, 121, 150, 160
intervention 20, 35–6, 78, 81–2, 94, 96
Iran 55, 64, 71, 78, 110, 114, 157
Iran–Iraq War 64
Iraq: containment of 1, 77, 95, 115–16, 121; disarmament of 75–7, 85–8, 90–1, 94, 96, 126, 132–3, 145, 158; economic embargo of 30, 36, 63, 65, 67; hostage-taking by 33, 37, 143, 169; invasion of Kuwait 25–7, 29,36, 49, 60, 67, 69, 73, 140, 142–3, 148; occupation of 119; post-war reconstruction of 107, 131, 138
Iraq Survey Group 155
Iraq War 2003 20, 108, 112, 119, 127, 159–60
Iraqi regime 24, 29, 43–4, 49, 51, 67, 71, 77, 84, 91–2, 107, 114, 120, 143
Israeli–Palestinian conflict 40, 155
Italy 30, 52–3, 74, 108, 110

Japan 22–3, 30, 32, 48–9, 51–3, 56, 58–63, 66, 69, 71–3, 108–14, 129–31, 135–41, 147–9; Air Self Defence Force 111; Constitution, Article 9 62; diet 113; Ground Self Defence Force 67–8, 111; United Nations Peace Corp Bill 62
Jordan 54, 56, 58–9, 80

Kaifu, Toshiki 58, 62
Keohane, Robert O. 9–10
Kindleberger, Charles P. 8–9
Kohl, Helmut 56–8
Koizumi, Junichiro 112–13
Korean War 43
Kosovo conflict 81, 83, 116–17, 125
Kurds (Iraqi) 155
Kuwait 24–6, 28–30, 33–4, 36–40, 42–5, 49–53, 59, 61, 63–5, 67–9, 110–11, 142–3, 151–2, 158; annexation of 33, 37, 42, 44; government, legitimate 28, 142; invasion of 24–6, 37, 49, 51, 53, 69, 106; liberation of 25, 29, 33, 37, 43, 45, 69, 142, 151–2, 158
Kyoto Protocol 1, 156

leadership *see* hegemony
leadership role, of international society 2, 16–17, 19, 21, 23, 44, 49, 62, 65, 76, 94, 106, 134–5, 142, 146–50, 153–4
leadership style 84, 94, 150–1
League of Arab States (LAS) 26–7, 92, 99, 148
League of Nations 28
legitimacy 2–5, 8–9, 11–14, 16, 18–21, 23–45, 48–9, 75–96, 134–5, 141–4, 146–60; as a form of power 19, 152, 154, 157–8; of a hegemonic order 25, 134; and hegemony 2, 4–5, 15–18, 19, 21, 24–48, 75–105, 141–7, 151–4
legitimate power 10
Lepgold, Joseph 50
Libya 81–2, 175
logic of appropriateness 15–16, 28, 45, 85–6, 152
logic of expected consequences 14–16, 45, 162
Luxembourg 48, 52, 109

Malaysia 27, 32, 38, 40, 42–3, 93, 144
Mearsheimer, John 6–7
Mérimée, Jean-Bernard 120
Mitterrand, Francois 63, 65–6, 140
Morgenthau, Hans J. 11

NATO 55–7, 66, 70, 73–4, 83, 109–10, 114, 116–19, 122, 131, 137–8, 140
Nazi Germany, appeasement of 140
naval coalition, Gulf War 1991 34, 38

Index 195

necessity, principle of 36, 38, 79–80, 90
'New World Order' 31, 42, 140, 144
'no-fly zones' (Iraq) 1, 130
Non-Aligned Movement 92–4, 99
norms 2–8, 10–11, 13–21, 27, 37, 43, 76, 90, 96, 134, 143, 147, 149, 153, 164–6; and international order 2, 16, 153
North Korea 61, 73, 113, 137–8, 157
National Security Strategy (NSS), United States 78–80, 82
nuclear weapons 71, 79–80
nuclear umbrella 61, 73, 137
Nye, Joseph 157

Obama, Barack 155–7, 159–60
Obama Administration 156–60
occupation, illegitimacy of 155
oil dependency 22, 50, 55, 59–60, 62–4, 68, 71–2, 106–7, 114, 118, 128, 133, 135–6, 149
oil price stability 50, 60, 69, 71–2
oil supplies 22, 50, 60, 63–4, 66, 69, 107, 114, 120, 128, 136
Oman 48, 52, 67, 74, 114
OPEC 50, 114
Operation Desert Fox 1, 77, 82–3
Operation Desert Shield 55–6
Operation Enduring Freedom 121
Operation Granby 68
order 2, 4, 6–9, 11–13, 15–17, 25, 64, 88–9, 117–18, 134–5, 143–5, 153–4, 159; hegemonic 7, 12–13, 16, 25, 134, 151, 153–4; rules of international 10, 15–16, 152
Organisation of African States 92
Organisation of Islamic Conference (OIC) 27
Osiraq nuclear reactor (Iraq) 80

Paris Club 119
Pasqua, Charles 120
peaceful settlement of disputes 28, 32, 37, 42–5, 48, 76, 81, 87, 92, 142, 144–5, 148, 150, 158
P'eng, Li 36
Persian Gulf Crisis 1990–1991 109
Pew Global Attitudes Project 155
Pickering, Tom 26, 31
Poland 28, 48, 74, 108, 110, 155
Powell, Colin 90, 121
power 1, 3–13, 15–16, 18, 20, 22–3, 26, 32–3, 51, 125–6, 128, 151–2, 157–8, 160; balance of 6, 59, 116; coercive 24; definition of 7–8, 162; illegitimate 10;

material 9, 94, 151, 157–8; smart 156–7; soft 157, 190; relationships 5–6; reward power 24
pre-emption, doctrine of 79, 80, 82–3, 87, 89, 92–3, 95–6, 122, 145–6, 150, 155
Preventive War 80, 90
proportionality, principle of 36, 38, 79

Qatar 48, 52, 74, 109–10, 114, 166, 171
Qichen, Quan 41

Reagan, Ronald 70
realism: classical 10–11; structural 6–8, 9; see also Hegemonic Stability Theory; hegemony: materialist approaches to
Red–Green coalition (Germany) 115, 117
regime change 23, 84, 88, 93, 95–6, 107, 115–17, 120–1, 123, 128, 130, 145, 147, 150, 152–3, 155; democratic 93–4, 158
research design 18–19, 21, 50
Resolution 655 (UNSC) 33
Resolution 660 (UNSC) 26, 29–30, 32–3
Resolution 661 (UNSC) 29–30, 34, 36–7
Resolution 665 (UNSC) 33–4, 36–8, 42–3, 143–4
Resolution 678 (UNSC) 40, 42–3, 83, 144
Resolution 687 (UNSC) 77, 83
Resolution 1199 (UNSC) 83
Resolution 1441 (UNSC) 76, 84–5, 87–9, 92, 94–5, 102, 113, 121, 123, 141, 145
Resolution 1483 (UNSC) 111
Resolution 1511 (UNSC) 119, 186
Rice, Condoleezza 123, 182
rogue states 2, 78–80, 82–3, 92, 108, 112, 131, 146
Romania 40, 74, 99, 111
Russian Federation 77, 83–5, 87, 89–93, 95–6, 98, 111, 114, 118–20
Rwanda 81, 184

Saudi Arabia 24, 36, 48, 51–3, 61, 63, 65, 67–9, 111, 114, 120, 143
Schröder, Gerhardt 116–18
Scowcroft, Brent 30
Self Defence Force (Japan) 62, 111
Senate Foreign Relations Committee (US) 56
September 11, 2001 1, 77–80, 115, 121, 127, 131, 156, 158
Shapiro, Jeremy 128
Shevardnadze, Eduard 35, 41
Shiites (Iraq) 155
Smit, Christian-Reus 17
Snidal, Duncan 163

196 *Index*

Social Democratic Party, SPD (Germany) 115, 141
Solomon, Richard 36
Somalia 81
Southern Rhodesia 31
sovereignty 27–8, 46, 53, 81–2, 90, 94–6, 104, 114, 119, 142, 146, 148, 150, 153, 158–9
Soviet Union 30, 34–6, 38, 41, 56–8, 60, 64, 73, 113, 125, 136, 149; invasion of Afghanistan 30
Spain 48, 74, 89–90, 108–9, 111, 155
'Special Relationship', the 70, 74, 125–6, 132, 137–8
Straw, Jack 126, 128, 138
Sunnis (Iraq) 155
superpowers 35–6, 42, 66
Syria 48, 53, 56, 74, 80

Tatsuo, Arima 113
terrorism, international 81, 92, 112–13, 130–1
terrorist attack 77–8, 81, 121
Thatcher, Margaret 30, 41, 67, 69–70, 140
theoretical framework 1–2, 4, 6, 8, 10–23
Tiananmen Square massacre 41
torture memos 159
Tunisia 65
Turkey 48, 54, 56, 58, 99, 101, 105, 111, 114, 118, 155

United Kingdom 22, 26–7, 30, 32–4, 36–7, 52–4, 67–72, 74, 83–5, 87, 90–1, 108–9, 123–6, 128–2, 135–41, 147–9; government 67, 126, 128, 132, 139; Ministry of Defence 124–5
Ukraine 109, 111
United Nations 1, 24–8, 31–40, 62–3, 76–7, 79–81, 84, 97–8, 109–11, 118–19, 141–3, 145–7, 149–51; credibility of 31–2, 37, 39, 69, 94, 142, 145; General Assembly 27–8, 32–3, 35, 45, 65, 78, 80, 82, 141, 148; Independent Inquiry Committee into the UN Oil for Food Program 119; UN inspections process 75, 77, 83–5, 89–92, 95–100, 102, 115–16, 121–2, 127, 141, 145; Military Staff Committee 4–6, 38–40, 45, 144
UN Security Council 24–34, 36–45, 62–3, 75–8, 80–8, 91–2, 94–8, 101–6, 122–3, 125–6, 142–3, 145–7, 150–2; authority of 37, 43, 87, 93, 143
United Nations Charter 17–18, 24–5, 27, 31–2, 34–5, 37, 39, 42, 44–6, 79, 81–3, 86–7, 93, 142–3, 158–9; Article 2(4) 27; Article 2(7) 27, 111; Article 39 24; Article 40 26; Article 41 39; Article 51 34, 41, 69, 79, 143
Unger, Danny 50
unilateralism 1–2, 17, 32, 34–5, 75–6, 82–4, 87, 95–6, 117–18, 121–3, 132, 146–7, 150, 156
United Arab Emirates 51, 63, 74, 109
United Nations Peace Corps Bill (Japan) 62
UNMOVIC 76, 85, 88–9, 93
UNSCOM 1, 77, 88–9
US Congress 24, 40–1, 52, 59, 61, 73, 109
US hostage affair in Tehran 30
use of force 2–3, 19–21, 27, 31–45, 75–6, 79–97, 102–5, 112–14, 123, 141–6, 148–50, 157–9
USSR *see* Soviet Union

Volker, Paul 119

Walt, Stephen M. 22, 51, 62, 70, 107–8, 112, 139
Waltz, Kenneth 6–8
Wendt, Alexander 14–15
West Germany 32, 53–7, 61, 72, 136–7
WMD 75, 78, 81–3, 85–6, 91–4, 102, 108, 112, 118, 120–1, 127, 130–1, 139, 141, 144–6, 156
World Bank 109, 111

Yemen 26–7, 29, 33, 37–8, 40–2, 104

Zaire 31, 37, 40, 44, 148